The Future of the South China Sea

The Future of the South China Sea

Disputes and Negotiations

Jiye Kim

University of Michigan Press
Ann Arbor

Published in the United States of America by the
University of Michigan Press
First published January 2026

A CIP catalog record for this book is available from the British Library.

Library of Congress Control Number: 2025025213
LC record available at https://lccn.loc.gov/2025025213

ISBN 978-0-472-07778-6 (hardcover : alk. paper)
ISBN 978-0-472-05778-8 (paper : alk. paper)
ISBN 978-0-472-90537-9 (open access ebook)

DOI: https://doi.org/10.3998/mpub.12472546

The University of Michigan Press's open access publishing program is made possible thanks to additional funding from the University of Michigan Office of the Provost and the generous support of contributing libraries.

Cover image: SpaceX Dragon capsule passing over Manifa, Saudi Arabia (December 8, 2018). Photograph by astronaut Alex Gerst, courtesy of NASA Earth Observatory.

The authorized representative in the EU for product safety and compliance is Easy Access System Europe, Mustamäe tee 50, 10621 Tallinn, Estonia, gpsr.requests@easproject.com

For those who inspired, encouraged, and supported this book.

And for those who devote their nameless commitment to diplomacy.

Contents

Digital materials related to this title can be found on
the Fulcrum platform via the following citable URL:
https://doi.org/10.3998/mpub.12472546

Illustrations

Maps

Figures

Tables

Abbreviations

ADB	Asian Development Bank
AIIB	Asian Infrastructure Investment Bank
ASEAN	Association of Southeast Asian Nations
BRI	Belt and Road Initiative
CBM	confidence-building measures
CLCS	Commission on the Limits of the Continental Shelf
CNOOC	China National Offshore Oil Corporation
COC	Code of Conduct
CPC	Communist Party of China
CPV	Communist Party of Vietnam
DOC	Declaration on Conduct of Parties in the South China Sea
ECS	East China Sea
EEZ	exclusive economic zone
FON	freedom of navigation
ICJ	International Court of Justice
IMO	International Maritime Organization
ITLOS	International Tribunal for the Law of the Sea
JMSU	Joint Marine Seismic Undertaking
JWG	joint working group
MFA	Ministry of Foreign Affairs
nm	nautical miles
PB	Politburo
PBSC	Politburo Standing Committee
PLAN	People's Liberation Army Navy
PRC	People's Republic of China
R2P	Responsibility to Protect
ROC	Republic of China

SCS	South China Sea
SCSPI	South China Sea Strategic Situation Probing Initiative
SLOC	Sea Lines of Communication
UN	United Nations
UNCLOS	United Nations Convention on the Law of the Sea
WTO	World Trade Organization

ONE

China's South China Sea Diplomacy

A Negotiation Perspective

In the 1970s, the littoral states surrounding the South China Sea (SCS) began defining and claiming their rights in the SCS. The United Nations Convention on the Law of the Sea was developing, and the People's Republic of China (China) was no exception in this relatively new drive—or nascent conflict—to seek maritime rights. Indeed, China proved to be the most willful power, as evidenced by the first interstate naval skirmish in the SCS—between China and South Vietnam—in 1974. Since then, China's foreign and security policies have been configured as cooperative, status-quo-oriented, or aggressive, although these categories have been neither clear-cut nor occurring in a distinct sequence. The configuration of China's cooperativeness, conservatism, and aggression constitutes a critical narrative of the failure or success of negotiations in the SCS. China has engaged in minor and major standoffs at the Paracel and Spratly Islands with SCS stakeholders including Vietnam and the Philippines. These standoffs invite a multilevel analysis that encompasses key individuals, domestic institutions and politics, changes in the regional order and in international regimes, and the balance of power.

In the hypothetical "orange quarrel" situation studied by Fisher and Ury (1991), two people argue over one orange. One person needs the flesh of the orange to eat, whereas the other wants the orange peel to bake a cake. The person who wants the peel has choices. They may give it away because they are not very desperate, preserve the status-quo condition where no one consumes the orange, or, in the worst-case scenario, maximize their aggressive tendencies and take the orange completely. If they attempt to seize the entire orange, negotiations will fail and lead to a zero-sum game. If there is a sufficiently capable external party, the status quo might be forced, or the orange may be split in half. However, in any zero-sum, status quo, or external mediation outcome, the fact does not change: having the orange peel to bake a cake was the *underlying interest*.

One of the early diplomatic efforts to manage the SCS disputes occurred in 1978 when the president of the Philippines, Ferdinand Marcos, disclosed that the visiting Chinese vice-premier Li Xiannian had confirmed that a dispute over the Spratly Islands should be settled through diplomatic negotiations. China's dominance in the SCS has been consolidated through substantial changes in the status quo in the disputed waters, including Sino-Vietnamese skirmishes and China's occupation of the Paracel Islands in 1974, China's takeover of the Spratly Islands from Vietnam and the Philippines in 1988, the Mischief Reef incident and the ensuing diplomacy between China and the Philippines in 1995, China's engagement in multilateral negotiations with ASEAN in 2002, and the standoff at the Scarborough Shoal in 2012 that culminated in the International Tribunal's Award denying China's "historic rights" in the SCS. Since then, SCS disputes have been largely determined by two distinct phenomena: (1) China's military power projection in the SCS and the freedom of navigation operations of the United States and allies, and (2) China's bilateral and multilateral diplomacy and the ongoing code of conduct negotiations. This book is about the past, present, and future of the latter: China's diplomacy and negotiations.

The major turning point in China's diplomacy and negotiation was the Declaration on Conduct of Parties in the South China Sea (DOC), signed between China and the Association of Southeast Asian Nations (ASEAN) in 2002. The DOC was signed on the sidelines of the 8th ASEAN summit at Phnom Penh in November 2002. The DOC was the first documented multilateral declaration in which China participated specifically regarding the SCS disputes. The DOC document and the process to reach the agreement are of research value because the DOC shaped China's later dispute management framework in the SCS. In 1992, ten years before the DOC was signed, there was a declaration similar to the DOC but it was signed only by ASEAN countries: the ASEAN Declaration on the South China Sea. By joining ASEAN countries' multilateral dispute management efforts, China became one of the signatories of the 2002 DOC and established itself as an actor in the multilateral management of disputes in the SCS. Likewise, upon signing the 2002 DOC, ASEAN recognized China as one of the claimants of the SCS disputes and a legitimate actor in multilateral negotiations concerning SCS disputes. If the 1992 ASEAN Declaration is the first version of multilateral dispute management, the 2002 DOC is the second version that engages China in the negotiation process.

It is important to note that dispute management and dispute settlement are distinct concepts with policy differences. Bilateral dispute settlement and multilateral dispute management have been the default framework of China's diplomacy in the SCS since 2002; therefore, the 2002 DOC—with China's participation—is about dispute management. Considering that China enacted the Law on the Territorial Sea and the Contiguous Zone in February 1992—which became a legal ground for China's official argument on indisputable sovereignty over the SCS—the DOC was a watershed event for China to extend its diplomacy into a multilateral platform for affairs relating to SCS disputes.

The ongoing SCS disputes arise from the overlapping sovereignty claims of six claimants: Brunei, China, Malaysia, the Philippines, Taiwan, and Vietnam. Scientific surveys initiated the disputes over marine resources since 1968 when an academic survey was undertaken by the United Nations.[1] The dispute escalated as these states' claims overlapped, and no international authority would effectively control their maritime activities. China has occupied the Paracel Islands in the SCS since 1974, and each claimant occupied some of the Spratly Islands; Vietnam occupies twenty-nine islands, the Philippines occupies nine, China seven, Malaysia five, and Taiwan occupies the largest naturally formed island in the Spratlys.[2] Taiwan also occupies the Pratas Reef group located in the northeast part of the SCS. Regarding their respective positions, the Spratly Islands have all six countries as territorial claimants, the Paracel Islands have two primary claimants—China and Vietnam—and the Macclesfield Bank has three: China, Taiwan, and the Philippines.

In 1996, China's series of ground-to-ground missile tests in the SCS was one of the most outstanding examples by which China showcased its power to maintain and preserve its national territorial integrity and sovereignty.[3] However, during the Taiwan Strait Crisis in 1995–96, it was demonstrated to the Chinese that their assertion of territorial claims might provoke US involvement in the region.[4] The possibility of the alignment of the other parties to SCS disputes with the US has also increased as ASEAN states became cautious about China's ascent after the Mischief Reef incidents in 1995.

China's use of diplomacy in the SCS reflects its consideration of the need for a stable political situation, to say nothing of the growing economic interdependency between China and neighboring states surrounding the SCS. Participation in regional cooperation and multilateral diplomacy is one of

China's most effective means to mitigate the suspicions of its neighbors.[5] In the early 2000s, China joined various multilateral regimes of economic cooperation, scientific exploration, joint development, and peaceful resolution of territorial disputes, such as the Treaty of Amity and Cooperation (TAC) in 2003 and the Joint Marine Seismic Undertaking (JMSU) in 2005.[6] In China's white paper published in 2011, it is argued that China has made a constructive proposal to "shelve disputes and seek joint development," and has done its utmost to uphold peace and stability in the SCS, the East China Sea, and the surrounding areas.[7]

The diversified diplomacy is closely related to China's attempt to secure its national interests by expanding its soft power over its neighbors to the southeast. China's policy initiatives such as "smile diplomacy," "public diplomacy," and "good neighbor diplomacy" have facilitated its pursuit of realizing national interests through varied diplomatic channels: bilateral (foreign aid and trade), multilateral (e.g., China-ASEAN Free Trade Agreement, ASEAN Regional Forum, ASEAN Defence Ministers Meeting-Plus), and track-two diplomacy (e.g., exchanges between civilians and Confucius Institutes).[8]

However, hopes for China's amicable diplomacy in the SCS fell as China resolutely associated its core interest with the SCS in the late 2000s.[9] China's core interests are described as state sovereignty, national security, territorial integrity and national reunification, overall social and political stability, and basic safeguards for ensuring sustainable economic and social development.[10] Furthermore, China's participation in many regional regimes in the SCS could not move on toward *resolving* the core of the dispute: maritime delimitation based on sovereignty. China has not found suitable diplomatic measures to repair its deteriorating image except by responding with "strategic ambiguity." Due to its strict adherence to its core interests, China's activity in the regional regimes has been limited to economic, scientific, and joint development alone, rather than direct negotiation on territorial issues.

It is interesting to contemplate the dynamics of China's diplomacy in the SCS in the light of the coexistence of its two diplomatic axes in the SCS: pragmatic diversified diplomacy and its principle of "indisputable sovereignty." Indisputable sovereignty is attached to two additional principles, namely shelving, or setting aside, the sovereignty issue and promoting joint development that appeared with Deng Xiaoping's initiative in June 1984. Chinese officials still use these three principles due to their high applicability to many different problems of clear priority. China's diversification in its diplomatic choices influences the status of SCS disputes. Therefore, the significance of the research is placed on the analysis of the two axes of China's diplomacy—indisputable sovereignty and pragmatism—in China's interactions with the various claimants in the SCS.

China in the Multilateral Disputes

This book explores China's diversified diplomatic approaches, which are unique compared to other historical major powers' diplomatic traditions. The US has been the sole and most influential superpower to fill the power vacuum since the dissolution of the Soviet Union, which was the end of the bipolar era. China's international behavior, including its diplomacy with its principles, invites discussion on an effective analytical tool that tells us how China ensures order while the US maintains power projection in East Asia. Changes in regional dynamics add significance to the SCS disputes concerning the research on the frontier of China. Following the Sino-Indian War in 1962 and the Sino-Soviet clash over the land border in 1969, the gravity of China's border dispute was located in the land border.[11] Since the beginning of the normalization of Sino–US relations in the early 1970s, the frontier of Chinese territory has also been extended from its interior lands to the eastern maritime border and beyond to China's remote islands in the SCS. Expanding China–ASEAN relations and increasing interactions with the ten ASEAN member states in the late 1990s further broadened the need for the present study in light of the scant scholarly attention observed in the early 1990s.[12]

The island subgroups in the SCS have particular implications for the history of the dispute. For example, the Paracel Islands involved China and Vietnam as primary claimants. Compared to the Spratly Islands—which have a greater number of claimants—the relatively few claimants over the Paracels made possible a different path for the dispute, as China forcefully occupied the Paracel Islands after conducting naval operations against Vietnam in 1974. China's early occupation of the Paracel Islands further strengthened its efficacy toward the upcoming operations held in the southern part of the SCS, that is, the Spratly Islands. In terms of setting the precedents for China's successful occupation and effective control in the SCS, the dispute history of the Paracels guided subsequent dispute trends and problems that affected the SCS claimants.[13] Clarence Bouchat calls the Paracel Islands dispute a "microcosm of the South China Sea disputes" because fewer participants and a relatively smaller maritime area are involved.[14]

The SCS disputes hold further significance as a research topic due to their relevance and geographic proximity to other regional flashpoints, such as the East China Sea and the cross-strait relations between mainland China (the People's Republic of China) and Taiwan (the Republic of China). These areas are all geographically interconnected, with China playing a central role in each. In the East China Sea, China and Japan compete for legitimacy, their relationship characterized by regional rivalry and a complex historical background. Unlike Japan, however, the other claimants in the South China Sea are not necessarily viewed by China as rivals or competing powers in the region. Given that all these areas have the potential to escalate into armed conflict, it is difficult to label any one area as inherently more serious or volatile. However, comparisons can be made by applying specific criteria over a certain period of time. Erica Strecker Downs and Phillip Saunders, for example, assess the severity of China's claims in the SCS, East China Sea, and Taiwan Strait using three key criteria: the symbolic value of the disputed territory to China's nationalistic narrative, the economic rewards of China's aggressive pursuit, and the relative power gap between the states involved. Their analysis concludes that, among these three cases, Taiwan holds the highest symbolic value for China, the SCS offers higher economic rewards than others, and China's power dominance compared to other claimants is most pronounced in the SCS.[15]

The SCS is surrounded by China's Southeast Asian neighbors. The varying power structures associated with the SCS and East China Sea disputes demand different analytical approaches. Furthermore, the multilateral nature of the SCS disputes offers insight into how China deals with multiparty interactions as a regional power. China's national interests and negotiations, therefore, appear in dynamic correlation over time. Research on the SCS has significance in that the SCS disputes have created cycles in Asian maritime affairs since the 1970s.[16] Considering that the maritime disputes in other parts of the world, such as in the Arctic Ocean, also involve multiparty claimants, China's diplomatic footprints and choice of actions potentially suggest its possible policy pursuit in future challenges elsewhere.

It is no surprise that Chinese academic interest in the SCS disputes is growing rapidly. According to the China National Knowledge Infrastructure academic journal article database, the number of academic journal articles written by Chinese scholars with keywords related to the SCS—Nanhai (South Sea) or Nanzhongguohai (South China Sea)—increased rapidly in the later 2000s under the specific categories of politics and military affairs. During 2002–6, the number was slightly higher than 100—but just ten years later, by 2016, that number had jumped to 1,000.

In the 2000s, China succeeded in addressing border disputes with its neighbors, including the China–Russia border dispute, which was settled in 2004. As Taylor Fravel persuasively argues, the path of land border negotiations between China and neighboring countries has shown a trend of reconciliation rather than escalation, which raises expectations for diplomacy and negotiation in the maritime dispute.[17] This book deals with the research problem that comes from China's multifaceted and complex diplomacy and negotiations to suggest a path for the future of China's SCS disputes. This book does not directly discuss whether China's or any other parties' claims in the SCS are legitimate. Instead, it focuses on China's diplomatic maneuverings that exercise and distribute its power and reasoning in negotiations.

How will the SCS disputes unfold over the next thirty years? This book seeks the answer in China's diplomacy and negotiations, suggesting that the end game China pursues to accomplish in the SCS is neither a monolithic nor an immutable goal. Specifically, this book argues that China's official claims and its bottom-line policies have become disjointed. China has insisted on absolute sovereignty over the SCS for the past seventy years; meanwhile, it has also participated in bilateral and multilateral negotiations with other SCS claimants for forty years. The discordance between official claims and the bottom-line agenda leads to China's evolving underlying interests in the SCS. China's underlying interests in the SCS have varied in urgency and focus, including economic, historical, domestic, and international concerns, and nontraditional security issues.

Underlying Interests in Negotiations

Traditional theories of international relations define the nature and causes of the SCS disputes by applying their respective theoretical assumptions. Realism, liberalism, and constructivism put forward that countries involved in the SCS disputes enter into conflict or cooperation with different motivations. Liberal institutionalists, for example, claim that countries seek to further national interests through institutions, thereby diversifying and expanding the framework of cooperation. Realists argue that countries manifest their SCS policy to pursue self-help and to ensure their nations' survival. Liberals admit that a non-zero-sum game is possible in the SCS disputes because countries seek absolute gains based on their specific needs—rather than relative gains, which focus on increasing power in comparison to others.[18] This section review delves into international relations theories, with a particular focus on how these frameworks explain the diverse interests of states that affect dispute management and settlement. The Chinese, as well as international scholars, are adopting and developing theories in research concerning China's diplomacy and the SCS disputes. This section discusses the differences between each theoretical paradigm, followed by a discussion of the gap in existing theories and the approach of this book.

From the classic work on realism, *The Peloponnesian War* by Thucydides,[19] to contemporary international relations theorists such as Hans Morgenthau, Kenneth Waltz, Robert Gilpin, and John Mearsheimer,[20] realism has evolved and found a more apt explanation on the subject matter of international conflicts. Realist theory argues that, first, nation-states are the key actors in an international system; second, domestic and foreign policy are separated; third, international politics is a struggle for power in an anarchic and self-help international environment; and last, states have different capabilities to achieve goals and defend interests. According to the realist's perspective, an ascendant China will expand its interests abroad.[21]

According to the core assumptions of realism, cooperation in the SCS is inherently challenging due to China's status as a rising power.[22] If Thucydides's expression is used, the SCS disputes are caused by the growth of Chinese power and ASEAN's fear (or the fear of the US and consequential intervention). Cooperation in the SCS is merely a temporary and intermittent occurrence; therefore, the balance of power is critical to maintaining a stable regional security order.

David Shambaugh uses realist logic to explain China's limited rise and low likelihood of becoming a global power.[23] The power structure in the regional order is one of the main reasons for a dispute. In Chinese literature, the "intervention" of the US in the region is often described as an obstacle to regional stability, while China is described in like terms in Western literature. For example, Yan Xuetong studies China's diplomatic effort to avoid the rebalancing of the US and the possibility of a clash in the SCS.[24] Since the 1980s, in order to avoid wartime economic disruptions, China has ceased to involve itself in large-scale military conflict. Yan expects that the possibility of military conflict in the SCS may emerge from US military aid to other SCS claimants in the region, which would threaten China's interests.[25] He concedes that the political negotiation suggested by China between the parties concerned was offered in order to prevent interference by other major powers. The difference between Shambaugh and Yan is in their analysis of China's diplomatic practices. Shambaugh argues that China helps even rogue regimes in Africa if they can fulfill China's appetite for resources; however, Yan argues that China has gained African countries' favor by providing aid without any political conditions, whereas the US has not received such a positive reaction from African countries.[26]

Zheng Zemin analyses the pattern of the SCS dispute from a strongly realist perspective.[27] He studies regional powers—China, US, Japan, Russia, India, and ASEAN—and their respective interests and influences in the SCS. For instance, the US (1) is the supreme power in the Asia-Pacific area, (2) would take actions to influence the dispute, and (3) is the most threatening external factor from the Chinese perspective. Cooperation among ASEAN states may also disturb China's actions in the SCS. Zheng's argument shows China's strong need for bilateral—not multilateral—communication with each claimant in the region, as such an approach may allow China to successfully pursue power diplomacy.

In the realist view, the sovereignty issue in the SCS is a significant factor as it is the right of independent states. It is also an indicator of how far a state's power can reach in the traditional international system. Barnard Cole associates China's sovereignty issue in SCS to its military power.[28] He argues that China has shown confidence in its ability to employ its maritime strength effectively at the turn of the twenty-first century—for example, the Mischief Reef incident in 1995, which solidified its sovereignty claim over the SCS. The writings of Liu Huaqing, also known as China's Alfred Thayer Mahan, supported this premise. In his posthumously published memoir, Liu wrote that the ultimate resolution for the SCS dispute was China's military presence in disputed locations.[29] Similarly, many Chinese scholars now argue in favor of China's complete sovereignty in the SCS, using various bodies of evidence in support of this advocacy, such as legal and historical justifications.[30]

Yuan Jingdong illustrates the neutral perspectives in his analysis of the SCS dispute.[31] He contemplates two main reasons for the dispute: the unresolved territorial claims and the pending great-power rivalry between the US (status-quo power) and China (rising power). Furthermore, he points out that the contention reflects claimant states' hopes that occupation or repeated claims will enable them to establish legitimacy. Therefore, the introduction and development of confidence-building measures are crucial in preventing maritime incidents. Regarding confidence-building measures, Bateman wrote that the essential requirement to cooperate in managing the SCS resources should be maritime confidence-building measures, which are distinct from military confidence-building measures and strategic trust.[32]

A realist perspective is often employed in literature on the causes of conflicts. The theoretical assumptions of realism are arguably deficient in explaining new agendas in the SCS and China's response. Realist agendas—such as power, sovereignty, and maritime delimitation—have competed in the scholarly debates with the issues of the interdependent regional system and China's diversified diplomacy.

In the liberals' view, the order of international society is largely affected by the growth of economic interdependence and the evolution of a transnational global society. International institutions such as the United Nations create conditions in which an entirely anarchical order is an insufficient characterization of the nature of international politics.[33] Liberal institutionalists appear curious as to how China's diplomacy in the SCS has responded to intensified interdependency in the regional order and complicated agenda structure.

The liberal explanation became more persuasive when China took responsibility for varied security tasks and proactively carried out strategic adjustments in its foreign policy in the early 2000s. In July 2002, in the ASEAN Regional Forum foreign ministers' meeting, the Chinese delegation stated that territorial disputes over land and sea would no longer stymie China's efforts in conducting cooperation, building relations, and jointly pursuing regional security with surrounding countries. Yu Xiaofeng analyzes the official statement in light of the emergence of nontraditional security.[34] Ju Hailong also argues that cooperation in nontraditional security would improve the relationships among the countries around the SCS.[35]

In the early 2000s, China actively participated in multilateral regimes in the SCS, such as the DOC in 2002. Even though it fell short of concluding a multilateral binding code of conduct, the DOC was one of the most important documents ever signed multilaterally between China and ASEAN countries.[36] Along with signing the DOC, China's diplomacy has entered into a number of formal and informal agreements in which the concerned parties would keep watch on China's endeavor to expand or fortify its sovereignty argumentation. In 2005, Wang Jianwei argued that China's attitude toward the SCS has become increasingly reconciliatory and cooperative since the establishment of the ASEAN+1 mechanism with China in 1997,[37] and the DOC was one of the achievements in the transformation. Similarly, Wu Shicun and Ren Huaifeng from the Hainan Research Institute for the South China Sea conclude that the DOC aims at forming more favorable political commitments by the parties that will preserve peace and stability in the region.[38] Furthermore, Luo Guoqiang focuses on the internal task of the DOC and provides suggestions for improved cooperation.[39] He argues that ASEAN should not constitute a united group to counter China.

Moreover, the negotiators should not be adamant about achieving success on all fronts in the process; rather, they should show a degree of flexibility in prioritizing various agendas to enhance the effectiveness and workability of the negotiations.

Experts from Western academia also find the DOC attempts attractive. Leszek Buszynski has pointed out that the theme of China's "lost territories" in the SCS lost its significance among the Chinese leadership in the 1990s,[40] as China wrestled with its desire to expand economic relations within the Asia Pacific region, which became more apparent in China's subsequent diplomacy. He assessed that the DOC was symptomatic of a trend toward adopting norms in the regulation of the dispute. This point of view is also found in Snyder's research on the transparency mechanism in the SCS in 2001:[41] in fact, one of Scott Snyder's suggestions were realized in the DOC.

However, Chinese scholars do not consider cooperation in the SCS to be an equal opportunity for all parties. Xiong Tao argues that the obstacle to the implementation of the Declaration is that, since the DOC was signed, ASEAN countries have nevertheless joined hands with powers from outside the region to exploit natural resources.[42] Su Hao, a researcher on Asia-Pacific studies with the China Foreign Affairs University, shares a similar view.[43]

The liberal perspective does not sufficiently credit China's selectivity in the negotiation process because, theoretically, the liberal perspective supports the possibility of negotiation across all issues. On the contrary, if China firmly considers a specific issue to be indisputable, its cooperation does not lead to resolution of the conflict; rather, it aids only in maintaining the status quo in the SCS. For example, in the case of a territorial dispute, the Chinese delegations' statement at the 2002 Asian Regional Forum did not address the territorial issues at all because economic cooperation was the chosen priority.

As described by constructivists, international relations are the interplay between diverse political actors and structures formed by social relationships. States, organizations, and rules shared between political agents are commonly constructed in the social context.[44] Research on constructivist theory is not as popular among Chinese researchers as liberalism and realism.[45] According to Xue Li and Xiao Huanrong, in 2006, the number of Chinese constructivist researchers was around forty, including Yuan Zhengqing, Fang Zhangping, Fan Juhua, and Qin Yaqing.[46] However, the number of scholars in constructivism in China has been growing incrementally since then.

In constructivism, *idea* and *identity* are the independent variables, much like *national interest* is the independent variable in realist theory. Marc Lanteigne argued that in a state's foreign policy development, its idea is equally important as its responsible internal institutions, its government, and other actors.[47] According to constructivists, ideas are being constructed that affect China's future foreign policy goals. Constructivists focus on the contents of policy ideas, arguing that what China wants depends on its national ideas about how to achieve foreign policy goals.[48]

Qin Yaqing, a constructivist in China, argues that the more positively a state identifies itself with international society, the more cooperative its strategic culture is and the less inclined it is to seek a zero-sum interpretation of security interests.[49] According to Qin, China's positive self-identification with international society shapes China's definition of its national interest as well as its international behavior. Qin further argues that in international relations, the idea of any debate should be plural in nature, whereby Chinese ideas and narratives can enrich the discussion by contributing new ideas to non-Western theories.

Qin's position is informed by social constructivism and Chinese philosophical traditions, and it is further motivated by two key Chinese ideas: *process* and *relationality*;[50] process plays a crucial role in international relations and relationality is the core concept in processual constructivism. The independent ontology of social processes plays a meaningful role in constructing international norms and state identities. Qin argues that social interactive processes and social relations have been neglected in the study of international relations after his critical review of Waltz, Robert Keohane, and Alexander Wendt.[51] He further argues that processes and relations are two important factors in the Chinese sociocultural context and key concepts of Chinese political philosophy.[52]

According to Qin, it is easier to understand why the DOC is considered an effective and meaningful development from the Chinese perspective in the midst of the SCS disputes. The overall assessment of achievements in the DOC is positive in the Chinese way of thinking. In an interview, Qin said that the ASEAN states wanted to set up a binding document, which they called a Code of Conduct on the SCS, but after a series of discussions, China and ASEAN set aside the binding force debate to increase the flexibility in cooperation. Qin further states that many Western scholars may think this type of regional process does not lead to regional integration. Counterintuitively, Qin stresses lesser-known Chinese ways of forming regional integration or cooperation: informal relations, processes, and nonbinding consensus.[53]

Lanteigne's argument is similar to Qin's; that is, China is much more sensitive to the manner in which its identity and its foreign policies are perceived abroad.[54] He explores the shift in China's approach to international institutions from suspicion to active participation. China has access to various tools in the international system that it can follow to promote the idea that the country is returning to the great-power status it once enjoyed centuries ago. The ways China identifies itself in international society and forms relations with other actors (states and global organizations) provide the framework for China's foreign policymaking.[55] Lai-Ha Chan further argues that China's approach to international norms or other types of institutions derives from rational *utilitarian* calculations, as observed in China's recognition of international norms.[56]

Yan points out that constructivism is not yet a mature discipline and remains stuck at the academic level.[57] He argues that the lessons of human authority and morality could lead China to a differentiated way of rising, and that China should not be hypocritical but instead openly recognize that it is one of the major powers to provide economic and philosophical guidance for developing countries. Yan suggests specific foreign policy in support of his arguments, such as zero tariffs in trade and the democratization of international relations.[58]

Opening a Black Box

In regards to the internal process of decision-making, Andrew Nathan and Andrew Scobell provide a comprehensive study. China's Politburo (PB) and the Politburo Standing Committee (PBSC) are the levels at which the country's significant foreign policy decisions are formed. The PBSC provides the final approval when the Central Leading Small Groups (CLSG) recommend policies, and it also consults with the CLSG on relevant issues. Among China's CLSGs, the Foreign Affairs CLSG and the State Security CLSG work across the fields of security, foreign affairs, and defense. Unlike the US National Security Council, the Foreign Affairs CLSG makes decisions rather than coordinating advice from other agencies.[59] However, at the Eighteenth National Party Congress Third Plenum in November 2013, it was proposed that the Chinese National Security Committee be formed to assume the role of coordination. The Committee was subsequently established shortly after the Plenum.

One of the earliest studies on the SCS focuses on China's overall policy toward the disputes over the Paracel and Spratly Islands from China's ocean policy viewpoint. Marwyn Samuels approached China's policy toward the disputes over the Paracel and Spratly Islands that were driven by a modified irredentist interpretation.[60] This analysis is related to a view that China's actions in the SCS will not be "expansive" but will instead constitute a relatively passive claim.

Even though there is comprehensive and general research on foreign policy and diplomacy decision-making processes, it is still challenging to connect a specific decision to a single event and its decision-making process due to outsiders' lack of access to the internal dynamics of such events. However, it is worth collating cases to deepen the analysis. To cite one clear example, when the US and China were negotiating President Richard Nixon's visit to China in 1972, the PB issued the negotiating instructions to Chinese diplomats. The PB also decided that China would conduct missile exercises in the East China Sea and the Taiwan Strait to resist the Clinton administration's allowing Taiwanese president Lee Teng-hui's visit to the US.[61] Liu Huaqing also wrote in his autobiography that the action to occupy six islets in the Spratly Islands in 1988 was an exclusive Central Military Commission decision approved by Deng Xiaoping.[62] Despite the existence of studies on the overall foreign policymaking process and authorities in China,[63] it is necessary to conduct further intensive and focused study on China's diplomatic action toward the SCS dispute—specifically the relevant internal decision-making process.

You Ji, and Ian Storey and Carlyle Thayer, conduct an inductive analysis of the SCS issue. In You Ji's research on China's maritime policy, he suggests a "one-plus strategy" by Xi Jinping's government.[64] This refers to the diplomatic stance that China takes only after receiving provocation from other claimants. Therefore, the assertiveness of China in the SCS should be analyzed from a different perspective. Assertiveness serves no Chinese vital interests at home and abroad, and Beijing is well aware of that. However, Beijing's concern for state stability always outweighs that of international perception. When state stability is threatened, China does not seek to achieve a benign external image by maintaining a peaceful attitude; at such times, its assertiveness becomes visible.

Storey and Thayer provide analyses of various incidents that occurred in the SCS region over more than two decades and analyze Chinese behavior inductively.[65] They observed continuity in Chinese assertive behavior despite the intentions of the 2002 DOC, which was meant to encourage self-restraint against dispute escalation. Interestingly, in their explanation of the Sino–Vietnamese friction in the SCS in the late 2000s, they argue that Beijing may have attempted to pressure Hanoi into accepting a joint exploration and production agreement covering energy fields located off the Vietnamese coast but within Vietnam's declared exclusive economic zone.

Storey and Thayer's approach toward China's diplomacy in the SCS contributes to research into intensified case studies and critical interpretation of political rhetoric.[66] For example, Storey and Thayer's observation provides a different interpretation of Deng's sovereignty-shelving formula. First, assertive enforcement is not exempted from feasible options in China's diplomacy to push joint development; in other words, the principle of joint development does not always mean peaceful cooperation. Second, joint development is not entirely separated from the sovereignty issue insofar as a claimant refuses to conduct joint development in the area over which its sovereignty is believed to exist. Storey and Thayer's study highlights the continuity of China's actions and rhetoric during the 1990s and 2000s. Further research into the changes and continuities in China's diplomacy with regard to the SCS is still required to approach the issue more comprehensively.

Dingding Chen and Jianwei Wang point out the role that interest groups within Chinese society play in China's foreign policymaking. In Chinese society, various social and interest groups put forward their opinions and seek to influence policy directions and outcomes in the policy circle.[67] Chen and Wang's analysis facilitates a reconsideration of China's political environment. They argue that China's foreign policy is an extension of China's domestic economy and social development.[68]

The *Qiushi Journal* is published by the Central Committee of the Communist Party of China and features studies on the SCS dispute. Around 60 percent of the articles in *Qiushi Journal* are written by Communist Party of China and state leaders as well as senior officials at the ministerial or provincial level.[69] The journal is introduced as "a platform for issuing and interpreting the policies of China's ruling party."[70] The English edition of the *Qiushi Journal*, which was launched in October 2009, describes itself as "a convenient channel through which Chinese and foreign readers can gain a better understanding of China's affairs."[71] It should be kept in mind that this journal presents official messages from the Communist Party of China. Table 1 shows the number of articles in the *Qiushi* English edition that contained "South China Sea" in their title or main texts more than once. The table further shows the contexts in which the keyword "South China Sea" was mentioned. Some of the following articles were not originally written in English and were translated from articles previously published in Chinese. The counted articles appeared in the English edition. The table indicates

Table 1. Articles Published in *Qiushi* Journal that Have "South China Sea" as a Keyword

Year	Issue	Title
2009	—	—
2010	—	—
2011	3 (4)	"The Formation of China's Sovereignty over the South China Sea Islands and the Origins of the South China Sea Dispute" (Li 2011)
2012	—	—
2013	—	—
2014	6 (1)	"Innovations in China's Diplomatic Theory and Practice under New Circumstances" (Yang 2014)
2015	—	—
2016	8 (3)	"China's Major-Country Diplomacy in 2015" (Wang 2016)
	8 (3)	"Pursuing Innovation in China's Diplomatic Theory and Practice to Achieve New Progress in Diplomatic Initiatives" (Yang 2016)

that the Communist Party of China initially focused on the sovereignty claim in the SCS—and later shifted toward a strategy of exercising effective diplomacy.

China's Diplomacy and Negotiation: A New Analytical Framework

The preceding discussion of the traditional international relations theories sought to define the nature of the SCS dispute by interpreting it through the basic assumptions of each theory. The deficiency of their interpretations is that these theories incorrectly assume that the relevant countries of the SCS disputes go through a process of conflict and cooperation to achieve the same goal. Institutionalists, for example, argue that China and related countries diversify and expand the framework of cooperation in pursuit of institutional achievements. Realists argue that each country's SCS policy is established for the sake of self-help and survival. Liberals acknowledge that countries can pursue absolute gains based on their specific needs so that a win-win game—rather than focusing on relative gains, which often lead to a zero-sum game—is possible. However, how the diversity of interests pursued by each country can result in dispute settlement is not the primary concern of liberals.

Roger Fisher and William Ury's previously described orange quarrel refers to a situation in which negotiations become locked in a stalemate because the negotiators focus only on positions that conflict with each other and fail to grasp the underlying interests that exist separately from positions. The positions raised by the negotiators are conflicting, but the premise exists that the underlying interests (desires and concerns) are complementary. As Fisher and Ury write, "A close examination of the underlying interests will reveal the existence of many more interests that are shared or compatible than ones that are opposed."[72] If all parties involved in the negotiation have the same interests (i.e., interests that are destined to conflict), the negotiation will inevitably break down. However, Fisher and Ury assert that such a situation "is almost never the case."[73] They argue that the interests of the parties involved in negotiation are very diverse and can be made into complementary combinations. For example, at the time of the Egyptian–Israeli peace treaty, the *positions* of Egypt and Israel were conflicting. Israel wanted to keep some of the Sinai for itself; Egypt, on the other hand, urged Israel to return the Sinai to Egyptian sovereignty. However, both parties' underlying *interests* were complementary. What Israel wanted was security and to be free from Egyptian troops' threat on the Israeli-Egyptian border. What Egypt wanted was different—to avoid ceding territory to yet another foreign conqueror.

One might say that the negotiating parties can quarrel over the same interest and inevitably end up in a zero-sum dispute. However, even if they have the same interest, the nature of an interest is different depending on whose it is. Even if China and Vietnam have the same interest motivated by economic considerations, if the economic interest for China is to gain international support for joining the World Trade Organization, the economic considerations for Vietnam could be signing free trade agreement between ASEAN and China. Even if China and Vietnam have the same economic considerations of potential natural gas resources surrounding an atoll, the two countries' objectives of developing and exploiting the natural gas may not be identical in every way.

The orange quarrel exemplifies the dynamic this book seeks to address. It is necessary to distinguish between China's positions and its underlying interests in the SCS disputes. Because the publicly available diplomatic documents are clearly designed for domestic and foreign audiences, the messages are based on positions. Nevertheless, these documents contain the collective underlying interests of the country without the bias that individual diplomats or politicians may have, and this book seeks to understand

China's underlying interests by analyzing objective records of diplomacy and negotiation without permitting that understanding to be colored by the leanings of individual officials.

In their seminal work on principled negotiation, Fisher and Ury state that "negotiation is a process of communicating back and forth for the purpose of reaching a joint decision."[74] For their part, Laurie Weingart and Mara Olekalns see that the negotiation process receives less definitional attention than the input (e.g., negotiator) and outcome (e.g., distribution of resources).[75] David Lax and James Sebenius, scholars who value process in negotiation, define negotiation as "a process of potentially opportunistic interaction by which two or more parties, with some apparent conflict, seek to do better through jointly decided action than they could otherwise."[76]

This book aims to achieve two research goals: first, to find the principles of Chinese diplomatic behavior; and second, to analyze and compare the negotiating patterns and efficiency of China's diplomatic efforts to maintain its claims and protect its interests in the SCS dispute. China's activities may be explained through an interpretation of China's establishment and management of diplomacy. The SCS dispute provides various combinations of negotiation between one regional power (China) and small- and medium-sized Southeast Asian states—combinations that constitute examples of China's maneuvers in different diplomatic settings.

The period after 2000 poses a couple of analytic points. Chinese foreign policy is symbolized by "harmony with difference" advocated by Jiang Zemin, which was followed by the broader concept of a "harmonious world."[77] Additionally, China sought multilateral approaches to the SCS disputes after 2000; however, it displayed a strategic shift into aggressive behavior in the late 2000s.[78] The period is critical to observe China's immediate diplomatic changes before and after it became the second-largest economy in the world in 2010—and beyond.

This book seeks to contribute to the current discourse on the SCS disputes by proposing a close connection between IR theory and China's diplomacy, claims, underlying interests, and patterns of diplomacy—from the Chinese point of view. This book focuses on the continuities in China's utilization of various sets of diplomacy, arguing that China has been involved in bilateral, trilateral, and multilateral diplomacy in the SCS disputes. Meanwhile, China has continuously maintained its indisputable sovereignty claim over the SCS. This book, therefore, approaches the bottom line of the claim as the diplomatic platform changes and the expected negotiating effects are varied.

The main purpose of diplomacy is to "enable states to secure the objectives of their foreign policies without resort to force."[79] Foreign policy, in turn, is established in accordance with the protection of national interests. The negotiation process as a tactical aspect of diplomacy is, therefore, intended to maximize China's bargaining capacity and protect its interests, reduce animosity, and create an environment conducive to China's rising without strengthening "China threat theory," which is the term often employed by the Chinese government to critique foreign countries' antagonistic approaches toward China. This study into China's diplomacy in the SCS context examines China's national and core interests, the evolution of the regional political situation, and China's diversification of diplomacy in the ever-changing security environment. China has initiated and participated in various diplomatic attempts—including bilateral, multilateral, track-one, and track-two diplomacy—to protect its national and core interests.[80]

The SCS—the geographic center of this research—is called *Nanhai* in Chinese (Mandarin), which means "South Sea." It is surrounded by six claimants—China, Taiwan, Vietnam, Philippines, Brunei, and Malaysia. The SCS consists of four groups of islands—the Pratas Islands (Dongsha Qundao in Chinese), the Paracel Islands (Xisha Qundao), the Macclesfield Bank (Zhongsha), and the Spratly Islands (Nansha). The SCS stretches from the Taiwan Strait in the north to the Malacca Strait in the south. Among the island groups in the SCS, the Macclesfield Bank has inspired few significant challenges in the claimants' interactions; moreover, it is permanently submerged. Therefore, the question of exercising control over the Macclesfield Bank has not been a matter of great practical concern.[81]

The year 2002 is significant in China's diplomatic history as the year when China signed the DOC in November 2002 on the sidelines of the 8th ASEAN summit. In the 1990s, Beijing began to interact more regularly with ASEAN members to discuss diverse issues following a period of strained relationships with ASEAN during the 1960s and 1970s; however, these efforts were not enough to ease anxieties among the ASEAN countries. Therefore, China had to face the consequence—that is, the proliferation of the China threat theory. By signing the DOC in 2002, China showed that it has increased its tactical flexibility in order to mitigate fear and suspicion among other disputants in the SCS.[82]

Indisputability of Sovereignty vs. Pragmatism

Fisher and Ury describe the principles that lead to successful negotiations,[83] but are their principles applicable to China's negotiations in the SCS? To find out, this book first investigates the underlying interests of China; and second, assuming that the underlying interests of China and other negotiating parties are complementary, it analyzes how the underlying interests of China are reflected in its negotiation process. A key question that emerges is which data can most effectively uncover China's underlying interests. Documents released before, during, and after the negotiations, publications including government position papers, and memoirs of related political figures are critical sources used in this study. Changes in China's bargaining behavior provide insight into understanding the country's bottom line. This book contains an analysis of negotiation documents that include China's bilateral code of conduct with the Philippines, the Chinese version of the code of conduct draft prepared for ASEAN–China negotiation, the Philippines' version of the code of conduct draft prepared for ASEAN–China negotiation, the ASEAN declaration on the SCS, and the ASEAN–China declaration on the SCS. The data used is categorized into bilateral, trilateral, and multilateral negotiation groups.

To effectively analyze these documents, process tracing is used for observing shifts in China's bargaining behavior by categorizing data over different periods. This approach is particularly useful for identifying changes in an actor's interests during negotiations by classifying and analyzing documents across various time frames. Negotiation documents serve as ideal sources for process tracing, as variations in these documents over time and differences in drafts demonstrate how each party's underlying interests have evolved.[84]

The simultaneous use of qualitative document analysis and process tracing is common in such studies.[85] In this book, collected documents are examined as text, process, and context. For instance, Agreement A signed by China in 1995 and Agreement B signed in 2002 offer valuable data for document analysis, allowing researchers to explore the background of each signing (process), the content of each agreement (text), and the Chinese government's evaluation over time (context). Through process tracing, the researcher can track how China's underlying interests have developed by noting which clauses or sentences in negotiation documents were retained, omitted, or newly added.

Fisher and Ury highlight a practical communication problem that occurs during negotiations, namely that negotiators "talk merely to impress third parties or their own constituency."[86] Robert Putnam conceptualized *constituency* as a win-set and used it to study negotiation behaviors between democratic and nondemocratic states. The audience issue is a significant constraint that influences the negotiation process from start to finish. Hence, the audience issue belongs to a constant variable. Tracking the change of negotiation documents over time is a valid approach, and this method continues to offer valuable insights into understanding China's underlying interests.

The research on China's SCS policy can be differentiated from the research domain investigating China's foreign policy in general and China's involvement in international conflicts in particular. First, from China's perspective, the SCS is not an international issue; like some of its other core interests (such as Taiwan, Tibet, and Xinjiang), the SCS is considered a domestic issue *within* China. However, the disparity arises from the different recognition of the fundamentals of this dispute. In contrast to the Chinese perspective, and due to the multiplicity of regional claimants as well as the variety of international actors interested in the SCS, other states perceive the SCS disputes to be international and consider China to be simply one of the claimants among other equals in this dispute. This is a massive gap in perception between Chinese and non-Chinese discourses. Therefore, SCS disputes can be defined as neither purely domestic Chinese issues nor as international conflicts. This complexity of the SCS disputes creates difficulties in finding explanations from theories of the Chinese foreign policy decision-making process. Therefore, this book collects relevant empirical sources to answer the research questions.

This book identifies the continuities and changes in China's diplomacy regarding the SCS. This research involves the interpretation that emerges from the collected cases with rearranged findings. Thus, the research attempts to create a holistic picture of historical episodes. These characteristics of inductive research are often associated with area studies.[87] The keywords in this book are China's diplomacy, negotiation, and the SCS disputes. As a diplomatic actor, China has various tools in the international system that it can employ to promote its strategic goals and simultaneously deter neighbors from following the so-called China threat theory. Drawing on experiences of the 1997–98 Asian Financial Crisis and gaining membership in various international organizations, China began to develop its capacity to employ diplomatic options. The SCS disputes, one of the keywords, are a prime example of multiparty conflicts, where various states have laid claims to small islets, their surrounding waters, seabed, and subsoil.[88]

Operationalization is significant in defining and measuring variables that consist of keywords. Literature on the analysis of diplomacy in general terms is spread over various sets of operationalization. Sorin Fetic suggests an example of dichotomous qualitative variables of defense diplomacy.[89] Practical analysis on diplomacy begins with choosing meaningful indices that adequately support an argument—in other words, "properties which are easy to measure are not always the most valuable."[90] Moreover, the most valuable patterns in phenomena are often difficult to distill into simple measurement units. In cases of dealing with variables that are barely operationalized, an arbitrary convention could be considered the rule of thumb. In this book, the primary purpose of the analysis is to explain diplomacy and negotiation, which often appear abstract and ambiguous, by breaking down their language into comparable elements to be assessed.

This research includes primary and secondary sources. Primary sources encompass Chinese official bodies, publications, memoirs, and public statements, as well as negotiation records and documents. Considering the balance of interpretation and perspective, primary sources from outside China—such as other disputants in the SCS—would be essential. Secondary sources disseminating analysis of facts from media, books, journal articles, conference papers, and columns will provide an understanding of the current research tendencies. In addition, material in the Chinese language is intensively surveyed to understand Chinese points of view on diplomacy.

This research proposes two main ideas to see if they are true. First, principles of indisputability and pragmatism in China's diplomacy have increased China's bargaining capacity and diversification of diplomacy in the SCS disputes. Second, the variance in China's diplomatic position toward the SCS disputes has turned these conflicts into dynamic entities, marked by both tension and cooperation.

The first proposed idea consists of two variables that make a set of causal relations. The independent variable is China's diplomacy, which is defined by its two main diplomatic principles: indisputability of sovereignty and pursuit of pragmatism in other issues. These principles were inherited from the axiom of "shelving dispute and seeking joint development," which was promulgated by Deng Xiaoping in the 1970s. The two pillars of China's diplomacy in the SCS disputes—indisputability of sovereignty and pragmatism—have continued to influence China's relations with the claimants and external actors beyond the SCS, although China's sovereignty claim has been further specified over time in accordance with the development of international norms.

The independent variable (i.e., China's diplomacy) is put in the first proposed idea as follows: principles of indisputability and pragmatism in China's diplomacy have increased China's bargaining capacity and led to diplomatic diversification in the SCS disputes. The first part of the dependent variables is China's diplomatic diversification and bargaining capability; *diversification* in China's diplomacy refers to its diplomatic channels as discussed in chapter 4, and *capability* is assessed by observing a China that achieves what it wants through such interactions. In order to assess capability, it is necessary to define the interests that China maintains in the SCS. In chapter 3, China's interests in the SCS are analyzed along with China's official claims and its underlying interests. China's official claims have not changed since the founding of the People's Republic of China in 1949; however, China's underlying interests in the SCS have had turning points in response to regional and domestic circumstances and needs. By identifying its national interests—both official and underlying—China's bargaining capability can be assessed in terms of how and whether China has been able to further those interests through diplomacy.

In order to assess the relationships between China's diplomatic principles and its bargaining capability, it is necessary to determine to what extent China has successfully advanced its national interests. China's bargaining capability can be assessed in terms of whether China has advanced its interests. This book discusses China's national interests in the SCS, and based on those interests, further assesses whether China's capability to achieve the objectives associated with those interests through diplomacy has increased or diminished. In order to test the first hypothesis, the book discusses whether the principles of indisputable sovereignty and pragmatism have affected China's capability to deal effectively with related actors through diplomatic means.

This book defines China's national interests in the SCS and identifies how its respective priorities have changed over time. Defining China's national interests necessitates a preliminary study before assessing China's bargaining capability. In order to identify China's underlying interests, this book separates China's official claims from its bottom-line claims. In both China's bottom-line and official claims, it is found that the principle of indisputable sovereignty has been pursued.

Another dependent variable is the changing patterns in the SCS disputes represented by cooperation and conflict. The fluctuation from stabilization to conflict escalation was affected by two different ways in materializing the principles mentioned above: increasing bargaining diversification and bargaining capability. In complementing existing literature, the book argues that, in a form of readdressing the hypotheses, Chinese effort in adopting contradicting principles of indisputability and pragmatism have increased China's diversification and bargaining capacity in the SCS dispute. Here, diversification is analyzed in various diplomatic platforms and bargaining capacity is operationalized by China's capacity to force its national interests through the diplomatic platforms.

TWO

History, Tradition, and Principles

> The three major tasks for the Chinese People in the 1980s are to make intensified efforts in the socialist modernization drive, strive to bring about reunification . . . oppose hegemonism and safeguard world peace.
>
> —Deng Xiaoping, 1982

> We do not seek to dominate regional affairs or establish any sphere of influence.
>
> —Xi Jinping, 2014

Diplomacy is the process designed to pursue coexistence among actors with different interests in the international system. Relations among countries and the international system change; therefore, the virtue of diplomacy in Western literature is described as innovation, creativity, and experimentation in finding ways and terms by which rival entities and ways of living can coexist and flourish.[1] This chapter focuses on the evolving idea and practice of diplomacy in China since Deng Xiaoping defined the framework of diplomacy that was integral to China's national development and economic plan—the reform and opening-up policy. Therefore, the discussion on diplomacy and diplomatic principles elaborated in this chapter focuses on China's historical context. From a strategic point of view, a country's diplomacy supports that country's national goals through negotiations under various conditions. No country pursues the same diplomatic strategy over time, and no country has the same national goals when it comes to the negotiation table. This chapter thus focuses on the framework of *principles* that support foreign policy decisions in China's diplomatic history.

The primary objectives of China's diplomacy in the mid-2000s were safeguarding national independence and state sovereignty, creating an international environment favorable to China's reform and opening up policy and modernization drives, maintaining world peace, and promoting common development.[2] The principle of indisputable sovereignty is one of two main principles, along with pragmatism, that form China's diplomacy. The norm of sovereignty is a relatively contemporary one in Chinese history. The context of interpreting the norm is important because it influences China's diplomatic principles. China endorses sovereignty and territorial integrity as part of its core interests. In the *Peaceful Development White Paper* published in 2011, China's core interests are specified:

> China is firm in upholding its core interests which include the following: *state sovereignty, national security, territorial integrity and national reunification, China's political system* established by the Constitution and overall *social stability*, and the basic safeguards for ensuring *sustainable economic and social development.*[3] (emphasis added)

State sovereignty appears first among the core interests listed in the *White Paper*. Indisputable sovereignty has emerged as China's fundamental principle in the South China Sea disputes since the 1980s.[4] Along with the sovereignty principle, China also backs territorial integrity in both domestic and foreign policymaking and when it responds to other states' policies. China's stance on other countries' domestic issues is intrinsically neutral because of the noninterference principle that is part of the Five Principles of Peaceful Coexistence and China's demand that other countries not intervene in Chinese domestic affairs. Therefore, on principle, other countries' domestic issues cannot possibly incur China's proactive response, including issues concerning Responsibility to Protect (R2P), such as political violence and crimes against humanity. However, if those domestic issues in other sovereign states affect the territorial integrity of China, the state reacts. A precedent-setting incident matters to China's territorial integrity.

Territorial Integrity and Territorial Expansion

Does the territorial integrity principle imply a policy of territorial expansion? Ryan Griffiths discusses that China holds its current territorial claims firmly and insists on its territorial integrity principle; and by the same logic, China would have little interest in claiming to supersede other states' sovereignty and their respective territorial integrity claims.[5] In other words, China upholds the principle of inviolable sovereignty and does not maintain a double standard regarding this principle. On his expectation of China's territorial expansion, Taylor Fravel also argues that the benefits to China of territorial expansion are limited, although the power transition theory and offensive realism indicate pessimistic views on China's future aggression in territorial claims.[6] His argument is based on the economic interdependence with neighboring countries on which China's current rising status heavily relies. Both Ryan Griffiths and Fravel indicate that China's territorial expansion is not a priority; however, disputed Chinese lands and waters make the meaning of territorial expansion far more complicated. China claims, for example, that the Paracel and Spratly Islands indisputably belong to China, and China's state sovereignty gives grounds for Chinese activities on them. On the other hand, other claimants view China's expansionism in the South China Sea as leading to claims and interventions affecting other littoral states' territorial integrity.

China's interpretation of the sovereignty norm showcases the peculiarity of Chinese diplomatic principle-building. From a specific country's point of view, it is difficult to find a balance between defining the distinctiveness of the country and making relevant connections with the existing discourse in the subject research area. Research on both the former and latter is equally critical to define the balance. The study of China's unique situation is not only pursued by Chinese scholars but also by non-Chinese researchers. For example, A. Doak Barnett in 1991 argued that "China will continue to undergo profound changes, but at its own pace and in its own distinctive way."[7] His argument aligns with the Chinese leader who assumed power two and a half decades later. In China under Xi Jinping, the pursuit of diplomacy has been redirected by the complexity of the peaceful development concept and the newly introduced idea—the Chinese dream—which represented the new leadership's vision of rejuvenating China in all dimensions, including diplomacy, while implying additional steps along with the previous leadership's harmonious world and peaceful development agendas. Xi Jinping pointed out that China's diplomacy highlighted the significance of choices to enable "the Chinese dream and enrich the strategic thinking of peaceful development."[8]

Quansheng Zhao argues that Chinese foreign policy behavior contains two contrary aspects: rigidity and flexibility.[9] He agrees that rigidity and flexibility are found in other countries' foreign policies; however, he focuses on "the Chinese style of political rhetoric," citing Lucian Pye's statement.[10] Realistic decision-making affects China's behavior, though what China considers its most prioritized interests could precipitate so-called Chinese characteristics. Different motivations lead to different foreign policy choices.

Zhao points out that economic issues tend to bring flexibility into China's policy options and these issues are pertinent to the least influential motivation. Meanwhile, China's domestic politics affect both the pursuit of flexibility and rigidity in foreign policy according to the degree of decentralization and centralization of political power.[11] Zhao's argument is appropriate and could be rephrased as stating that Chinese national interests affect its external behavior; however, different motivations lead to different policy choices. The prioritization of those different motivations requires the analysis of Chinese diplomacy with Chinese characteristics. Yaqing Qin studies the continuity of China's international strategy through its changes.[12]

As socialism with Chinese characteristics gained significance during Deng's era, "Chinese characteristics" became a flexible term adopted in various development domains. For example, Yizhou Wang describes the economic achievement of China's reform and opening up as a competitive market economy with Chinese characteristics.[13] Tingyang Zhao, an influential philosopher at the Chinese Academy of Social Sciences, writes that China could become a new kind of great power—one that is responsible for the whole world, but in a different way than other empires in history.[14] Feng Zhang agrees with the necessity of studying China's diplomatic philosophy and notes that the "attempt to define China as a new great power is part of the larger political and intellectual project to . . . develop a Chinese diplomatic philosophy for its foreign relations."[15] The nature of Chinese foreign policy is "unidentifiable" according to Ashok Kapur. Kapur argues that "the development of China's diplomatic thought is still a work in progress since the mid-1800s" and the "proper role of diplomacy, military force and core interests remains unsettled in the thinking and practices of China's leaders post-Mao, post-Deng Xiaoping and post-Hu Jintao."[16]

Peaceful Coexistence: One Side of the Coin

China claims that the state holds the principle of inviolable sovereignty without double standards, in other words, China adheres to the norm of sovereignty and does not interfere with other states' sovereignty and their territorial integrity claims. Where does this tradition come from? How China treats other states based on the norm of sovereignty is reflected in the Five Principles of Peaceful Coexistence. The Five Principles were born during an interstate dispute involving China and India in the early 1950s. Premier Zhou Enlai suggested peaceful coexistence to Jawaharlal Nehru, prime minister of India, in the talks on Tibet that were held from December 1953 to April 1954. The joint statement between China and India referred to as the Five Principles of Peaceful Coexistence consists of five clauses: first, mutual respect for territorial integrity and sovereignty; second, mutual nonaggression; third, noninterference in each other's internal affairs; fourth, equality and mutual benefit; and, lastly, peaceful coexistence.

Shortly after the birth of New China in 1949, Chairman Mao Zedong stated many times that China was ready to establish diplomatic relations with all countries that were willing to observe the Five Principles. These principles were expounded in the Common Program adopted by the First Session of the National Committee of the Chinese People's Political Consultative Conference on September 29, 1949. Mao also stated the principles at the proclamation ceremony marking the founding of the People's Republic of China (PRC) that embodied the major content of the Five Principles of Peaceful Coexistence. The formation of the Five Principles was influenced by China's relations with neighboring India and Burma. The Five Principles were initially adopted to guide relations with these two countries. After China and India established diplomatic relations in 1950, the Tibet issue arose between the two countries. The PRC government insisted that all the privileges inherited by India in Tibet should be revoked. In a spirit of good neighborliness and guided by the policy of peaceful coexistence, China agreed to negotiate with India on their relationship to Tibet.

The Sino–India meetings were held in Beijing from December 31, 1953, to April 29, 1954. Zhou Enlai put forward for the first time the Five Principles of Peaceful Coexistence. In response, Jawaharlal Nehru agreed that the Five Principles should be taken as the guiding principles for the negotiations. This was incorporated into the "Agreement Between the People's Republic of China and the Republic of India on Trade and Intercourse Between Tibet Region of China and India" signed on April 24, 1954, in Beijing. The Five Principles were affirmed in their entirety as principles guiding China's international relations for the first time.

In June 1954, Zhou Enlai visited India and Burma—both of which share land borders with China. The Joint Statement of the Prime Ministers of China and India was issued on June 28 and the Joint Statement of the Prime Ministers of China and Burma was announced on the next day. Both statements affirmed the Five Principles as guiding elements of their bilateral relations. The Ten Principles for conducting international relations adopted in the Asian–African Conference convened in Bandung, Indonesia, in 1955 were a continuation and development of the Five Principles. The Five Principles are opposed to the power politics that dominated international relations.[17]

The diplomatic implications of the Five Principles can be found in Mao Zedong's remarks:

> To achieve *a lasting world peace*, we must further develop our friendship and co-operation with the fraternal countries in the camp of socialism and *strengthen our solidarity with all peace-loving countries*. We must endeavour to establish normal diplomatic relations on the basis of *mutual respect* for territorial integrity and sovereignty and of equality and mutual benefit with all countries willing to live together with us in peace. We must give active support to the national independence and liberation movement in countries in Asia, Africa and Latin America as well as to the peace movement and to just struggles in all countries throughout the world.[18] (emphasis added)

> The Five Principles are suited to the conditions of *China, which needs a lasting peaceful environment*. . . . To us, *stability is preferable*. There should be *stability* within our countries as well as internationally.[19] (emphasis added)

The first quotation indicates the abstract and general goals of the Five Principles while the second quotation shows a more specific and detailed need to initiate the Principles. In the first quotation, Mao said China must develop relations not only with other socialist countries but also with all countries in Asia, Africa, and Latin America. These regions were the third-world region that Mao and Zhou identified.

This practical necessity was related to China's other diplomatic strategy, "leaning on one side." After Mao Zedong's declaration of "leaning to one side" in 1949, from 1949 to 1952 China's foreign policy interests focused exclusively on Communist nations and associated revolutionary forces. Under the anti-communist strategy of the United States, China maintained the Soviet Union's support to survive and overcome its economic and technological backwardness. Only in late 1952, under the Five Principles, did China begin to cultivate unofficial relations with different groups abroad. As seen in Mao's 1954 quote on China's preference for stability, the meaning of *stability* implies a broadly applicable agenda. The call for stability continued in the post-Mao era, though for a different purpose to pacify international relations and for China to focus on reform and opening up policy. The Five Principles were also promulgated against the background of the deepening Cold War, unresolved tensions from unsettled borders, Tibet's status remaining a source of dispute between India and China, and the immediate aftermath of the Korean War.[20] The Five Principles were eventually agreed upon between India and China in 1953–54 to ease tensions.[21]

China criticized other countries' actions by invoking the Five Principles. In 1963, a Chinese newspaper editorial blamed India for not following the Principles.[22] It stated that China had consistently consolidated and further developed peaceful coexistence and friendly cooperation with countries in Asia, Africa, and Latin America. The author of the editorial argued that China had waged appropriate and necessary struggles against countries such as India that violated or wrecked the Five Principles. Premier Zhou Enlai tried to persuade Indian Prime Minister Nehru to recommit to the Principles and reiterated the Principles in 1959 before the border dispute occurred that led to the Sino–Indian War in 1962:

> As the Sino-Indian boundary has never been delimited and it is very long and very far or comparatively far from the political centres of the two countries, I am afraid that, if no fully appropriate solution is worked out by the two Governments, border clashes which both sides do not want to see may again occur in the future. And once such a clash takes place, even though a minor one, it will be made use of by people who are hostile to the friendship of our two countries to attain their ulterior objectives. There is a history of long-standing friendship but no conflict of fundamental interests between our two countries, and our Governments are initiators of the Five Principles of Peaceful Coexistence. We have no reason to allow the tension on the border between our two countries to continue.[23]

The Five Principles were even the foundation for criticizing the Soviet Union. During Sino–Soviet conflicts, differing interpretations of the Principles between China and the Soviet Union caused deep anxiety in China, increasing China's mistrust of the Soviet Union. The Communist Party of the Soviet Union, concerned about the dangers of nuclear war, saw coexistence with the West as in the mutual interest of both systems. However, according to the Chinese perspective, this was a sign of capitulation. China condemned the Soviet Union for seeking coexistence with the main enemy of world peace and the main aggressive force.

Former Chinese Premier Zhao Ziyang defined the meaning of peaceful coexistence clearly:

> If the Five Principles of Peaceful Coexistence are adhered to, countries with *different social systems* can live in harmony and maintain amicable cooperation, but if not, even countries with similar social systems may come into sharp confrontation or even conflict. Whether relations between countries are good or bad depends on whether or not they strictly adhere to these principles.[24] (emphasis added)

The emphasized part of Zhao's remarks implies that there are no superior or inferior social systems under the principle of peaceful coexistence. This theory further indicates why China disagrees with peaceful evolution and democratic peace theory. "Peaceful evolution" is a term that the Chinese government uses when critiquing Western nations' infiltration activities in other countries aimed at undermining communist regimes. "Democratic peace theory" is the liberalist idea that democracies do not go war against with one another, and that the spread of democracy ensures stability.

In post-Mao China, the Five Principles have been adopted as guiding principles in foreign policy. However, the context of interpreting the Five Principles has been transformed under the country's new circumstances. Under Jiang Zemin's leadership, the Five Principles reappeared in the form of the New Security Concept; this was first developed at the ASEAN Regional Forum summit in 1996 that drew heavily on the Five Principles. These Principles experienced a renaissance in the late 1980s and early 1990s due to international humanitarian interventions exemplified by the first Gulf War and interventions in the former Yugoslavia, Somalia, and Haiti during the 1990s. The Five Principles and later the New Security Concept were normative protections for China against such potential interventions and abuses.[25] Hu Jintao continued to maintain the Five Principles at the core of foreign policy, but he further reconciled them with his interpretation of the near-term and long-term trends of Chinese history.

The Five Principles continue to provide China with fundamental guidance in foreign policy. They have also appeared in China's recent white papers and government publications.

> China is committed to promoting peace and stability in this region. It follows the path of peaceful development and the mutually beneficial strategy of opening up, and pursues friendly cooperation with all countries on the basis of the Five Principles of Peaceful Coexistence.[26]

> They [China's armed forces] uphold *the Five Principles of Peaceful Coexistence*, conduct all-round military exchanges with other coun-

> tries, and develop cooperative military relations that are non-aligned, non-confrontational and not directed against any third party.[27]

> China unswervingly pursues an independent foreign policy of peace and promotes friendly cooperation with all countries on the basis of *the Five Principles of Peaceful Coexistence*.[28]

> It [China] resolutely protects its national independence and sovereignty and opposes foreign interference; seeks to establish and develop extensive, friendly relations with all the world's countries on the basis of *the Five Principles of Peaceful Coexistence*[29]

Based on the understanding of China's continual endorsement of the Five Principles from the 1950s to the present, the Five Principles generally have four practical applications in China's diplomacy. First, China propagates its pacific image using historical ideas. Its concern is how to successfully tackle the China threat theory suggested by Western countries. Second, China tries to defend its pattern of development with the noninterference principle. China worries about so-called peaceful evolution through Westerners' influence on internal issues such as humanitarian problems and reform of the Chinese political system. Third, the Five Principles grant China historical justification for its sovereignty and territorial concerns. Fourth, the Five Principles give normative grounds for China to advocate a multipolar international system under the equality principle.

However, in China's circumstances in the late 2000s, the Five Principles were not its ultimate guiding principles. China collides with neighboring countries on territorial and sovereignty issues such as the Sino–Indian border disputes, SCS disputes, and the East China Sea (ECS) conflict with Japan. On those occasions, we argue, the mutuality of the Principles has disappeared and unilateralism rules China's interpretation and application of the Five Principles. Therefore, any understanding of the Five Principles must stand on the understanding of historical and political contexts. Repetition of the Principles in official statements and speeches does not guarantee their coherent interpretation or application.

The philosophical roots of peaceful coexistence can be found in China's inclusivism and exclusivism. Feng Zhang raises questions regarding the traditions of Confucian foreign policy and identifies two major conceptional components: inclusivism and exclusivism.[30] Further, he argues that these components are derived from the Chinese theory of human nature, *inclusive humanism*. Zhang concludes that this inclusive tradition from history could explain contemporary Chinese foreign policy. Significantly, Zhang critically views the role of Confucianism as intellectual propaganda advocating pacifism and argues that inclusivism and exclusivism are major traditions in the history of Confucian Chinese foreign policy.

In the SCS disputes, China's peaceful coexistence principles drew unfavorable assessments. The so-called Chinese new assertiveness in the SCS in the late 2000s significantly increased doubts about the practicality of the peaceful coexistence principle.[31] However, peaceful coexistence is more closely related to China's maintenance of nonexpansive territorial policy than to a willingness to be unassertive in any issue.

Does China pursue territorial expansionism in the SCS, or is it simply being assertive? The difference between territorial expansionism and assertiveness lies in an assessment of whether China is encroaching on *new* territory that previously did *not* belong to it or is it securing territory believed to belong to China in the past and present. The difference between territorial expansionism and assertiveness is important because it could be a way to understand whether China's peaceful coexistence principles are being practiced, at least from the Chinese point of view, in the context of the SCS.

For example, in an edited book, *Power Politics in Asia's Contested Waters*, most chapters dealing with China's policies in the SCS disputes identify China's assertiveness as one of the major factors that upset the status quo.[32] However, although not all chapters of this book raise concerns about Chinese territorial expansionism, Srini Sitaraman and Alexandra Sakaki share a view in their chapters on the "Chinese army's repeated intrusions" into the Himalayan boundary with India and China's "creeping expansionism in the maritime domain" in the South and East China Seas.[33] Among China's land and maritime neighbors, India and Japan seem concerned about China's territorial expansionism. On the other hand, the other chapters in *Power Politics in Asia's Contested Waters* do not necessarily raise concerns about a territorially expansionist China. The perception of the "China threat" and, more particularly, China's expansionism is shaped by different contexts and focuses depending on other countries' geographical proximity to China and historical experiences with China.

Core Interests: It's Not All About the Nine-Dash Line

China's so-called core interests are another side of the coin of peaceful coexistence principles. China's core interests have been marked in its white papers as state sovereignty, national security, territorial integrity and national reunification, maintenance of China's political system and overall social stability, and basic safeguards for ensuring sustainable economic and social development.[34] China's core interests were mentioned by State Councilor Dai Bingguo in the US–China Strategic and Economic Dialogue in July 2009. He stated that core interests were a necessary principle of China–US relations, saying that "ensuring the long-term healthy and stable development of Sino–US relations, it is important to (pursue) a mutual understanding, respect and support each other, to protect their core interests."[35] He implied that the US has critical interests as China does and that China–US relations would be enhanced if the parties recognized and respected each other's core interests. A year later, China's core interests provided a rationale for its aggressiveness toward neighboring countries, and the expectation of China's amicable diplomacy in the SCS drastically decreased as China associated its core interest with the SCS in the late 2000s.[36]

One commonly suggested argument regarding China's policy toward the SCS disputes is that China's core interests and China's historical nine-dash line in the SCS are treated the same. The nine-dash line refers to a U-shaped line that encompasses most areas in the SCS and forms a critical part of China's historical claim in the region. The line appeared in a Nationalist government publication in 1947 as an official map and was later recognized by the PRC after its establishment in 1949 (see map 1). However, the core interests narrative has been highlighted in Chinese official documents since the 2009 US–China Strategic and Economic Dialogue and reappeared in China's white paper on *Peaceful Development* in 2011. In his memoir, former Chinese foreign minister Tang Jiaxuan wrote about the 2001 China–US air collision incident (when military aircraft from both countries collided over the SCS) and added that China and the US can develop their bilateral relations if they "fully respect and take into account each other's core interests."[37] Therefore, China's core interests were initially part of China's negotiating targets, particularly with the US in the context of preparing the "new type of great power relations" Xi Jinping suggested to Barack Obama later in 2013. It is unclear whether the "core interests" China suggested in 2009 were a sort of test to see the US response; however, the suggestion of a new type of great power relations clearly indicated that the two powers should respect each other's core interests.

On the other hand, China's nine-dash line claim was publicized in response to territorial claims in the South China Sea. Richard Heydarian argues a causal relationship between China's decision to disseminate its nine-

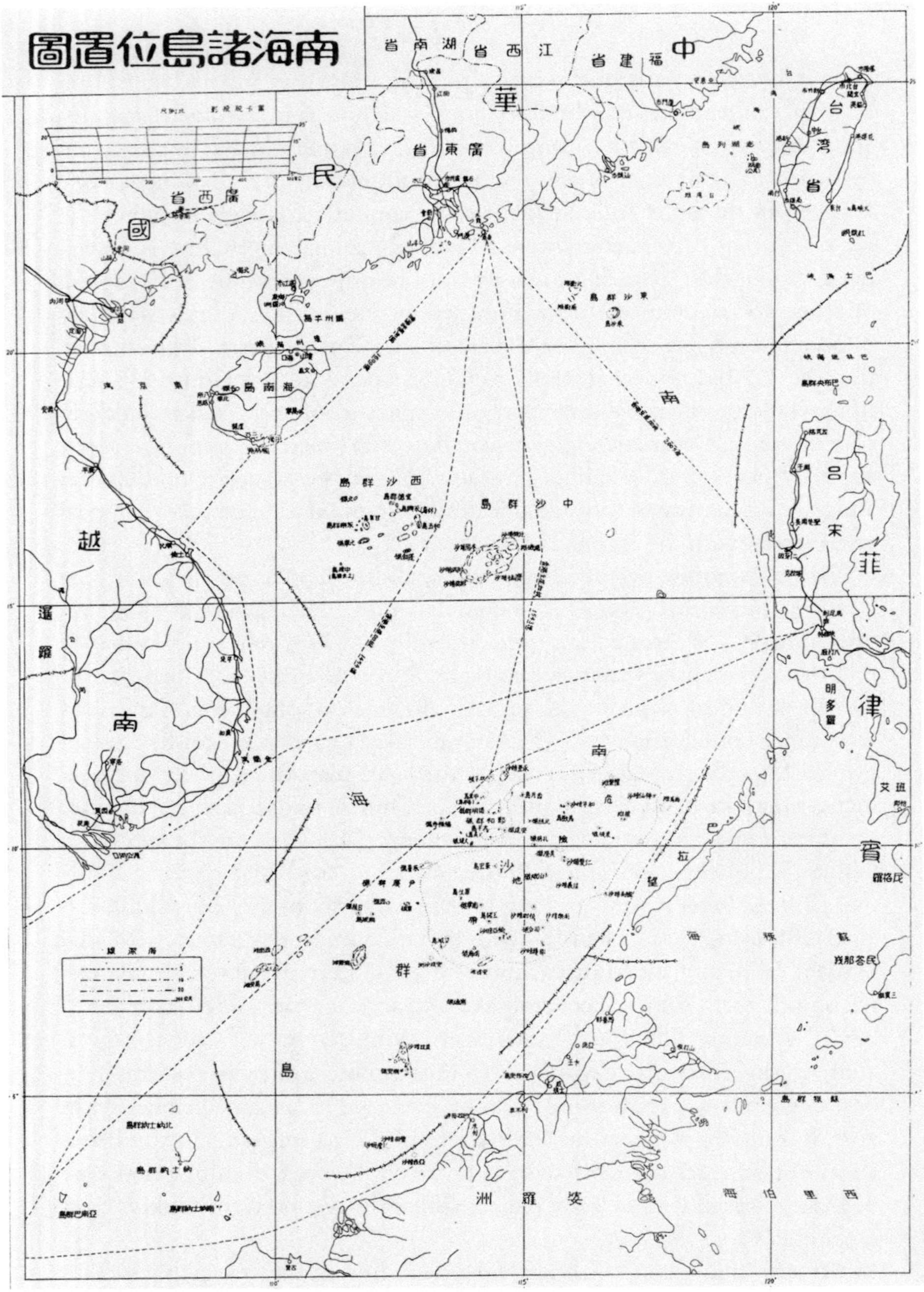

Map 1. The map of eleven dashed lines issued by the Republic of China

dash line and the external factors that catalyzed China's decision. He argues that in 2009, the joint Malaysia–Vietnam submission of their extended continental shelf claim in the South China Sea to the United Nations "irked" China and "Beijing responded by publicizing its controversial 'nine-dash line' claim" in China's officially submitted note verbale to the UN.[38]

Chinese core interests have a practical impact on regional security because the core interests refer to the "areas or issues that Beijing would be willing to employ armed force to defend."[39] In 2003 and 2004, China began to use the core interests narrative in its official sources as terminology relevant to China.[40] Before then, according to Michael Swaine, the core interests narrative had been used concerning other countries, not China.[41] A few sources identify the SCS as one of China's core interests. One of the primary sources comes from US secretary of state Hillary Clinton's remarks in 2010. In an interview regarding the Strategic and Economic Dialogue between the US and China, Clinton stated that the US did not agree with China's stance on the Tibet and Taiwan issues nor with China's argument that these were part of Chinese core interests.

> We've made it clear to the Chinese that we will not agree with them, but we're going to continue to press them. . . . And when China first told us at a meeting of the Strategic and Economic Dialogue that *they viewed the South China Sea as a core interest*, I immediately responded and said we don't agree with that. (Was that Dai Bingguo that said that to you?) Yes, yeah.[42] (emphasis added)

The official Chinese state news agency, Xinhua, disseminated a commentary that China was enabled to secure its maritime security and strategic waters "by adding the South China Sea as a 'core interest.'"[43]

China raises its core interests in the context of foreign relations and diplomacy. At the US–China Strategic and Economic Dialogue in 2009, China officially argued that the core interests should be mutually respected between the two countries. In Xi Jinping's historic visit to Kazakhstan and the following proclamation on constructing the new Silk Road Economic Belt, Xi mentioned "rendering each other firm support on major issues concerning core interests such as sovereignty, territorial integrity, security and stability" as a prerequisite condition to form a "strategic partnership."[44] In other words, China claiming its core interests in its diplomacy implies that China also mutually acknowledges its diplomatic counterparts' core interests. Therefore, China's core interests are one side of the coin that bears peaceful coexistence on the other side. In this logic, the US adhering to freedom of navigation, for instance, cannot be mutually respected by China because the US does not consistently claim that freedom of navigation operates as one of the US's internal core interests.

China's approach toward the land border and maritime territorial disputes divides into three phases based on the transformation in China's strategic interests: first, China prioritized "security" considerations before the 1970s; second, China put importance on "regional stability" in the reform and opening-up period; and, last, after 2009, China showcased "core interests" as its priority in border and maritime disputes while still protecting regional stability in balanced diplomacy.[45] However, a tautological error could be found in arguing that the SCS is important to China *because* it is a core interest. An elaboration on the existing value of the South China Sea could underpin the argument by providing the linkage and correlation between the interest and significance in the South China Sea to the core interests of China.

Evolving Tradition: Leaders and Beliefs

Since the Third Plenary Session of the Eleventh Central Committee of the Chinese Communist Party in 1978, the country's domestic tasks required setting the stage for the new period and readjusting its foreign policy.[46] The principles of shelving, or setting aside, disputes and seeking joint development appeared in Deng's speech in 1984, followed by another speech during his visit to Japan in 1986.[47] Since then, Premier Li Peng, Foreign Minister Qian Qichen, and former foreign ministers Tang Jiaxuan, Li Zhaoxing, Yang Jiechi, and Wang Yi have continuously underscored the principle of shelving disputes in their public speeches.[48]

In the *Peaceful Development* white paper published in 2011, the Chinese government proposes its solution for maritime disputes as follows:

> China . . . calls for settling disputes over territory and maritime rights and interests with neighboring countries through dialogue and negotiation. For instance, China has made a constructive proposal to *shelve disputes and seek joint development* and done its utmost to uphold peace and stability in the South China Sea, East China Sea and the surrounding areas.[49] (emphasis added)

Shicun Wu and Keyuan Zou argue that the pragmatic position can extend to China's commitment in the SCS. For example, they suggest that China and other claimants need to move a step further from the commitment to "setting aside disputes for joint development of resources" to "setting aside disputes for joint maintenance of maritime security."[50]

Officially, China's diplomacy follows the guidance of the leadership of the Chinese Communist Party and advocates theories of Marxism–Leninism, Mao Zedong thought, Deng Xiaoping theory, and Xi Jinping thought.[51] Mao's thoughts formed the basic principles of China's diplomacy: maintaining independence, opposing hegemony, peaceful coexistence, and a policy of good neighborliness.[52]

However, Marxist–Leninist and Maoist ideology have been gradually losing their functional ability to explain the ruling Party's behavior. Chinese calls for adhering to the socialist road have been largely devoid of corresponding economic content and have therefore become rhetorical.[53] Andrew Kennedy analyzes Mao Zedong's diplomatic cautiousness and military boldness and argues that Mao's national efficacy beliefs are congruent with these characteristics.[54] Mao's diplomatic concerns did not repeatedly appear after Deng's reform and opening up; however, studies define China's strategic tradition throughout the shift from Mao to Deng's era.[55]

Deng's reforms demonstrated shifts in China's identity, both in terms of how it saw itself and how other countries should treat it. Considering Alexander Wendt's theory of the international system as a social construction, during the Dengist period, China sought sweeping changes in its foreign policies and the international system's perception of the state. Yaqing Qin argues that the more positively a state identifies itself with international society, the more cooperative its strategic culture is and the less it embraces a zero-sum interpretation of security interests.[56] According to Qin, this identity shapes China's definition of its national interest as well as its international behavior. He believes that not only the constructivists but also other theoretical approaches since 1979 have reflected China's identity factor vis-à-vis international society since the Opium War in 1840.[57]

China's perception of the international system and foreign policy in the first thirty years since the establishment of the PRC in 1949 shifted in Deng's era, which was driven by the reform and opening up.[58] The Great Proletarian Cultural Revolution (1966 to 1976) marked the darkest time in China's engagement with the international system because the Cultural Revolution did not allow interaction with foreign actors. After Stalin's death in 1953,

Khrushchev did not support China's attempts to retake Taiwan by military force in 1954–55 and 1958, as well as the Sino–Indian border disputes in 1962. As a result, in the middle of the 1960s China was isolated from both East and West and Mao was concerned that, after his death, he might suffer the same fate as Stalin—condemnation by his Communist comrades and successors. This led to the Great Proletarian Cultural Revolution in 1966. Mao wanted to secure leadership that no one could threaten and eliminate political opponents within the party by promoting a strong and entirely independent China. Professing itself to be independent, that is, isolated, the country drastically reduced foreign relations.[59]

Before this policy of isolation, China took a "leaning to one side" approach and relied heavily on the Soviet Union while negatively perceiving international organizations and the US. At that time, the PRC was closely aligned with the Soviet Union and exported the communist revolution with a strong suspicion of the West, especially the US, which had supported the Nationalist government and Chiang Kai-shek until 1949. The PRC's pessimistic view of the West was also affected by its unsuccessful initial attempt in 1949 to join the UN. Mark Lanteigne argues that these negative ideas affected China's foreign policy.[60] The Korean War was another reason for China to distrust the UN. The temporary Soviet withdrawal from the UN Security Council resulted in US-led forces fighting Chinese troops up to the China–North Korea border.

Deng's view on the SCS dispute—shelving disputes and seeking joint development—was reiterated by other significant figures in China's foreign policy, such as Huang Hua, who served as Chinese foreign minister from 1976 to 1982. Moreover, Deng's approach appeared in the draft of the Code of Conduct prepared by China in 1999: "The countries concerned shall, in a spirit of 'putting aside disputes and engaging in joint development,' explore or carry out" their activities.[61]

Since the 2000s, the Chinese government has attempted to defuse tensions over the SCS and diversify its diplomatic efforts. Dai Bingguo, the state councilor in 2010, focused on preventing Chinese policy from being hijacked by aggressive nationalism in China.[62] Chinese diplomatic policy was based on the idea that China could rise peacefully soon if other countries acknowledged and welcomed its advancement and treated it as a reasonable world leader.[63]

In the 2000s, China's diplomatic initiatives helped ease neighboring countries' concerns about its assertiveness by pursuing a variety of diplomatic channels: bilateral (summit meetings, foreign aid, trade), trilateral (joint exploration), multilateral (China–ASEAN Free Trade Agreement), and extended multilateral (ASEAN Regional Forum, ASEAN Defence Ministers Meeting-Plus) platforms as well as track-two diplomacy (establishing Confucius Institutes and exchanging civilians).[64] China's utilitarian view of diplomacy constitutes its expectation and practice of diplomacy with various actors in negotiations at different levels of value and importance to China. Compared to Mao's totalitarian drive, China's foreign policy since Deng Xiaoping came to power has been guided by economic reforms and development.[65] Since Deng, China's foreign policy was driven by a utilitarian approach and multifaceted national interests were reflected in China's foreign policy aims.

Agenda-setting is given much weight in China's diplomacy and leads the discussion with the principles that China endorses. Yan has envisaged that China would prepare principles to manage territorial disputes and avoid obstacles in its cooperation with ASEAN, and his assumption was demonstrated to some extent when the Chinese foreign minister Wang Yi introduced the "Four Respects."[66]

Four Respects: The New Face of the Indisputable Sovereignty Principle

In September 2014, Foreign Minister Wang Yi visited Australia for the second annual China–Australia Diplomatic and Strategic Dialogue and introduced China's "Four Respects" principles in the South China Sea dispute. The first respect is that the dispute over the sovereignty of some reefs in the Spratly Islands is a problem of historical precedent, and historical facts should come first in handling the dispute. Second, other countries should respect international laws, specifically the United Nations Convention on the Law of the Sea (UNCLOS). Third, direct dialogue and consultation between the countries involved should be respected. Last, the joint efforts of China and ASEAN have been made to maintain peace and stability and these efforts should be respected.[67]

The Four Respects indicate that China suggests and positions the agenda in the dispute to lead negotiations in its favor. Among these four principles, China's advocacy of UNCLOS came as the second statement. In the third and fourth principles, Wang emphasized that direct dialogue and consultation between the countries involved should be respected. If Wang Yi listed the four principles in order of priority, that indicates China's diplomatic focus has expanded its focus from history to international law, diplomacy with claimants, and multilateralism, at least in its public statements.

These principles are comparable with those mentioned in China's 2011 white paper on peaceful development, which put forth the directive to "shelve disputes and seek joint development" as guidelines for upholding peace and stability in maritime areas.[68] Shelving disputes and seeking joint development also appeared in Deng Xiaoping's speech in 1984 and his subsequent speech during his visit to Japan in 1986.[69] Since then, Premier Li Peng and Foreign Ministers Qian Qichen, Tang Jiaxuan, Li Zhaoxing, Yang Jiechi, and Wang Yi have continuously underscored the shelving principle in public speeches. However, Deng's "shelving disputes and seeking joint development" proposal was too abstract to lead to any effective negotiation, especially when the Declaration on Conduct of Parties in the South China Sea failed to maintain the status quo in the region. In the early 2000s, China joined various multilateral agreements for economic cooperation, scientific exploration, joint development, and peaceful resolution of territorial disputes, such as the Treaty of Amity and Cooperation and the Joint Marine Seismic Undertaking.[70] However, the expectations for amicable diplomacy in the SCS drastically lowered as China firmly associated its core interest with the SCS in the late 2000s and demonstrated a "growing pattern of assertiveness" as observed by Western scholars.[71] Furthermore, China's participation in many regional regimes in the SCS kept the country from resolving the core of the dispute: maritime delimitation based on sovereignty.

The Four Respects proposed China's priorities regarding the SCS disputes and these priorities and principles are becoming more evident. Since the DOC was signed in 2002, China's diplomatic power has accumulated and has been tested by various attempts to change the status quo. Therefore, China's diplomatic maneuvering in the SCS utilized the Four Respects to proactively conduct bilateral negotiations and condition the involvement of external actors such as the US.

The Four Respects, of course, are not new and have been mentioned by Chinese diplomats partially and frequently over the years. In 2012, Foreign Minister Yang Jiechi placed a high priority on these principles regarding the SCS during the ASEAN Regional Forum Foreign Ministers Meeting. Yang stated that "countries concerned should first resolve their territorial disputes over the Nansha (Spratly) Islands and, on that basis, proceed to resolve the issue of maritime delimitation in the SCS in accordance with international law, the UNCLOS included."[72] Wang Yi also asserted China's sovereignty in "the South China Sea islands and their adjacent waters" during a meeting with US secretary of state John Kerry in February 2014.[73] Therefore, as long as the islands in the Spratly and their adjacent waters are considered Chinese territory, China is willing to discuss the maritime delimitation issue in the SCS, according to the UNCLOS.

China explicitly argues, through the Four Respects, that, first, the country acknowledges international law and abides by it as a legal signatory of UNCLOS. Second, China provides the littoral states with the opportunity to negotiate the waters *outside* the Spratly Islands and their adjacent waters. China has stubbornly held to indisputable sovereignty since the 1980s;[74] however, the principle of indisputable sovereignty has been more specified by the Four Respects. The possibility of engaging in negotiation as a result of discussions with the littoral states is also increasing as China concentrates its diplomatic power on prioritized targets.

China's approach toward international norms or other types of institutions has derived from rational utilitarian calculations, as observed in other cases that showcase China's recognition of international norms. These utilitarian calculations are built upon three priority blocks. First, sovereignty should be respected. Second, China should be able to make state-centric decisions. Lastly, Chinese national interests should be guaranteed at an advantage. The utilitarian view is useful to analyze China's behavior as it became a signatory of UNCLOS. China's intention to become a member of UNCLOS is indicated in its statement made upon the ratification of UNCLOS in 1996, which will be discussed in detail in chapter 5.[75] According to this statement, China seeks to "enjoy sovereign rights and jurisdiction" over the land territory in the SCS and their exclusive economic zone (EEZ) and continental shelf. China further articulates that it will conduct consultations on the "delimitation of the boundary of the maritime jurisdiction" if issues arise regarding overlapping maritime areas.

China's view, presented in the 1996 statement, has reappeared in various sources since then. China's declaration in 2006 further clarified what the country wanted to obtain by being part of UNCLOS and what consequent compulsory engagements articulated by UNCLOS China wanted to avoid. In the 2006 declaration, China made it clear that it "does not accept any of the procedures" "with respect to *all the categories of disputes* referred to in paragraph 1 (a) (b) and (c) of Article 298 of the Convention" (emphasis added). "All the categories of disputes" refers to (1) the territorial sea, (2) the EEZ, and (3) the continental shelf, and further "historic bays or titles," which refers to a coastal state's claim to certain maritime areas based on historical usage and sovereignty. Therefore, China, as a signatory of UNCLOS,

Table 2. China's Stance on Diplomacy Presented over Time

Sources	Year	China's Expectations of Diplomacy[a]
Statement on ratification of UNCLOS	1996	"The People's Republic of China will effect, *through consultations, the delimitation of the boundary of the maritime jurisdiction* with the States with coasts opposite or adjacent to China respectively on the basis of international law and in accordance with the principle of equitability" (UN Division for Ocean Affairs and the Law of the Sea 1996)
Declaration on the Conduct of Parties in the South China Sea (DOC)	2002	"The Parties concerned undertake to resolve their *territorial and jurisdictional disputes* . . . through friendly consultations and negotiations by sovereign states *directly concerned*, in accordance with universally recognized principles of international law, including the 1982 UN Convention on the Law of the Sea" (DOC 2002)
Declaration under article 298 of UNCLOS	2006	"The Government of the People's Republic of China *does not accept any of the procedures* provided for in Section 2 of Part XV of the Convention with respect to all the categories of disputes referred to in paragraph 1 (a) (b) and (c) of Article 298 of the Convention" (UN Division for Ocean Affairs and the Law of the Sea 2006)
Four Principles	2014	"China insists on *upholding the international laws on territorial disputes* and the UN Convention on the Law of the Sea. . . . *direct dialogue and consultation* between the countries involved should be respected. It has proven to be the most effective way to solve the dispute" (CCTV 2014)

[a]Emphasis added to statements on China's expectations of diplomacy.

does not accept compulsory dispute resolution procedures relating to the territorial sea, the EEZ, the continental shelf, and "historic titles."

China was able to declare such rights because UNCLOS permits member countries the privilege to do so. Article 298, "Optional exceptions to the applicability of section 2," suggests that "when signing, ratifying or acceding to this Convention or at any time thereafter, a State may, . . . declare in writing that it does not accept any one or more of the procedures . . . with respect to one or more of the following categories of disputes." Not only China but thirty-six other members of UNCLOS declared a similar intent to avoid this type of arbitration.[76]

China's setting of principles and forcing them on other claimants in the SCS dispute is another example of a peculiarly Chinese approach. Before starting negotiations, China urges its partner to understand its principles, which are usually listed by priority, as the Four Respects demonstrate. A similar example is China's Eight Principles, which were proposed to Africa. This practice enables an analysis based on China's exceptionalism. Feng Zhang argues that Chinese exceptionalism is an essential part of China's worldview.[77] He pointed out the fundamental importance of historical thinking in Chinese policymaking circles. China puts historical arguments before any other priorities in the SCS disputes, including international law, direct consultation with claimants, and China–ASEAN cooperation.

China and the One China Consensus

Taiwan (the Republic of China, ROC) has been involved in the sovereignty contest in the SCS as one of the claimants of the disputed waters for the last decades. Taiwan's involvement in the SCS disputes adds another layer of complexity to the multifaceted disputes. This section discusses how China's diplomatic principles have affected cross-strait interaction in SCS disputes and further limited Taiwan's activities in the SCS. Taiwan's claims in the SCS are similar to those of China, with a few different expectations and interpretations of international regimes and cooperation. This section also addresses the Republic of China's claims regarding the SCS disputes, its relevant activities and initiatives, and how these have been limited by China's diplomatic principles. The relevance of the One China Consensus between China and Taiwan to the SCS disputes must be examined because the One China Consensus affects the Republic of China's foreign interactions. Taiwan's initiative to stabilize the SCS is also analyzed in light of Taiwan's efforts to strengthen its position in the region.

The 1992 One China Consensus needs to be understood, particularly in relation to its impact on the SCS disputes. This consensus between China and Taiwan sets preconditions on Taiwan's foreign engagements, shaping its interactions on the global stage. In the 1992 One China Consensus, an approach of "One China" was agreed to between China and Taiwan. The Consensus was significant as it marked the beginning of efforts toward "the gradual institutionalization of the cross-strait relationship" with twenty-three signed agreements.[78] Taiwanese president Ma Ying-jeou (2008–16) reaffirmed that the One China principle is the cross-strait consensus that should be supported by the president of the ROC, "whoever that may be."[79]

Taiwan's voice in the international community has limited impact while providing Taiwan with a complicated sovereignty status. The One China Consensus bars Taiwan from participating in international and regional regimes and dialogues, including the United Nations Convention on the Law of the Sea.[80] In 2002, there was an agreement between China and ASEAN on the Declaration on the Conduct of Parties in the South China Sea that excluded Taiwan as a member state. Taiwan expressed "its protest and discontent to ASEAN and the PRC for . . . signing the Declaration on the Conduct of Parties in the South China Sea without inviting the government of the Republic of China to participate in the discussion."[81]

Despite the ROC's limited access to international dialogues concerning the SCS disputes, there are some positive exceptions. One example is the Workshop on Managing Potential Conflicts in the South China Sea. In July 1991, Taiwan, China, and Vietnam joined the Second SCS Workshop.[82] The workshop solicited participants who attended as individuals, not as representatives of countries, which enabled Taiwan to participate.[83] Taiwan has maintained its participation in the workshop through the Twenty-Fourth Workshop, which was held in 2014.

Taiwan and China share commonalities of position as well as disparities. Both Taiwan and China claim the legitimacy of nine-dash lines and their historical sovereignty. Both countries share a common ground for territorial claims, which they have maintained in the SCS over the past seven decades.[84] However, their status in the international community and their interpretation of international standards vary. Taiwan's South China Sea policy faces a dilemma: it closely aligns with China's stance, yet Taiwan seeks to uphold international standards that align with the expectations of the US-led order and global institutions.[85] The divergence between Taiwan and China toward the SCS is apparent in their stance on the US. President Ma Ying-jeou delivered a statement during his visit to Taiping (Itu Aba) Island, the largest naturally formed island in the SCS and occupied by Taiwan since 1956, in which he declared that Taiwan's activities would not contradict the US appeal for "three halts," referring to a moratorium on further land reclamation, the construction of new facilities, and the militarization of disputed features.[86]

Taiwan promulgated laws in 1998 and subsequent years regarding its maritime claims: the Law on the Territorial Sea and Contiguous Zone of the Republic of China (1998), the Law on the Exclusive Economic Zone and the

Continental Shelf of the Republic of China (1998), the Notice to Mariners on Territorial Sea Baseline, Outer Limits of the Territorial Sea and Contiguous Zone (1999), and the Marine Pollution Control Act (2000).

These laws are, in general, consistent with the UNCLOS.[87] Article 6 in the 1998 Law on the Territorial Sea states, "In the event that the territorial sea of the Republic of China overlaps with the territorial sea of adjacent or opposite countries, the delimitation shall be the *equidistant median line*" (emphasis added). Article 6 complies with Article 15 of UNCLOS, which declares that "neither of the two States is entitled . . . to extend its territorial sea beyond the median line every point of which is equidistant from the nearest points on the baselines."[88] In overlapping EEZs and the continental shelf, similarly, the ROC's relevant article in the 1998 Law on the Exclusive Economic Zone complies with the UNCLOS equivalent addressing provisional arrangements between concerned countries.

Taiwan further specifies the baselines of maritime features in the SCS that provide the measuring points for the territorial sea (12 nautical miles from the baseline), the contiguous zone (24 nm), the EEZ (200 nm), and the continental shelf (200 nm). Taiwan claims specific baselines for three areas: the main island of Taiwan and its appurtenant islands, the Pratas Islands and Macclesfield Bank.[89] The Pratas and Macclesfield Bank are located in the middle and eastern part of the SCS. Regarding the Spratly Islands, which have been the subject of prolonged disputes, a Notice to Mariners in 1999 announces that "all islands and atolls of the Nansha Chiundau (the Spratly Islands group) surrounded by the Chinese traditional U-shape lines are the territory of the Republic of China. The delimitation of the baselines in this region . . . shall be promulgated in the future."[90] Taiwan made its sovereignty claim clear while avoiding specifying baselines surrounding the Spratly Islands. The Paracel and Scarborough Reef are not listed in the baseline chart provided by the Notice to Mariners; however, they are also claimed by ROC.[91]

The ROC's claim in the SCS has repeatedly appeared in its official statements and government documents. The ROC claims that "in terms of either historical, geographical or international legal perspective, the Nansha (Spratly) Islands, Shisha (Paracel) Islands, Chungsha (Macclesfield) Islands, Tungsha (Pratas) Islands, as well as their surrounding waters, their respective sea bed and subsoil belong to . . . the Republic of China"[92] as "an inherent part of the territory."[93] Therefore, the ROC "does not recognize any claim to sovereignty over, or occupation of, these areas by other countries."[94]

The nine-dash U-shaped line constitutes the foundation of Taiwan's historical claim over the SCS. Taiwan claims historical sovereignty of maritime regions located far distant from the main island's baseline. The ROC has endorsed the line through formal and informal routes. The original line appeared in 1914 on a map by the Chinese cartographer Hu Jinjie.[95] In December 1946, eleven discontinuous U-shaped lines were presented in a map issued by the Department of the Territories and Boundaries of the Ministry of the Interior of the ROC (see map 1 above).[96] In 1947, the Nationalist Government of the Republic of China's Ministry of the Interior issued the *Location Map of the South China Sea Islands* showing an eleven-dash line covering whole waters of the SCS.[97] In 1948, the government declared its sovereignty and rights of maritime resources over the islands and reefs within the line. The line was also recognized by the PRC government when it was established in 1949.[98] The current nine-dash lines were set down when the PRC government removed two dashes in the Gulf of Tonkin in 1953.[99]

The U-shaped lines define the boundary of Taiwan's current claim. In the Policy Guidelines approved by the Executive Yuan (the executive body of the ROC) in 1993, the lines were "the historic water limit," and the whole area of the SCS within the lines was viewed as the "historic waters" of the ROC. The SCS was again defined as a "body of water of the Republic of China" in the Ministry of Foreign Affairs' 1999 statement.[100] However, subsequent maritime legislation enacted by the ROC and official statements no longer suggest these views on the historical waters.[101]

Slight changes and variations have occurred in Taiwan's claim. Kuan-Hsiung Wang, from National Taiwan Normal University, says Taiwan's claim has come to focus on the islands, their surrounding waters, and the continental shelf, not the whole body of water in the U-shaped line. In the South China Sea Peace Initiative proposed by the ROC government in May 2015, Taiwan's claim was more explicit, specifying that "the Nansha (Spratly) Islands, Shisha (Paracel) Islands, Chungsha Islands (Macclesfield Bank), and Tungsha (Pratas) Islands, as well as their surrounding waters, are an inherent part of ROC territory and waters."[102] The same position has been represented in most of the SCS-related official statements from the ROC government.[103]

According to Wang, "it would be difficult to claim the water body within the U-shaped lines as internal waters or territorial sea" in reality for the ROC.[104] The slight change in Taiwan's claims indicates that Taiwan has adopted an ambiguous strategy toward the SCS. Taiwan "suspended its claim to the entire waters" within the U-shaped line in December 2005 while advocating ownership of land features within the line.[105]

Taiwan's claim is practically backed by its occupation of the largest inhabitable island—Taiping Island (also known as Itu Aba Island). Taiping Island currently amounts to the ROC's most important physical asset in the SCS to prove its active administration of the maritime feature and protect its activities by providing stable access. Taiwan firmly maintains that Taiping Island undeniably fulfills the definition of an island provided by UNCLOS Article 121. UNCLOS describes an island as "a naturally formed area of land, surrounded by water, which is above water at high tide," differentiated from rocks that "cannot sustain human habitation or economic life."[106]

Taiwanese presidents and officials have visited Taiping Island to reiterate and promote their claim in the SCS. Chen Shui-Bian was the first president to visit Taiping Island when he made a trip on February 2, 2008, to assert Taiwan's sovereignty over the island and propose a "Spratly Initiative."[107] The ROC's interior minister, Chen Wei-zen, visited Taiping Island on December 12, 2015, with a group of government officials to reassert sovereignty despite the ongoing dispute in the SCS. The renovation of the island's wharf and airstrip and the construction of a lighthouse had been completed around the time of his visit to the island.[108]

On January 28, 2016, Ma Ying-jeou visited Taiping Island with government officials and scholars and promoted the roadmap of the South China Sea Peace Initiative and peaceful use of Taiping Island.[109] Before he visited Taiping Island, the Philippines raised an argument that Taiping Island is a rock that cannot sustain human habitation.[110] Ma demonstrated the island's favorable soil and water conditions and the potential for human habitation and sustainable economic life during the visit in response to the Philippines' argument.[111] Ma took another one-day trip to Taiping Island two months later in March 2016 and repeated Taiwan's firm stance on the island's status as a naturally formed island.[112]

The differentiation of rock from island is significant in maritime disputes because UNCLOS Article 121 rules that "rocks which cannot sustain human habitation or economic life of their own shall have no exclusive economic zone or continental shelf." Accordingly, Ma argued that "as Taiping is an island as defined by the UN Convention on the Law of the Sea, in addition to 12 nautical miles of territorial waters, the Republic of China is entitled to claim a 200-nautical-mile exclusive economic zone and a continental shelf" in his visit to Taiping Island.[113]

The Taiwanese Coast Guard Administration currently manages the island's defense instead of the Marine Corps, which concluded its duty on the island in 2000. Taiwan continues to renovate facilities on the island and, in 2015, completed the renovation of a wharf that can accommodate 3,000-ton ships.[114] When the presence of fresh water and natural vegetation on Taiping Island and its status as an island was questioned, Ma provided historical and scientific evidence opposing this argument.[115]

Taiwan's activities in the SCS have included conflict and cooperation with the concerned states. There are six claimants in the SCS disputes: Taiwan, China, Vietnam, the Philippines, Brunei, and Malaysia. Over the decades, Taiwan has experienced fluctuating relationships with the claimants, especially in the Spratly Islands. Vietnam and the Philippines have frequently come into conflict with Taiwan as they compete for sovereignty over the overlapping areas.

The Taiwanese Ministry of Foreign Affairs explains its standardized diplomatic response at any events relevant to infringement on its claim in the SCS.[116] For example, in May 2009, Vietnam and Malaysia filed a joint submission to the Commission on the Limits of the Continental Shelf of the United Nations proposing outer continental shelf limits beyond 200 nautical miles. Vietnam also filed an individual submission to the commission before the joint submission. The Taiwanese Ministry of Foreign Affairs then issued a statement on its claim and urged Vietnam and Malaysia to abide by the principles agreed in UNCLOS to peacefully resolve the dispute.[117]

Taiwan and Vietnam have further disagreed over Taiping Island (Ba Binh Island in Vietnamese). Vietnam's Ministry of Foreign Affairs stated, in November 2007, that Taiwan's construction of an airstrip on Taiping Island violated Vietnamese sovereignty. Taiwan argued that it had long stationed troops on the island and possessed actual control.[118] In April 2012, when three Taiwanese Kuomintang lawmakers visited Taiping Island, Vietnam opposed the visit by asserting its sovereignty over the island. Taiwan's Ministry of Foreign Affairs reiterated its sovereignty over Taiping Island while additionally claiming the SCS islands and their surrounding waters.[119] In January 2013, the Taiwanese Ministry of Foreign Affairs opposed Vietnam's Law on the Sea, which placed the Paracel Islands and Spratly Islands under Vietnam's sovereignty and jurisdiction.[120]

Taiwan also criticized the Philippines' domestic and foreign activities. For instance, Taiwan released statements following the election held by the government of the Philippines for the village chief of the Kalayaan Islands (the northeastern area of the Spratly Islands) in the SCS in 1997.[121] Furthermore, in 2009, when the Philippines passed bills incorporating Huangyan Dao (the Scarborough Shoal in English) into the Philippines, Taiwan restated its claim and urged the Philippines to abide by the UN Charter,

UNCLOS, and DOC.[122] Taiwan also opposed the Philippines' claim of its right to construct a wharf on Thitu Island in the SCS, which the ROC considers part of its territory.[123]

One of the intense conflicts between Taiwan and the Philippines occurred in January 2013, when the Philippines initiated international arbitration proceedings against the PRC at the International Tribunal for the Law of the Sea in accordance with UNCLOS Annex VII. The Philippines' legal challenge sought to invalidate the nine-dash lines and reaffirm the Philippines' maritime jurisdiction in the disputed waters.[124]

The arbitration initiated by the Philippines has caused Taiwan concern because, first, Taiwan was not invited as a concerned party in the arbitration. Secondly, in addition to Taiwan's objection against the Philippines' pursuit of international arbitration, the ROC protested an argument presented during the second hearing at the Permanent Court of Arbitration in November 2015 that denied Taiping Island's status as a naturally formed island.[125] Immediately after the circulation of the hearing result, the ROC denounced the argument through various diplomatic channels. Shen Lyu-shun, the representative of the ROC to the US, claimed that Taiping Island was a role model for SCS islands because it is a natural island with fresh water from four wells producing sixty-five metric tons of freshwater at 99 percent purity. He emphasized that Taiping Island corresponded to the UNCLOS definition of an island.[126] During the meeting with the former Philippine president in Taipei, President Ma invited the Philippines' representatives to visit Taiping Island and investigate the claims themselves.[127]

Taiwan's activities in the SCS are conducted predominantly for civilian purposes amid rising concerns regarding the militarization of maritime features and potential clashes in the region. In July 2010, Taiwan's Ministry of the Interior established the Tungsha (Pratas) Atoll National Park Management Station to support its marine research and promote its actual administration of the Pratas Atoll. This was followed by mapping mining areas for oceanic surveys around Pratas Island and Taiping Island in 2011. Since then, Taiwan's Ministry of National Defense and the Coast Guard Administration have organized civilian events to enhance awareness among civilians of the significance of the Pratas and Spratly Islands. Since November 2013, the Ministry of Transportation and Communications has constructed transportation infrastructure jointly with other departments on Taiping Island and a communications network has been completed. Taiwan facilitates regular and emergency communications for international humanitarian rescue operations under the guidance of its civilian administration.[128]

On May 26, 2015, the Taiwanese government proposed the South China Sea Peace Initiative (the SCS Initiative). In the initiative, Taiwan underscored its claim to the SCS islands and surrounding waters. Taiwan recognizes the San Francisco Peace Treaty and the Treaty of Peace between Taiwan and Japan that in the early 1950s officially ended the state of war arising from World War II. These treaties "reconfirmed that the islands and reefs" in the SCS "should be returned to the ROC."[129] Ma further explicated the SCS Initiative through short-term, mid-term, and long-term plans when he visited Taiping Island in January 2016. Ma said the SCS Initiative presented a "viable path" for "shelving disputes, integrated planning, and zonal development."[130]

The SCS Initiative further led to the Agreement Concerning the Facilitation of Cooperation on Law Enforcement in Fisheries Matters between the ROC and the Philippines on November 5, 2015.[131] Before the agreement, Taiwan and the Philippines agreed to refrain from the use of force to prevent unfortunate incidents such as the killing of a Taiwanese fisherman by the Philippine coast guard in 2013.[132]

The SCS Initiative was motivated by the East China Sea Peace Initiative (the ECS Initiative), which was proposed by Taiwan in 2012.[133] The ECS Initiative was recognized and supported by the US when Daniel Russel, US assistant secretary of state, found it aligned with the US effort to ease maritime tensions, although the initiative lacked favorable circumstances in which to grow.[134] Ma explained that the ECS Initiative "de-emphasizes the territorial nature of the dispute and focuses on resource sharing and cooperation," therefore, it applies to the SCS.[135] He claimed the fisheries agreement with Japan in 2013 as a successful development from the ECS Initiative.[136] Likewise, the SCS Initiative is expected to be grounds for future provisional arrangements between Taiwan and the SCS claimants, affirming the belief that "while sovereignty cannot be compromised, resources may be shared."[137]

Despite the restrictive conditions imposed by the One China Consensus, Taiwan's claims and activities have been represented in its statements and individual discussions. Taiwan's actual control of Taiping Island and the enlargement of the island's infrastructure have significantly contributed to its claim in the SCS disputes. Taiwan affirms the viability of its SCS Peace Initiative with its previous experience managing cooperation in the East China Sea. After her landslide victory in the presidential election of 2016, President Tsai Ing-wen of the Democratic Progressive Party insisted on Taiwan's sovereignty over Taiping Island.[138] As Yann-huei Song elaborates, Taiwan's dilemma comes from the peculiar status of possessing a similar position to China while pursuing internationally corresponding standards.[139] The dilemma of the ROC's policy is constant through the leadership changes in Taiwan.

In summary, Taiwan's involvement in the SCS must be examined within the framework of the One China Consensus. Taiwan is a critical part of China's territorial integrity claim and goal of national reunification; therefore, China's diplomatic principles have decreased in flexibility regarding cross-strait relations in the SCS and furthered Taiwan's position as a claimant in the disputes.

THREE

Evolving Underlying Interests

> The allegation that China claims all waters within the dotted line as its internal waters and territorial sea is a deliberate distortion of China's position.
>
> —Chinese foreign minister Wang Yi, August 4, 2021[1]

The previous chapter examined the historical and diplomatic principles attached to the SCS concerning China's bargaining practices and negotiations. This chapter analyzes China's underlying interests in the SCS, which have varied in content and urgency, in the context of *bargaining capacity*. Bargaining capacity refers to a party's "ability to bargain over issues of interest to rank-and-files and to regulate those issues."[2] Similarly, Urs Luterbacher and Detlef Sprinz note that "bargaining power derives from their ability to hold out for a better agreement."[3] Thomas Schelling further states that "'bargaining power,' 'bargaining strength,' and 'bargaining skill' suggest that the advantage goes to the powerful, the strong, or the skillful."[4] Taylor Fravel observes that a state's bargaining power in territorial disputes comprises two components: the amount of contested territory that it occupies and its ability to project power against its opponent over the contested areas.[5] If the criterion of bargaining power in the SCS disputes is the number of occupied maritime features, China and Vietnam rank as the top two powers in the SCS. This narrow definition of bargaining capacity constrains a state's diplomacy in order to obtain underlying interests. Table 3 shows the number of occupied maritime features by each claimant in the SCS and the features remaining unoccupied.[6] The number of features counted by the low threshold includes islands, rocks, submerged features, and low-tide elevation.

China's bargaining capability is closely related to critical questions about its underlying interests. What are the national interests underlying China's negotiations and bargaining practices with other SCS claimants? Does

Table 3. Occupation Status of Island Features in the SCS

	Paracels	Spratlys	*Total*
China	22	7	29
Vietnam	0	29	29
Taiwan	0	1	1
Malaysia	0	5	5
Philippines	0	9	9
Unoccupied	13	92	105

Note: Data from Asia Maritime Transparency Initiative, "Island Features Occupation Status in the South China Sea," 2020, https://amti.csis.org/scs-features-map

China have enough power to acquire its interests by force? Does China have the ability to do so in any other way, either in a coercive or charismatic manner that leads others to voluntarily follow China's desires as the outcome of China's soft power?[7] This chapter addresses these questions by contemplating the underlying interests of China in the SCS, which have manifested on various occasions. These occasions are governed by hard power, such as economic statecraft and military force, or soft power, such as China's cultural influence and regional leadership.

The conceptualization of bargaining capacity is an important process for analyzing China's underlying interests. If "bargaining power derives from (a claimant's) ability to hold out for a better agreement,"[8] the "better agreement" refers to one that is closely aligned with the claimant's interests. How do we know that a particular actor's negotiation activity occurred successfully? Hypothetically, to conclude that its negotiation was successful, the actor's interests are known to the other parties at the moment of negotiation. However, state actors intentionally choose to be ambiguous about their interests and objectives throughout bargaining processes. The degree of success of China's negotiations and the strength of its bargaining capacity go hand in hand with the country's underlying interests. The challenge is that national interests continually change and are not transparent; there is consistent intervention by political elites and domestic institutions, and the regional and international balance of power influences the outcome as well.

A bargaining process shaped by ambiguous underlying interests can deceive other parties into believing that they won a favorable deal. Schelling makes clear that "bargaining power has also been described as the power to fool" other parties.[9] A news report issued after the Mischief Reef incident in

1995 stated that "analysts wonder whether China's main interest is the vast oil resources beneath the shoals or control of a strategic regional nerve centre. Neither, they conclude, is reassuring."[10] In the face of major confrontations, including the Mischief Reef incident, the Sino-Vietnamese skirmishes in the Paracel and Spratly Islands, and the Sino-American encounters in the air and waters, China's concerns and underlying interests have been in doubt and subject to debate. The underlying interests of China present a research puzzle concerning the country's negotiation capacity and flexibility. In this book, this puzzle is explored with the hypothesis that China does not compete for precisely the same interests as other claimants of the SCS disputes. If each claimant is vying for the same interests simultaneously, then the negotiation does not continue, and the balance of power will determine the results of the dispute. However, if the claimants vie for distinct interests, negotiation progresses because of trade-offs. While China's interests in the SCS justify why the SCS is valuable for China, these interests change over time.

This chapter discusses what interests China pursued over time through its diplomacy for the SCS disputes. China's underlying interests in the SCS are elaborated in consideration of each critical theme: economic interest and historical rights. The section on historical rights consists of two subsections that examine the topic in detail, focusing on themes of sovereignty issues in Chinese history and the role of domestic politics in the historical rights narrative. Before discussing each theme, a conceptual approach applicable to analyzing them will be discussed in the following sections. These sections will demonstrate China's official claims and its bottom-line policies and how they have become disjointed.

The Bottom Line

Is the bottom line of China's claim identical to the indisputable sovereignty principle? The indisputable sovereignty principle is a broad concept and is not associated with a particular action. The principle is a guideline for China's default position about the SCS disputes; it does not constitute China's underlying interests per se. Nevertheless, the bottom line of China's claim in the SCS provides evidence that closely relates to China's national interests in the SCS and priorities within those interests. What is the right approach to analyze the bottom line of China's claims in various SCS negotiations? China's bottom line refers to the smallest demand that China would accept.

Scott Kastner discusses the bottom line and its relationship with a potential military conflict in the Taiwan Strait.[11] Kastner's case study is cross-strait relations, and he uses the term "red line" to describe the critical issues most likely to provoke a military response from China. The bottom line means the minimum content (in the form of geographical ambit) that China must achieve from a specific deal that is directly or indirectly linked to its underlying interests, as developed in the next section.

Like a negotiator who deceives other parties regarding what agenda, priorities, and options are available under the table,[12] China's ambiguity in its negotiation agenda is a strategic measure. However, being ambiguous is both strategic and risky if the negotiation is part of diplomacy among states that share the same regional space for security. Ambiguity can even cause a security dilemma due to the "difficulties states have in gaining security" without transparent communication.[13] What China eventually wants to acquire has been unclear; therefore, China's activities in the SCS have caused more concern from other claimants.

Sovereignty has been regarded as the central claim in China's position in the SCS disputes. Is the sovereignty claim by China in the SCS built upon the same understanding of sovereignty as the claims of other states? If not, how is China's sovereignty claim different from that of other claimants? According to the deputy director of the China Institute for Marine Affairs, China's sovereignty over the maritime features in the SCS should be given priority.[14] Yu Jia's argument appears to be the same as the Western idea in the sense that sovereignty over land territory is a prerequisite for maritime jurisdiction.[15] Disputes over contested waters are fights for certain rights, but ultimately, these rights are located within a specific geographic area that is measurable and demarcated. If sovereignty is the predominant and substantial claim of China, then the next question is over which particular area sovereignty is claimed.

In the same article, the deputy director of China Institute for Marine Affairs claims that the question of the status of maritime features in the SCS does not have any implications "if the sovereignty is not made clear first." He argues that "terra nullius is not entitled to any maritime rights, so it will be nonsense to discuss the maritime rights of a feature."[16] In other words, the question of defining these features—for example, if they are island, reef, or low-tide elevation—is to be discussed only after the sovereignty issue is clarified. His article defended China's position when the Philippines initiated an arbitration at the Permanent Court of Arbitration in 2013. The Philippines argued that the reefs claimed by China were low-tide elevations that could not be claimed as part of the territorial sea, EEZ, and continental shelf. The deputy director's opinion implies that China's concern and interests are neither geographically demarcated waters such as the territorial sea and EEZ nor marine resources in the form of the continental shelf and subsoil. Instead, China's most significant concern is the sovereignty issue; its rights to the territorial sea, EEZ, and continental shelf are secondary—though crucial—to this issue. When ASEAN foreign ministers issued a statement outlining ASEAN's Six-Point Principles on the South China Sea in July 2012, as a response to it, the Chinese Foreign Ministry spokesperson clarified that "the core of the South China Sea issue" was ultimately two issues: first, the disputes between relevant countries "concerning the sovereignty" over the Spratly Islands, and second, the "demarcation of their adjacent waters."[17]

The sovereignty issue has not been part of the negotiable agenda for China. When the Philippines initiated the arbitration on disputes with China according to Annex VII of UNCLOS in 2013, the Philippines' primary concerns were not about the sovereignty issue. Indeed, the Philippines side stated that it was "not asking this Tribunal to rule on the territorial sovereignty" aspect of its disputes with China.[18] The Tribunal settled issues regarding the legitimacy of China's historical rights claim in accordance with the UNCLOS. However, the Tribunal's Award on Jurisdiction and Admissibility, announced two years later in 2015, was more than enough to provoke China because it denied China's historical rights in the SCS.

Another relevant study provides a different idea of China's bottom line in the SCS. In 1994, Chinese president Jiang Zemin stated that China only claimed the islets and their adjacent waters within the dotted lines, not entire waters within the lines in the SCS.[19] Does this mean that China's bottom line in the SCS extends to islets or rocks or even permanently submerged rocks? Richard Heydarian argues that "it is still unclear whether China is treating the disputed waters as a virtual internal lake, or, alternatively, only laying claim to individual features."[20]

Different agreements have mentioned the sovereignty issue in different contexts. In the ASEAN Declaration on the SCS of 1992, ASEAN members confirmed that "the South China Sea issues involve . . . [the] sovereignty" of each claimant. Until signing the 1992 ASEAN Declaration, ASEAN members agreed that the nature of the SCS disputes was a sovereignty dispute, that is, their respective sovereignty was the center of the contest in the SCS. The concept of contested sovereignty included in the 1992 ASEAN Declaration did not appear in the following agreements on the SCS disputes between the claimants and China. For example, the sovereignty issue did not appear in the SCS Code of Conduct signed between the Philippines and China in 1995. As the 1995 Code of Conduct between China and the Philippines was prepared and signed immediately after the Mischief Reef incident, the agreement's focus was specifically on avoiding similar incidents in the future.

The Philippines reincorporated the sovereignty problem in the draft ASEAN–China Code of Conduct in the SCS circulated among China and ASEAN member states in 1999. The draft by the Philippines states that "disputes relating to sovereignty and jurisdiction in the South China Sea shall be resolved by peaceful means . . . on the basis of sovereign equality." The Philippines draft in 1999 stated that the Philippines recognized that, first, sovereignty was being contested, and, second, all sovereign states were equal actors.

The Chinese version of the Code of Conduct draft was also circulated among ASEAN members in the same year (1999) and explicitly stated the Chinese government's understanding of the SCS disputes:

> Disputes relating to the *Nansha Islands* shall be resolved by the sovereign states directly concerned through bilateral friendly consultations and negotiations, in accordance with universally recognized international law, including The 1982 UN Convention on the Law of the Sea.[21] (emphasis added)

The Chinese draft specified that it did not argue that the *whole* SCS was being contested but rather that the Nansha Islands (Spratly Islands) were. China's successful occupation of the Paracels in 1974 explains this approach. Furthermore, the Chinese draft stipulated that "disputes relating to the Nansha Islands shall be resolved by the sovereign states." China used the word "sovereign" states to be claimants in the context of the qualification, while the "sovereignty" issue did not appear in the draft. For China, sovereignty is not a source of the conflict, but being a sovereign state is a requirement for being a valid claimant at the negotiation table and provides authority to direct claimant state actors—not to a third party, including international institutions. In the Chinese draft, the 1982 UNCLOS was mentioned as an international legal regime that provides the state signatories with the right to solve disputes.

Why did China affirm that the Spratly Islands were subject to disputes? The reason can be found in China's discomfort with the 1992 ASEAN Declaration on the SCS. When the ASEAN members signed the declaration in 1992, China disagreed with it. China maintained that the groups of islands in the SCS other than the Spratlys—that is, the Pratas and Paracels Islands—were not related to ASEAN's affairs. The Chinese government was concerned that the formal declaration might compromise China's claim over the southern part of the SCS—that is, the Spratly Islands. According to Qian Qichen, the Chinese foreign minister in 1992, Beijing was not prepared or willing to enter into such negotiations and would only do so when the conditions were ripe.[22] However, in 2002, China was able to force its position in the Declaration on the Conduct of Parties in the South China Sea signed with ASEAN.

Both the draft by the Philippines and the Chinese draft made in 1999 were reflected in the 2002 DOC. Concerning the sovereignty issue, the Chinese position in the 1999 draft was moderated and included in the 2002 DOC. For example, ASEAN countries were not required to agree that only the Spratly Islands were disputed. Still, sentences concerning "contested sovereignty" were not incorporated in the 2002 DOC. The quotation below indicates that sentences from the 1999 Code of Conduct draft prepared by China appeared in the 2002 DOC:

> The Parties concerned undertake to resolve their territorial and jurisdictional disputes [through] negotiations by sovereign states directly concerned, in accordance with universally recognized principles of international law, including the 1982 UN Convention on the Law of the Sea.[23]

Similarly, the content of the Code of Conduct between China and the Philippines on the SCS signed in 1995 was largely repeated in the draft prepared by China in 1999. The 1995 Code of Conduct between China and the Philippines emphasized bilateral negotiations. Furthermore, the 1995 Code of Conduct considered relations between the two countries and associated the SCS dispute with overall bilateral relations, especially economic relations:

> In the spirit of expanding common ground and narrowing differences, a gradual and progressive process of cooperation shall be adopted with a view to eventually negotiating a settlement of the bilateral disputes. . . . The two sides agree to settle their bilateral disputes in accordance with the recognized principles of international law, including the UN Convention on the Law of the Sea. . . . They noted the successful conclusion of the 18th Philippines-China Joint

> Trade Committee Meeting. (COC between China and the Philippines, 1995)

The following excerpts demonstrate another way in which the 2002 DOC was a compromise between the Philippines draft and the Chinese draft of 1999. The 1999 Philippines and Chinese drafts pointed out what to avoid in actions in the SCS:

> The Parties undertake to exercise self-restraint in the conduct of activities in disputed areas . . . refraining from new occupation of presently unoccupied islands, reefs, atolls, shoals, cays or other features in disputed areas. (Philippines COC draft, 1999)

> The parties . . . refrain from taking actions that will complicate or magnify the disputes. (Chinese COC draft, 1999)

> The Parties undertake to exercise . . . refraining from action of inhabiting on the presently uninhabited islands, reefs, shoals, cays, and other features. (DOC, 2002)

The prohibited actions described in the 2002 DOC were moderated compared to that of the 1999 draft submitted by the Philippines. In the draft, the Philippines stated that "new *occupation* of presently unoccupied islands" (emphasis added) should be refrained. However, the 2002 DOC adopted a more neutral tone regarding changes to the status quo, stating that "inhabiting on the presently uninhabited islands" should be refrained from. By avoiding the stigmatization of potential conflict, this phrasing redirected the audiences to focus to the positive outcomes of the agreement. The Philippines' draft in 1999 was the most specific of the three documents in describing the prohibited actions; on the other hand, the Chinese draft in 1999 had the most ambiguous expression on this matter. The 2002 DOC blended the sentences of the Philippines and China into the agreement.

There were two different drafts of the Code of Conduct prepared by China and the Philippines in 1999. The draft prepared by the Philippines implied that there *was* a sovereignty dispute, and the parties *knew* the existence of the dispute. It stated that "refraining from new occupation" of maritime features should be agreed upon, and *maintaining* the status quo in the waters is crucial. On the other hand, the 1999 draft prepared by China includes a different point of view toward the COC. For example, language often employed by China was used, such as "good-neighborliness" and "harmonious." Further, in the Philippines' draft, the UNCLOS was branded as the international rule to abide by. By contrast, China's draft included the Charter of the United Nations and the Five Principles of peaceful Coexistence as the guiding rules to follow. The UNCLOS was also mentioned in China's draft, but in a different context:

> Disputes relating to the Nansha Islands shall be *resolved by the sovereign states* directly concerned through *bilateral* friendly consultations and negotiations, in accordance with universally recognized international law, including *The 1982 UN Convention on the Law of the Sea.* (COC draft by China, 1999; emphasis added)

This quotation provides insights into China's rules of the game. China attempted to reassure other claimants in the SCS disputes that only the Nansha Islands (Spratly Islands) were disputed—not the whole waters and features in the SCS. Since the 1974 naval clash in the Paracel Islands with Vietnam and Chinese victory followed by actual control of the islands, China did not view the Paracels as contested. China attacked the western Paracel in January 1974, marking the first interstate naval clash in the SCS, resulting in hundreds of casualties, as detailed in Chapter 5 of this book. Leszek Buszynski and Christopher Roberts note that "China's claim to the Paracels may be supported by international law if China can satisfactorily demonstrate continuous" and "effective occupation."[24] Also, China argued that "disputes . . . shall be *resolved by the sovereign states* . . . through *bilateral* . . . negotiations, in accordance with . . . *The 1982 UN Convention on the Law of the Sea*" (italics added). China brought up the UNCLOS to advocate "bilateral" solutions between directly concerned "sovereign states."

On the other hand, the Philippines suggested in its COC draft that all parties had "sovereign equality," which was irrelevant to the *sovereign state first* position that China proposed. As indicated in the COC draft suggested by the Philippines, the Philippines' concerns regarding sovereignty were different from that of China. What concerned China, as far as the COC draft by China indicated, was that complicated international laws and rules interfere with sovereign states' rights to decide their foreign relations and related disputes. On the other hand, the Philippines was concerned that aggressive states' behavior would intervene in nonaggressive states' sovereignty if no regionally or internationally agreed rules regulated the resolution of disputes. Hasjim Djalal endorses the Philippines' interpretation of the sov-

Table 4. Sovereignty Issue and Statements on Agreed Actions in South China Sea Agreements since 1992

Agreements					
ASEAN Declaration on the South China Sea (among ASEAN members only)	Code of Conduct between China and the Philippines on the South China Sea	ASEAN-China Code of Conduct in the South China Sea (drafted by Philippines)	ASEAN-China Code of Conduct in the South China Sea (drafted by China)	Declaration on the Conduct of Parties in the South China Sea between China and ASEAN (DOC)	The Guidelines for the Implementation of the DOC (China and ASEAN)
Year					
1992	1995	1999	1999	2002	2011
Sovereignty					
"Recognizing that the South China Sea issues involve . . . *sovereignty* and jurisdiction of the parties" "Emphasize the necessity to resolve all *sovereignty* and jurisdictional issues" "Resolve (disputes), without prejudicing the *sovereignty* and jurisdiction of countries . . . to explore the possibility of cooperation in the South China Sea relating to the safety"	(*sovereignty issue not mentioned*)	"Disputes relating to *sovereignty* and jurisdiction in the South China Sea shall be resolved . . . on the basis of *sovereign equality*" "Without prejudice to existing claims of *sovereignty* . . . the parties concerned shall . . . build trust and confidence" "Without prejudice to existing claims of *sovereignty* . . . the parties concerned may explore or carry our cooperation through bilateral or multilateral agreement"	"Disputes relating to the *Nansha Islands* shall be resolved *by the sovereign states* directly concerned through bilateral friendly consultations and negotiations, in accordance with universally recognized international law, including the 1982 UN Convention on the Law of the Sea"	"The Parties concerned undertake to resolve their territorial and jurisdictional disputes [through] negotiations by *sovereign* states directly concerned, in accordance with universally recognized principles of international law, including the 1982 UN Convention on the Law of the Sea"	(*sovereignty issue not mentioned*)

Agreed action					
"Emphasize the necessity to resolve . . . by peaceful means, without resort to force"	"Frank discussions on Mischief Reef ('Meiji Reef') were held. . . . They agreed to hold further consultations in order to resolve their differences."	"The Parties . . . *refraining from new occupation* of presently unoccupied islands, reefs, atolls, shoals, cays or other features in disputed areas"	"the parties . . . *refrain from taking actions* that will complicate or magnify the disputes"	"The Parties undertake to exercise . . . refraining from action of *inhabiting* on the presently uninhabited islands, reefs, shoals, cays, and other features"	"The implementation of the DOC should be carried out in a step-by-step" "on a *voluntary* basis"; "activities or projects as provided for in the DOC *should be clearly identified*"

Note: Emphasis added. Developed from Kim and Druckman (2020), 39, 43.

ereign rights guaranteed by the UNCLOS. According to Djalal, "The state parties to UNCLOS have obligations to . . . exercise their rights . . . in such a way that would not constitute 'an abuse of rights' (Article 300) . . . against the territorial integrity or political independence of any state."[25]

The differences between China and the Philippines further highlighted different expectations of the role of international law. Both desire substantial sovereign rights in due course of the competition. However, one—China—insinuated that international laws advocate sovereign states' right to conduct negotiations with complete autonomy. Another—the Philippines—believed that international laws protect nonaggressive or weaker state's sovereignty from an aggressive sovereign actor.

Limits in the Seas

Limits in the Seas is a series published by the United States Department of State on maritime states' claims and maritime borders. In 2014, the report analyses what exactly is being claimed by China in the nine-dash line and the reasons China gives for its claim's consistency with the UNCLOS. The report questions the inconsistency of the nine-dash line claim in Chinese official government publications. The Permanent Mission of the People's Republic of China to the United Nations submitted a note verbale to the UN Secretary-General in 2009 following Vietnam's submission to the commission on the Limits of the Continental Shelf proposing outer limits of the Vietnamese continental shelf beyond 200 nautical miles. The Chinese note verbale attached the SCS map with the so-called nine-dash line. *Limits in the Seas*, published by the United States Department of State in 2014, points out that the nine-dash line appears differently in maps published in 1947 by the Nationalist government and in 2009 by the PRC. As per *Limits in the Seas*, the dashes in the 2009 PRC map came closer to the littoral states' coasts, and each dash was shorter in length.[26] Another problem pointed out in the report was that the symbology used in modern Chinese maps to depict the nine-dash line is same as the symbology used for depicting international boundaries, which leads to interpretation that China treats the nine-dash line as its national boundary—despite many unresolved questions, including inconsistencies between the line's appearance in 1947 and 2009.

The *Limits in the Seas* report says that UNCLOS contains articles for "historic" bays or titles—but only in two instances. Article 15 states that if "it is necessary by reason of historic title," either of the two neighboring/

opposite states can "extend its territorial sea beyond the median line," which is "equidistant from the nearest points on the baselines." But this article is applied only to the territorial sea and cannot support China's historical claim beyond its territorial sea, which extends twelve nautical miles from the baseline. The report points out that "Articles 10 and 15 are strictly limited geographically and substantively," and they are not applied in "areas of EEZ, continental shelf, or high seas."

The report further notes that China's claim on "land" (islands)—not "waters"—in the nine-dash line is evident according to its 2009 note verbales and its 1992 territorial sea law. The report reviews China's 1958 Territorial Sea Declaration in which China claimed its sovereignty over only "islands" and did not claim the whole maritime area within the nine-dash line. In the 1950s, international law had not introduced the concept of EEZs or the continental shelf yet. However, in its 2009 note verbales, China claims its sovereignty and jurisdiction over not only the islands but also the "adjacent waters," the "relevant waters," and the "seabed and subsoil thereof." The report suggests that the "adjacent waters" refer to the 12-nm territorial sea, and the "relevant waters" means the EEZ, and the "seabed and subsoil thereof" is the continental shelf. In other words, China renamed its existing traditional claims according to the concept of EEZs and the continental shelf as defined by the UNCLOS—the contemporary international law. From the context of Chinese exceptionalism, Feng Zhang views the historical narrative and legal interpretation as example of Chinese exceptionalism to counter structural pressures from the international system discursively.[27]

Following the analysis above on the possible interpretation of international law in China's claim, the report addresses the remaining and more critical problems. Even if China claims only islands, those islands are still subject to disputes with littoral states because they would overlap with other littoral states' maritime zones. China has not clarified which features it considers to be "islands" and "rocks." The difference between islands and rocks is significant because rocks do not create EEZs and the continental shelf under UNCLOS Article 121(3). Rocks are entitled to a 12-nm territorial sea, but its practical impact is insignificant.

A couple of questions raised through the *Limits in the Seas* report provide an in-depth analysis of the nine-dash line and UNCLOS inconsistency. The report examines whether the Chinese claim to historic waters and rights in the nine-dash line has a basis under international law. "Historic rights" are used as important grounds for China's claim over the SCS; however, it has been controversial what exactly China claims on historical grounds. The report answers this question, arguing that "China has not actually made a cognizable claim to either 'historic waters' or 'historic rights' to the waters of the South China Sea within the dashed line."[28] On the contrary, Guifang Xue, director of the Institute for the Law of the Sea at Ocean University of China, argues that the waters within the nine-dash line are neither international waters, territorial waters, nor high seas, but waters with a historical attachment that the UNCLOS does not define in its articles.[29] Hence, the UNCLOS Article 15, which is about "historic title" and states that it is not applicable beyond a claimant's territorial sea, remains relevant to the case of China's historical waters narrative.

Islands, Waters, or Seabed?

How clearly do Chinese government documents identify the ambiguous bottom line that China has in the SCS disputes? The Chinese note verbale submitted to the UN in 2009 states:

> China has indisputable sovereignty over the islands in the South China Sea and the *adjacent waters*, and enjoys sovereign rights and jurisdiction over the *relevant waters* as well as the *seabed and subsoil* thereof.[30] (emphasis added)

In the 1950s, before the EEZ and continental shelf were introduced, China claimed its sovereignty over only islands and did not claim the waters within the nine-dash line.[31] In 1951, Zhou Enlai wrote in the statement about the US-British draft peace treaty with Japan and the San Francisco Conference Statement that

> The Nanwei (Spratly) *Island* and the Sisha (Paracel) *Islands* have always been part of China's territory. These vital *islands* in the South China Sea are outposts of China's national frontiers.
>
> The Sisha *Islands* [. . .] location is very important, as they link China with the South Seas as well as with the main sea routes between Europe and Asia.
>
> Nanwei *Island* [Spratly Island] is the main island of the Nansha Islands [the group of Spratly Islands]. [. . .] It is important in a com-

> munication as well as in a military sense, as it is located in a central position between the Philippines, Borneo, Malaya and Indo-China.[32]

The US-British draft stated that Japan surrendered rights over the Paracels and Spratlys; however, how and to whom the sovereignty of those areas should be returned was not indicated. Zhou further argued that any decision made by the US and British would not affect Chinese sovereignty over the SCS *islands*.[33] Zhou's description of the significance of islands focused on their role as maritime communication chokepoints and as objects of strategic occupation, while the waters and seabed themselves were not mentioned as part of China's interest. This contrasts with China's 2009 notes verbales, which claim sovereignty over the islands, the waters and the seabed as a whole.

The ambiguity in the Chinese claim in the SCS increases when it comes to the so-called nine-dash line. The nine-dash line is referred to by other names, including the "nine-dotted line," "cow's tongue," and "U-shaped line." The dashed line in the SCS was originally composed of eleven dashes. In 1952, the socialist bonhomie between China and North Vietnam enabled their mutual agreement on a concession to Vietnam in the Gulf of Tonkin area in 1953.[34] Therefore, two lines out of eleven lines over the Tonkin Gulf were eliminated and the current nine-dash line was formed. A recent report issued by the US Department of State points out the inconsistency between the dashed line maps published by Chinese authorities in different years.[35] The ambiguity of the interpretation of the SCS has been pointed out by Chinese scholars, including Xue Li from the Chinese Academy of Social Sciences. Xue argues that China should clarify the meaning of the nine-dash line to create a favorable effect in the tribunal initiated by the Philippines in 2013.[36] Not all Chinese scholars would agree with the idea that the nine-dash line and the UNCLOS are entirely separate.

The implication of China's official claim in the SCS has been an increasing concern in the region. Will China be satisfied with its current degree of control over the SCS? Will China make its successful control over the SCS into a precedent for pursuing further territorial expansion? Two different approaches suggest relevant answers. From the perspective of general theories on state behavior, a rising power pursues competition with the existing power. Eventually, it attempts to maximize its power beyond a certain level of self-defense capability.[37] Theoretically, China would seek to balance against the current order made by the US regardless of to what extent China respects other states' sovereignty and their territorial integrity. This balancing activity would also include territorial expansion and offshore balance.

In contrast, the combination of China's peaceful coexistence principle and China's core interests would instead enable an expectation that China would respect other states' core interests, including their sovereignty and territorial integrity. China's peaceful coexistence principle adheres to the significance of noninterference in foreign relations. China advocates its core interests, namely state sovereignty, national security, territorial integrity, national unification, and the integrity of its political system.[38] China's stance on *other* sovereign states' domestic issues is neutral, and it would not interfere with other states' sovereignty and their territorial integrity claims.[39] China claims the SCS as part of its core interests and domestic affairs—not international ones. This perspective leads to an argument that China will be satisfied when it secures its superior status in the SCS and will not pursue further territorial or maritime intrusion.

Economic Interests

Does China tend to negotiate for economic interests? Does the SCS contain an economic value that the SCS claimants vie for, and are China's underlying interests inherently economic? Possession of the islands is the precondition to obtaining benefits from them. The islands have only negligible physical value in themselves; however, countries that own those islands will be entitled to enormous wealth from the sea. These islands could be the basis for claiming a large sea area as either territorial sea or EEZ, including the seabed beneath. The economic value of the SCS is divided into various types: buried natural energy resources, trading, and sea lines of communication, tourism, the fishing industry, and other economic activities.

Each type of economic benefit differs in its value, utilization, and impact. Among the various economic values of the SCS, its role as one of the world's key sea lines of communication remains crucial, not only for China but also for many other global economies. In fact, given the SCS's significance as a vital maritime route, China's expectation that the SCS disputes should remain a regional issue is unrealistic. This importance is underscored in official documents from the world's top ten major economies. The White House's *National Security Strategy* in 2022 describes the SCS as "a throughway for nearly two-thirds of global maritime trade and a quarter of all global trade."[40] Similarly, the UK's *National Strategy for Maritime Security* in 2022 notes that "60% of all global maritime trade passes through Asia; of that, one-third passes through the South China Sea, equating to 2.5% of the entire global economy."[41] Japan's *Diplomatic Bluebook 2023* highlights the region's importance, stating, "As a stakeholder that relies on the South China Sea, the issue is critical for Japan, which depends on sea transportation for most of its resources and energy."[42] Germany's *Strategy on China* published in 2023 emphasizes the need for "stability, security, and navigability of this vital transit route [referring to SCS] for the international transport of goods and raw materials."[43] *Strategy on China* further states that "Germany and the EU have interests in the South China Sea, where challenges in upholding international law, security, foreign trade, climate change mitigation, and biodiversity conservation intersect."[44] The common thread in these key documents from various economic powers is clear: The South China Sea is an indispensable trade route with immense economic value.

In the case of energy resources, on the other hand, the main issue surrounding the oil and gas resources in the SCS is the potential profitability of these resource fields. While the value of the SCS for sea lines of communication safety is enduring, the value of the SCS from energy sources is less likely to lead to widespread conflict today than in the past. During the oil boom, oil reserves indeed had significant political ramifications, and China's aggressive actions in the SCS at the time were frequently driven by its immediate economic interests. In relation to China's interest in the economic resources in the SCS, China's oil consumption continues to grow to approximately 11.1 million barrels per day, and the oil production in domestic land and offshore oil fields was 4.5 million barrels per day in 2013. In the same year, the Philippines initiated arbitration at the International Tribunal for the Law of the Sea against China after the Scarborough Shoal standoff in 2012. As of January 2014, China held 24.4 billion barrels of proven oil reserves, and China's yearly consumption reached 4 billion barrels.[45] These numbers are comparable with that of the expected buried oil capacity of the SCS examined by the United States Geological Survey. The SCS contains an estimated 11 billion barrels of oil and 145 trillion cubic feet of natural gas that have yet to be surveyed.[46] China imported 6.2 million barrels per day in 2013 because of limited domestic oil exploitation and supply, and imports have been increasing after China became a net importer in 1993.[47] Therefore, oil is considered a potential strategic vulnerability as China's dependence on imports is growing.[48]

Meanwhile, oil makes up 20 percent of the country's energy requirements, with coal as the primary energy source in China, accounting for around 70 percent of total consumption in the 2010s. China has been a net coal importer since 2009, but coal imports do not constitute a significant portion of total coal consumption.[49] Oil's value has increased as the Chinese government plans to cap coal use to reduce heavy air pollution. Chinese coal consumption fell for the first time after 2010. China's gross domestic product growth and coal consumption have decoupled, suggesting a structural shift in the Chinese economy.[50]

The Chinese have long hoped for an oil boom since economic development became the national goal in the reform and opening-up period, so it is not a new phenomenon that China has focused on exploiting marine energy resources.[51] According to Chinese law, domestic companies have a right to cooperate with foreign enterprises in offshore petroleum exploration and exploitation. Because it did not have advanced technology in oil and gas exploration, China has cooperated with overseas corporations since the 1980s.[52]

In 1983, British and Chinese ministers discussed the possibility of UK offshore firms developing the oil in the SCS. In a meeting with the British energy secretary Peter Walker, the Chinese petroleum industry minister said "the expertise of the UK offshore industry . . . would be of special importance to China." China did not possess the technology and skills required to do oil exploration and drilling in the ocean; therefore, this necessitated cooperation with foreign corporations while hoping for an oil boom.[53] In April 1984, Esso/Shell corporation conducted oil exploration to the east of Hainan Island in the SCS and found oil in mud samples. However, according to the managers of the oil exploration companies, it was too early to confirm or deny the "rumour" of potential undersea resources and tell whether it was "commercial." Not all the international exploration cooperation was successful. In January 1984, BP abandoned its exploration well in the SCS after finding only limited amounts of oil, which indicated less possibility of a commercial discovery.[54] China, at that time, conducted a geophysical survey of the SCS together with the US, obtained samples from the seabed, and produced data on geological conditions in the SCS.[55]

The primary concern regarding the oil resources in the SCS is the profitability of the possible oil fields there other than the Pearl River Mouth Basin. The same concern could also apply to other types of natural resources buried in the overall disputed waters in the SCS. By May 2006, the China National Offshore Oil Corporation had signed 172 contracts with 75 oil companies worldwide to build 23 gas and oil fields in the SCS.[56] In 2014 China also developed an independent oil field in which the China National Offshore Oil Corporation held a 100 percent interest as a sole operator.[57]

Bill Hayton provides evidence that the SCS used to be China's "blue ocean" for energy supply at one moment of its history and may continue to be at present.[58] Hayton delves into a story of an American entrepreneur who skillfully bought and sold oil fields in the SCS and increased China's hope for energy resources extraction from the SCS. According to Hayton's study, Chinese authorities enacted the Law on the Territorial Sea and the Contiguous Zone of the People's Republic of China in 1992 to provide domestic and legal grounds for the oil exploration and extraction from the SCS. Buszynski also sees relevance between the Law on Territorial Sea passed on February 25, 1992 and the joint cooperation on the Spratlys with the American Crestone Energy Corporation that started a few months later, in May 1992.[59] The studies indicate that it is not correct to say that China's claim in the SCS has always been out of China's economic calculation; instead, depending on the time period, economic expectations for the SCS have sometimes been heightened and have faded at other times.

This phenomenon is similar in the East China Sea (ECS)—contested waters between China and Japan. In the 1960s and 1970s, China moved proactively when a UN report investigated natural gas in the South and East China Seas and caused an oil rush in the region. The survey reports in the 1960s by the United Nations Economic Commission for Asia and the Far East suggested that vast reserves of oil were likely to be found under the seabed of the SCS.[60] The reports affected China and other states surrounding the SCS. One of the initial research reports on the SCS disputes was published at that time.[61] Other SCS claimants also responded to this big news. The Philippines reported the discovery of oil and gas reserves off the Reed Bank in early 1976.[62] Vietnam had disputes in the SCS with China and other regional actors such as Malaysia and Indonesia. The disputes with other maritime neighbors occurred starting in the 1980s, when the expectation of buried energy resources in the SCS increased. Vietnam proposed to Indonesia to jointly explore an area of the continental shelf in the SCS between two countries; however, Indonesia rejected the proposal. After that, the ownership of a 400,000 square kilometer area in the SCS was disputed between Vietnam and Indonesia.[63]

In the 1970s, China claimed sovereignty over the continental shelf in the ECS. China was criticized for claiming "the entire continental shelf in areas (of the East China Sea) contiguous to Japan and South Korea which also enjoy similar rights as coastal states."[64] At that time, the major international law was the Convention on the Continental Shelf that came into force in 1958—not the UNCLOS, which came into force only after 1994. The Convention on the Continental Shelf, which was signed in Geneva, Switzerland, provided that the coastal state exercised sovereign rights over the shelf "to a depth of 200 metres or beyond that limit to where the depth of the waters admits of the exploitation of natural resources."[65]

China's interests in the ECS affected its diplomacy as well. In the early 1970s, China supported a few other underdeveloped countries to justify China's interpretation of the Convention on the Continental Shelf. China's urgent need to ensure its rights over the continental shelf in the ECS came from the direct economic benefits from the ECS. China released official statements to support Latin American countries that could not "invoke the Geneva agreement to protect their offshore seas from exploitation." China defended the right to fix limits "to meet the needs of using their own resources rationally." At that time, China did not support the convention that limited the rights in the continental shelf and defended Latin American countries that were not entitled to have the continental shelf in accordance with the convention.[66]

When promising reports appeared on the potential energy buried in the SCS, China's moves certainly were driven by those economic interests. However, it would be more accurate to argue that China's particularly aggressive behavior in the SCS often followed a pattern driven by relatively urgent economic interests. When the potential economic benefits are substantial, China frequently finds itself at odds with other claimants and countries in the SCS. As numerous reports of the SCS resources became available in the 1970s and 1980s, China prepared its domestic laws while pushing for assistance from domestic and foreign companies.

Recent studies objectively analyze the explanatory power of economic factors in the SCS disputes by comprehensively comparing and judging the economic determinants with other variables of the disputes. Brendon Taylor argues that the SCS is comparatively the least dangerous compared to other potential flashpoints in Asia because the SCS disputes do not meet the political-military crisis criteria: urgency, possible benefits of engaging in military conflicts, and *economic interests*.[67] According to Taylor's test of Michael Swaine's definition of crisis, the Korean Peninsula and the East China Sea meet the criteria of the political-military crisis. You Ji dismisses the idea that the East China Sea and SCS resources have motivated Beijing to up the ante in the dispute, due to the extraction and transportation costs as well as low commercial value.[68] Further, Beijing inherited the "nine-dotted line" in the SCS from the pre-PRC regimes long before potential energy reserves in the region attracted local and foreign oil companies.[69]

Hayton notes that the SCS is "not particularly rich in oil and gas resources," while other frequently cited beliefs surrounding the SCS dispute are also controversial.[70] It would make better sense to buy the crude oil from the international market if the exploitable resources buried under the Spratly Islands are not profitable in terms of exploration, exploitation, transport, and even diplomatic costs.[71] Xuetong Yan further argues that the value of natural resources has decreased dramatically as a catalyst for creating national prosperity, whereas science and technology have appreciated more.[72] These studies show how the narrative and importance of economic values in the SCS in analyzing China's underlying interests have changed over time.

As one of the major sea lines of communication, the SCS links the Indian and Pacific Oceans that would well emerge as the strategic center of the twenty-first century and the world's primary medium for the transportation of energy and the geographic center of Indo-Pacific visions shared by major powers.[73] The maritime trade is regarded as farming on the sea, comparable to arable fields. The Chinese long aspired to obtain resources from the sea when mercantile activities were flourishing in the late sixteenth and the early seventeenth century. Eleven million barrels per day are transported through the SCS; 35 percent of the world's total seaborne oil trade passes through the Strait of Malacca. This is second only to the Strait of Hormuz, the gateway for 40 percent of the world's seaborne oil trade.

Various Chinese sources discuss the sea lines of communication from a broader security point of view. In an article published in the *China Defense Journal*, safeguarding maritime sea-lanes was vital in protecting the "economic security of China."[74] In 2014, Chinese foreign minister Yang Jiechi pointed out at the ASEAN Regional Forum Foreign Ministers Meeting that "the South China Sea is an important shipping route. China is a big trading nation, and 60 percent of China's external trade goes through the South China Sea."[75] Hu Jintao also expressed his concerns over this issue by defining the issue as the "Malacca Dilemma" (*Maliujia kunju*). Alfred Mahan, the nineteenth-century American maritime strategist, described sea power as the ability of a country to use maritime communication for national advantage. Nations seek sea power as a "great highway."[76] The seaborne trade has often led to an increase in vulnerabilities and threats, therefore "who controls not just the production of oil and gas but also the supply will dominate the world."[77]

The *objective* value of the sea route can bring two different potential interests to China. First, China can secure its seaborne trade by strengthening stability in the SCS, *not* by inflicting instability in the region. Second, China threatens others with its capacity to blockade the sea lines of communication. Historically, a naval blockade has happened a few times in contemporary history, including Egypt's closure of the Suez Canal between 1967 and 1975.[78] The option of a naval blockade is historically uncommon because a naval blockade poses significant mutual risks due to strong economic interdependency among the regional states, and China is not an exception in the interdependent Asian economic community. Benjamin Goldsmith argues that interdependency is the most significant determinant that prevents a military conflict in Asian contexts compared to Western history.[79]

The Sovereignty Issue in Chinese History

Shicun Wu, the president of the National Institute for South China Sea Studies, headquartered on Hainan Island, admits that "the UN Convention on the Law of the Sea contains no provisions dealing with the definition of historic rights." Wu, however, further argues that "nevertheless, history cannot be overlooked, and nation-states cannot be expected to abandon such rights upon ratifying UNCLOS."[80] Merriden Varrall from the Lowy Institute in Australia argues that China's position in the SCS derived from its pursuit of a historical position in the world. She analyzes China's assertiveness after 2009 and the historical rationale behind it. "China's recent actions in the South China Sea and possible future actions reflect a strongly held sense in China that history is destiny."[81] Chinese actions in the SCS reflect the gradual resumption of its rightful and respected place in the world with their memory of the Century of Humiliation beginning with the Opium Wars in the mid-1800s. This section suggests two perspectives to approach China's historic rights: historical presence with historical facts and history as the heritage of China's dominant position in the region.

The historical argument is currently considered the ultimate rationale in China's claim over its sovereignty of the islands and waters in the SCS. Chinese scholars advocate China's sovereignty in the SCS with evidence such as legal and historical explanations.[82] Chinese foreign minister Wang Yi suggested the Four Respects to guide the SCS dispute in September 2014, which gave the top priority to historical perception—the dispute is a matter left over by history—followed by international laws, direct dialogue with claimants, and the role of external actors.[83] Gungwu Wang from the National University of Singapore notes that, for that Chinese, the role of history lies in its offerings to myth-making.[84] As far as China's history explains their ancestors' activities in the SCS, the region is regarded as the descendants' "arms and legs" that they never want to cut off, as Chinese admiral Shengli Wu metaphorically asserted.[85]

The nine-dash line constitutes the central part of the Chinese historical argument. China has endorsed the line through government officials as well as nongovernmental platforms. The original line first appeared in 1914 on the Chinese cartographer Hu Jinjie's map.[86] The map published by the Nationalist government in 1947 was composed of eleven dashes and entitled "Locations of the South China Sea Islands."[87] The 1947 document was the "first modern use of the dashed line."[88] In 1948, the Chinese Nationalist government declared its sovereignty and the rights of maritime resources over the islands and reefs within the line. The line was recognized by the PRC after its establishment in 1949. Later, in 1953, the PRC government took out two dashes in the Gulf of Tonkin, and the current nine-dash line was settled. From the Chinese point of view, the SCS littoral states and the international community were in a tacit understanding before the 1970s that China had sovereignty over the SCS, and there was no objection.[89]

The root of the historic rights argument is found in China's irredentist policy pursued at the national establishment of the PRC in 1949. China's first premier, Zhou Enlai, argued in his 1951 statement on the US-British draft peace treaty with Japan and the San Francisco Conference that the Pratas, Paracel, and Spratly Islands were originally Chinese territory for which China's inviolable sovereignty applied. Even though Japanese imperialists had occupied them, China had regained them when Japan surrendered.[90]

Domestic support is strong for the national and historical arguments in China. The Chinese government did not do enough to rein in China's nationalists until it seemed to harm Beijing's larger goals.[91] China controlled online and offline nationalistic demonstrations to prevent the strong public sentiment from encroaching on the realm of decision-makers and worsening the relationships with neighboring countries. However, this perception toward nationalistic opinion changed as the Chinese, "who are realists in essence," sensed the elevation of its status and China's relative power in the international system during the 2008–9 global financial crisis.[92]

Nationalism was not a constant phenomenon that appeared throughout Chinese history since the establishment of the PRC in 1949. For nearly three decades after 1949, communism was the predominant ideology in Chinese society. When the discussion and teaching of historical narratives and cultures were banned nationally, communism and the proletarian class identity ruled Chinese opinion. Nationalism, in theory, presumed a deep, horizontal comradeship among an "imagined political community," which cannot coexist with the class theory.[93]

It was only in the early 1990s that "China's nationalist turn began."[94] Quansheng Zhao, a US-based Chinese scholar, forecast in 1993 the continual influence of Chinese nationalism on its international behavior while witnessing less ideologically driven decision-making in its foreign policy.[95] Chinese leaders had sought a two-pronged policy that supported top-down patriotic nationalism and prevented bottom-up nationalism. However, popular nationalism has enjoyed more generosity from the Chinese government since the late 2000s.[96] Meanwhile, the risk of an "intersection of nationalism and the politics of discontent" in Chinese society has always been in Chinese leaders' concerns since nationalism based on an historical narrative was infused in domestic political dynamics.[97]

Hayton argues that China traditionally governed people, not space, and suggests the existence of maritime nomads (*Nusantao*) and anthropological research on the formation of the SCS culture. Hayton argues that "there's no archaeological evidence that any Chinese ships made trading voyages across the SCS until the tenth century CE."[98] Research on the history of other littoral states also challenges China's position.[99] In response to these counterarguments, Chinese governmental bodies conducted underwater archaeological surveys to salvage relics and drew a map pointing out sites.[100] China's geographical survey and mapping also aim to clarify the nine-dotted line's specific locations by setting their longitudes and latitudes.[101]

Shicun Wu, the president of the National Institute for South China Sea Studies, argues that sovereignty in the modern Westphalian system similarly existed in the Sinocentric tributary system before Chinese supremacy was encroached upon by foreign powers.[102] "The Chinese concept of sovereignty" was pursued in different rules that the tributary system and Confucius mentality guided.[103] In this order, rulers ruled people, not space.[104] Sovereignty in the Westphalian system requires particular territory within borders claimed by the sovereign state to be legitimate. However, in the Sinocentric world, Chinese sovereignty became legitimate once its tributaries agree to be China's subordinates. The question of whether China controlled those subordinate kingdoms was not significant in this so-called Sinocentric order because "the place would be included as part of the ruler's property too."[105] Therefore, the nine-dash line is legitimate because China maintained its sovereignty since territorial control did not count to legitimate sovereignty.[106] China became aware of the modern sovereignty concept only after the nineteenth century when Western powers challenged China. Wu's study indicates that sovereignty in the Chinese claim has a different connotation that the modern concept of sovereignty does not embrace.

A similar argument has been suggested by Western scholars as well. Buszynski argues that "China is today engaged in an effort to transform what was a frontier zone outside the dynastic state into national territory, just like Taiwan or Tibet."[107] China's state formation required it to regain maritime borders that were often vague in the form of frontiers in the decolonized world.[108] He explains two findings in his historical analysis on the origin of Chinese-defined sovereignty. First, the SCS was not formally incorporated in Chinese dynastic territory—it was the "modern concept of sovereignty . . . (that allowed China) to declare full title over an area" that used to be part of vague frontiers.[109] Second, why does China want to resolve maritime borders? China was "awakened by French and Japanese intrusion . . . in the 1930s," and was forced to take the "unresolved issue" of sovereignty over islands in the SCS after the Japanese occupation due to "the inability of the (San Francisco) conference" in 1951 to resolve it.[110] However, Buszynski's conclusion is different from Shicun Wu because Buszynski argues that Permanent Court of Arbitration and International Court of Justice cases have created precedents that continuous administration takes precedence over historical claims to disputed islands. Therefore, China's claim based on historical rights is legally not acceptable.[111] In other words, at least in terms of legality under the system of UNCLOS, there was no hope for China to secure its historical sovereignty throughout the power vacuum after the Second World War.

In China's white paper, *Peaceful Development*, state sovereignty and territorial integrity are integral to China's core interests, that is, national security, national reunification, integrity of the political system and overall social stability, and the basic safeguards for ensuring sustainable economic and social development.[112] Therefore, China is adamant not only about its current territory but also about "*regain*[ing] what it has lost to the foreign powers" (emphasis added) since the era of humiliation in the nineteenth and twentieth centuries.[113] Wu's interpretation implies that China benefited from the Sinocentric order and wants to restore that order in the current international state system.[114]

The Sinocentric order China established was similar to the suzerainty system in that the suzerain did not exert actual control on the territory of the tributary vassal state while giving the tributaries autonomy in domestic affairs. China was not able to secure its neighboring tributaries, such as

Vietnam, Korea, and Japan, in the turmoil of power contests in the nineteenth and twentieth centuries; however, for the maritime area, the period of a vacuum of norms and power continued until the Convention on the Territorial Sea and the Contiguous Zone in 1958. During this transitional period, the newly established Communist China gained time to safeguard what remained from the old system.

Domestic Politics and Historic Claims

Territorial disputes are often utilized to mobilize popular support in domestic politics. To what extent does China's domestic politics influence the formation of the country's underlying interests in the SCS? Jing Huang and Sharinee Jagtiani argue that "claimant countries have used sovereignty disputes as rallying points to solidify the legitimacy to govern their own people."[115] Is this argument applicable to political leaders and elites in China and how do they deal with "rallying points" in the SCS disputes? More importantly, do domestic political goals of mobilizing popularity through nationalistic foreign policy constitute China's underlying interests in the SCS negotiations? China has been claiming its historic rights since its national establishment as the PRC in 1949, and Chinese leaders also consistently utilize the same rhetoric. Various cases presented by Chinese leaders pursued distinct foreign policy goals that distributed different weights between diplomatic solutions and coercive measures.

Public opinion does exist in China. It does not mean that the role of public opinion in China's one-party political system functions like that of consolidated democracies. The expanding position of public opinion in China is more reasonably explained by the technological advances that have enabled rapid public opinion formation. The difference between public opinion in China and liberal democratic states is found in what sort of public opinion the Chinese are encouraged to shape. China's central party leaders and ordinary Chinese citizens are more familiar with nationalistic public opinion than democracy-oriented discourses. Consciously or subconsciously, the Chinese government did not act enough to prevent China's nationalist and hawkish sentiments "until it became clear that the negative reaction from the international community could endanger and impact Beijing's larger foreign policy goals."[116]

Domestic politics and historical claims in the SCS frequently meet at the corner of nationalism. One of the bestselling books in China in 2009,

Unhappy China, edited by Xiaodong Wang, shows that many Chinese believe that "China has been too compliant and weak" over time and needs to overcome this weakness with more robust politics.[117] *Unhappy China* taps into a widespread public sentiment of disgruntlement with the West and urges China to venture into militarily and diplomatically daring policies, and in other ways grasp its great power status in history.[118] Suisheng Zhao defines popular nationalism as a public opinion voluntarily formed without the government's intent. Chinese people with this popular nationalism are disturbed by a Western agenda of slowing down or even stopping China's rise, therefore, they are more vocal and emotional.[119]

Some scholars see books like *Unhappy China* as a rising sign of democracy in China. What Suisheng Zhao defines as "popular nationalism" expresses a desire to eventually participate in the state's foreign policy. Zhao lists three elements in China's calculations in making foreign policy: first, the domestic priority of economic modernization.[120] Second, the formation of a Great Chinese Economic Community, referring to a regional circle including China, Taiwan, Hong Kong, and Singapore. Third, benefiting from its relations with various states while not leaning or relying on one country. Regarding China's SCS policymaking, Kerry Brown from the University of Sydney focuses on the time scope and leadership variable since the appointment of Xi Jinping as general secretary of CPC in 2012. He argues that the CPC under Xi allowed voices within society to formulate policy, and the "South China Sea . . . occupies an important space in domestic politics."[121] Marc Lanteigne's observation supports this analysis. Since 2012–13, when Xi Jinping started his presidency, China's maritime policies in the SCS were further accelerated, denominating the SCS as China's "blue national soil" (*lanse quotu*).[122]

According to Brown, nationalism and national pride give new resources for legitimacy to the Chinese leadership under Xi Jinping. National dignity and "the public's emotions of now being a strong, rich country" are resources as well in an era in which China is the second-largest economy in the world with stagnated gross domestic product growth.[123] Brown's analysis provides linkages between the SCS and China's domestic politics. First, China's transition to becoming the world's second-largest economy in 2010 made the central leadership realize that the Peaceful Rise doctrine, which dictated that China would rise economically through peaceful means, was not suitable anymore. Second, Xi Jinping differentiated his leadership from his predecessor Hu Jintao by showing that he was willing to do something rather than just speak, and the Chinese people supported him. Brown sees that the change from rhetoric to action offered "a new source of legitimacy for the Communist Party," especially when China experienced falling gross domestic product growth followed by jeopardized domestic politics and stability.

There is a convincing argument that the explosive nationalistic power in Chinese public opinion is milder in the SCS dispute than in the East China Sea. Kheng Swe Lim believes that "the role of nationalism in the South China Sea dispute seems mild by comparison" "in the face of the strong emotions that the East China Sea disputes generate."[124] Vietnam and the Philippines are certainly not considered friendly countries by China when it comes to the SCS disputes; however, the historical hatred of the Japanese has always contained more explosive power for Chinese public opinion. This historical hatred was found in Chinese public opinion regardless of changes in China's leadership throughout Mao's communist regime, Deng's reform and opening up, and most recently, the era of the great rejuvenation of the Chinese nation represented by Xi's Chinese Dream.

China's domestic politics and nationalism find a historical basis in the narrative of the "century of humiliation." David Scott points out that China's century of humiliation left lasting imprints on the country's national identity.[125] In the context of the SCS disputes, Zanel Garcia and Christine Bianco argue that China's "century of humiliation" narrative is a key factor shaping its territorial claims. They explain that the unequal treaties with the West that China endured and China's historical view of the West's interventions in China fueled China's irredentist policies, leading to the resurgence of major maritime disputes in East Asia, including the SCS. The revived "cartography of national humiliation" as part of China's interpretation of its modern history has "led to the evolution and solidification of China's SCS claims."[126] The century of humiliation is a crucial sentiment for understanding China's modern diplomacy and a keyword for grasping China's stance across various diplomatic agendas in contemporary and current diplomatic practices, not just in the SCS. This narrative, along with nationalist domestic politics and shifts in public sentiment, does not constitute the underlying interests per se that China seeks to advance through negotiations in the SCS, though it provides a strong clue to understand China's official historical claims in the SCS.

Regional Order and Stability

How critical is the benefit of maintaining a regional security order that favors China among other interests it aims to achieve in the SCS? Under what conditions does the interest of the regional balance of power become more significant to China? There are two different approaches to assessing China's interests: first, China pursues a *stable* regional order; second, China pursues a regional order in which China has the role of leading power and eventually *competes* with the US in the region. If the first assumption is correct, stability is China's main interest in the SCS. If the second assumption is correct, the hierarchical structure in the region headed by China would be the first priority for China to pursue in the SCS.

In 2015 Xi Jinping pointed out that "China is now striving for the goals and tasks set by the 18th National Congress of the Communist Party of China and therefore requires peaceful and stable surroundings."[127] A state cannot choose its geographic neighbors. In the course of becoming a regional or global power, diplomatic challenges are given to a rising power to maintain stability in the region. Quansheng Zhao pointed out that "external pressure may also encourage Beijing to be more pragmatic and less rigid in its behavior' which is proved through the case of DOC."[128]

P. K. Ghosh from Observer Research Foundation argues that "it is apparent that the Chinese struggle to gain control over this vast area is not just about energy resources, but also about gaining strategic space in the region."[129] His argument is based on the US Environmental Impact Assessment report stating that none of the proved and probable oil and gas reserves in the SCS lie anywhere near the Spratly Islands. Ghosh asserts that China has drawn its own strategic lesson from the 1823 Monroe Doctrine, applying its logic to China's regional circumstances by attempting to limit external influence and assert control over the East and South China Seas, effectively treating these waters as Beijing's strategic backyard.

An analysis shows that China pursues a balance between its core interests and regional stability in the SCS. According to Chang Hee Park, China prioritized "security" when approaching maritime territorial disputes from 1949 to the 1970s. In the era of reform and opening up, "regional stability" was the primary concern of China in the SCS. After 2009, when the balance of power was reshaped as China became the second-largest economy in the world, China advocated its "core interests" while finding a balance in a way that did not interfere in the "regional stability" that it had pursued since the reform and opening up era.[130]

The perspective from regional supremacy suggests that the SCS possesses a strategic value that China should protect as a rising power in the current order. This perspective views the competition between China and the US as a significant factor worsening the SCS dispute. The SCS issue has gone beyond territorial claims and access to energy resources because the region has become a focal point for China-US rivalry in the western Pacific.[131]

Xi Jinping has accordingly mentioned that the US should let Asia's security be handled by Asians, when he spoke at the Conference on Interaction and Confidence Building Measures in Asia, a security forum initiated by China.[132] The Chinese University of International Relations has published a report pointing out that the US advocated reinforcing the "China Threat" theory and promoted a military buildup in Japan, the Philippines, and Vietnam. The report claims, in the same context, that an external power has strengthened its intervention in maritime and territorial disputes in the East China Sea and SCS.[133]

During the Obama administration, the US publicly recognized that it did not have a direct interest in the SCS while maintaining its principal position of freedom of navigation. These key points, that is, the US as a non-claimant and willingness to continue the freedom of navigation operations, were presented as the US stance on the SCS at a time while Xi Jinping was actively pushing the New Type of Great Power Relations as a new framework of China-US relations. The US stance was driven by Obama's strategic rebalance to Asia (also known as the Asian pivot) and the US's need to avoid explicitly antagonizing China while half-heartedly dealing with Xi's offer of the New Type of Great Power Relations that sought to ensure that each other respected their core interests. Xi sought Obama's agreement on the New Type of Great Power Relations to reassure mutual interests by demarcating boundaries, which was an aim reflected in its formal definition and principles including "no conflict or confrontation," "mutual respect," "mutually beneficial cooperation," and "control disagreements,"[134] The enduring factor that applied to both the Obama administration and his successors was that the US never ceased the freedom of navigation operations in the SCS. The US freedom of navigation operations was formally established in 1979 in both diplomatic and naval operational dimensions to safeguard the military of US forces. Their role in the SCS is to conduct naval operations against "excessive maritime claims."[135]

During the Trump and Biden administrations, the freedom of navigation operations were further strengthened within the context of the increasingly antagonistic US-China relationship in general. What changed most noticeably was that the narrative of "the US not being a party to the conflict" lost its power in US policy. The US response to the SCS disputes entered a new phase, with the US not only strengthening the freedom of navigation operations but inviting regional and even extraregional countries to participate in joint operations in the SCS. Secretary of State Michael Pompeo's statement, "The world will not allow Beijing to treat the South China Sea as its maritime empire," symbolically framed the SCS disputes within the broader context of the global rivalry between the US and China.[136]

China publicly supports the idea that each country's navigational and flight freedom in the SCS under international law should be fully guaranteed, as freedom of navigation in the SCS is already closely associated with the robust economic growth of the Asia-Pacific region.[137] The main concern for China is that the US has a different purpose in promoting the freedom of navigation principle. From the Chinese perspective, what the US wants is to maintain its leading position by using the SCS disputes to rationalize its intervention in regional affairs.[138]

Yan Xuetong adds to the literature by writing that what China pursues in the SCS is the initiative in the region. His analysis shows that the international security environment became unfavorable to China when the Secretary of State Hillary Clinton declared America's return to Asia in the 2009 ASEAN Regional Forum, which formally introduced the US strategic rebalance. That change is one of the considerations redirecting Chinese foreign policy, and China has started scrambling for leadership in the region.[139] Yan's interpretation explains the motivation behind China's aggressive attitude in the SCS since 2009. In this rivalry game, China's rise cannot mutually exist with the long-established American positions throughout Asia, as Robert Jervis has identified in the security dilemma.[140]

The geographical features of the SCS can support this point of view. According to Toshi Yoshihara and James R. Holmes the SCS is equipped with geographical elements that other historical powers enjoyed in their most prosperous times. The US, for example, aimed at securing strategically important waters, like the Caribbean Sea and the Panama Canal, from the maritime hegemony of Europe to consolidate a dominant position in the Western Hemisphere. However, the US did not have any other goals than this strategic purpose. If China is trying to achieve a dominant position over the SCS and the Strait of Malacca for a strategic reason, then the current disturbance in the SCS could be viewed as a natural process as similarly observed when the hegemony moved from Western Europe to the US.[141] However, the SCS still has its peculiar geographical features of various straits that could be used to enter into it. This feature creates an environment where a monopoly on transportation control and management is difficult, affecting China's strategy in the SCS.[142] A Chinese scholar also suggested that China needs to explore alternative transportation routes through the Sunda and Lombok Straits in Indonesia, which provide deep water alternatives to the Strait of Malacca.[143]

Robert Kaplan points out the military rivalry between the United States and China in the SCS.[144] Geostrategically, he compares China's position vis-à-vis the SCS with the US's position vis-à-vis the Caribbean Sea in the nineteenth and early twentieth centuries.[145] According to him, "China's effective capture of Taiwan [i.e., a reunification by China] in the years to come will allow Chinese naval planners . . . to finally concentrate their energies on the wider SCS."[146]

When it comes to China-US relations, China calibrates its use of force in accordance with its relatively expansive judgment of the sometimes-threatening intentions of the US in the region. The engagement of the US in the SCS with aircraft and warships means that China would not be the sole power in the region. Since the early 2000s, China has watched the military involvement of the US in the SCS. China's civil and military responses toward those cases of military engagement indicated China's interpretation of the US motives and the seriousness of the actions. China must judge whether a respective intervention intends to maintain the status quo by demonstrating US power or aims to extort specific intangible and tangible resources from China. China's default reaction to the former appears to be "defensive" while it would take an "offensive" posture to the latter.

Most maritime disputes between the US and China have taken place in the exclusive economic zone off China's coast. This zone extends 200 nautical miles offshore and is an area where China has special—but not exclusive—rights. As a result, confrontations here are less provocative than those in territorial waters that extend twelve nautical miles from the coastline.

In 2001, a Chinese F-8 fighter collided with a US EP-3 surveillance plane off the island of Hainan, and a Chinese pilot died from this incident. Former Chinese foreign minister Tang Jiaxuan describes this incident precisely in his memoir.[147] Tang finds that this incident "seemed accidental, but actually it had a certain inevitability in it" because the US continued its reconnaissance flights "along the edge of China's waters."[148] In the same year, the USS *Bowditch* was challenged by Chinese patrol vessels. The first such incident in Obama's term occurred when Chinese vessels blocked and surrounded the USS *Impeccable* in 2009. In 2013, a US missile cruiser, USS *Cowpens*, was blocked by a Chinese naval ship during its operation in international waters in the South China Sea.

The US argues that exclusive economic zones are part of international waters—meaning foreign vessels should have freedom of navigation. Chinese law also allows for freedom of navigation in the exclusive economic zone. However, it warns that China "has the power to take necessary measures against acts violating laws" within the zone.

While risky, the recent freedom of navigation exercises may have crucial foreign policy benefits for the US. They could build up trust between the US and its partners in the South China Sea, like the Philippines, or even Japan or Korea with current—or potential—maritime disputes with China. For the US, these benefits probably outweigh the risks.

US defense officials were open about the fact they sent a guided-missile destroyer within twelve nautical miles of a Chinese artificial island in the SCS on October 27, 2015. In response, Chinese president Xi Jinping asserted "islands in the South China Sea have been China's territory since ancient times" while US defense secretary Ashton Carter promised more such freedom of navigation exercises in the future.

Sailing within territorial seas has meaning beyond just advocating freedom of navigation. The move was a way for the US to express its repudiation of any territorial claims China had to seven new islands they have been building up over the years. With the US pursuing a "pivot to Asia" under the Obama administration, it was also a way to underscore the US commitment to keep trade routes open to other countries like Vietnam, the Philippines, Taiwan, and Malaysia.

The actions of the USS *Lassen*, in sailing near artificial islands created by China in the SCS in 2015, however, came as no surprise to China. Defense Secretary Ashton Carter raised the possibility of sending US Navy ships near the islands in May. Then, in September, the US sent a stronger signal of its firm will to "sail, fly and operate" near Chinese artificial islands during Xi Jinping's visit to the White House.

Notably, the US and China continued military-to-military dialogue despite tensions over US freedom of navigation exercises. This level of communication was possible because of confidence-building measures developed over many years. These were measures designed to "increase transparency and predictability and reduce risk of unintended incidents." The US and China agreed to these measures during a summit meeting held in November 2014. According to their agreement, "encounters between naval surface vessels" are limited by mutually accepted rules.

The effort to establish confidence-building measures between the US and China goes back to 1998 when the Military Maritime Consultative Agreement was signed between the Chinese defense minister and the US defense secretary. Since then, the Agreement has been maintained with regular contacts as an effective mechanism between the two parties. The contacts include nine annual meetings, two special meetings, and fifteen working group meetings. Recent events suggest that the US-China military-to-military confidence-building measures help build understanding and prevent the situation from becoming uncontrollable by providing channels to restore relations quickly.

The management of maritime confrontation in the SCS is part of China's long-term plan to reframe US-China relations. In a 2010 speech, the Chinese ambassador to the US referred to the two states as "great countries" that "should respect the other's major interests and concerns." Respecting each other's core interests is one of the critical elements of the new relationship ushered in by strategic and economic dialogue in 2009. The US showed respect for China's core interests when President Obama clearly stated that the US was "not a claimant" in the South China Sea dispute. He further "encouraged a resolution between claimants in these areas."

These statements indicated that the US would not attempt to directly take part in the resolution of the disputes in the SCS as one of the claimants. That would be welcoming to China. China would prefer direct negotiations with other direct claimants to the SCS, like Brunei, Malaysia, the Philippines, Taiwan, and Vietnam. The Chinese defense minister reaffirmed that the disputes should be solved by "bilateral negotiations between the parties directly involved." The US has a difficult road ahead—balancing moves that reaffirm its own and other countries' rights to navigate the SCS without raising China's ire by stepping in to broker long-term agreements.

Chinese concerns about nontraditional security are another factor that brings its footprint in the SCS. Addressing nontraditional security issues is relevant to regional economies, and nontraditional threats will cause severe damage to global trade if they cannot be resolved promptly. The US Defense Department report recognizes that China's military modernization has become increasingly focused on a range of missions beyond China's coast, including sea lane security, counterpiracy, peacekeeping, and humanitarian assistance/disaster relief. The idea of multilateral cooperation is highlighted by scholars because such nontraditional threats create vulnerabilities but have a far-reaching influence on all relevant parties. China, therefore, needs to embrace multilateral dialogues with the concerned parties to counterpiracy incidents, and to overcome misunderstandings on the security issues. Nontraditional security is an integral part of China's interest in the SCS. However, it is mainly discussed in cooperative and multilateral interactions, while other sensitive issues such as historical rights and regional supremacy bring difficult tasks in diplomacy.

Piracy legally refers to illegal acts which occur in the international sea according to the UNCLOS or the outer waters of any jurisdictional maritime zones. Piracy acts that occur in the territorial sea or EEZ are not treated as piracy. In UNCLOS, Article 101, this definition applies only to any of the described illegal acts committed either on the high seas or outside the jurisdiction of any state. Illegal acts that take place in ports or territorial waters are defined as "armed robbery against ships" by the International Maritime Organization.[149]

One of the first diplomatic efforts in the SCS disputes management appeared in 1978 when Philippine president Ferdinand Marcos disclosed that visiting Chinese vice-premier Li Xiannian had agreed that the dispute over the Spratly Islands should be settled through diplomatic negotiations. China's dominant power in the SCS has been consolidated through substantial changes in the status quo in the disputed water—the Sino-Vietnam skirmishes and China's occupation of the Paracel Islands in 1974, China's takeover of the Spratly Islands from Vietnam and the Philippines in 1988, the Mischief Reef incident and the subsequent diplomacy between China and the Philippines in 1995, China engaging in multilateral negotiations with ASEAN in 2002, the standoff at the Scarborough Shoal in 2012 that culminated in the International Tribunal's Award denying China's historic rights in the SCS. Since then, the SCS disputes are largely described by two distinct phenomena—first, military-driven changes to the status-quo, including China's military power projection in the SCS and the freedom of navigation operations of the United States and its allies; *and* second, diplomacy-led changes, including China's bilateral and multilateral code of conduct negotiations.

China's underlying interests in the SCS are not clearly ordered in priority and seemingly change over time. These interests are shrouded under the cover of historical concerns inherited from the country's irredentist policy since its national establishment in 1949. Nonetheless, it is relatively recent that the Chinese government sources and related analyses discuss the SCS as one of its "core interests."[150] With China becoming the world's second-largest economy in 2010, the diplomatic and military repercussions of its actions have significantly increased. The wariness of neighboring countries and major powers outside the region about China's policy and diplomacy in the SCS has also intensified. Compared to other SCS littoral states, China's overwhelming economic and military power has allowed it to expand its diplomatic maneuvers.

This chapter discussed how the narrative and importance of values in the SCS disputes and China's underlying interests have changed over time. China's strategic priorities and interests have changed, and the narratives regarding those interests have also changed in the domestic political discourse in China. While underlying interests have shifted, the rhetoric of indisputable sovereignty has neither changed nor weakened. However, China's evolving interests were reflected in its diplomacy through the various platforms that chapter 4 explores.

FOUR

Diplomacy

Bilateral, Trilateral, and Multilateral

On July 11, 2021, marking the fifth anniversary of the Arbitral Tribunal Ruling on the South China Sea, US secretary of state Antony Blinken issued a statement announcing that "an armed attack on the Philippines . . . in the South China Sea would invoke US mutual defense commitments under Article IV of the 1951 US–Philippines Mutual Defense Treaty." Historically, the Philippines has not always secured US protection over the disputed islands. In June 1978, President Ferdinand Marco signed a presidential decree claiming that the islands and islets in the South China Sea located within the Kalayaan Island group (part of the Spratly Islands) must be deemed subject to the Philippines' sovereignty. US officials at the time did not acknowledge that the US was obligated to protect the Philippines-claimed Spratly Islands under the US–Philippines defense pact.[1] While the Philippines' ally was keeping its distance, China reached out to the Philippines diplomatically. Three months before the Philippines' presidential decree was signed, Chinese vice premier Li Xiannian visited the Philippines and affirmed with President Marcos that the dispute over the Spratly Islands should be settled via diplomatic negotiations.

The outcome of the Sino–Philippines talks in 1978 and the subsequent negotiations between China and other claimants over four decades did not bring permanent peace and stability to the South China Sea. Nevertheless, the negotiation process reveals substantial evidence about what the claimants want and their essential goals. This chapter deals with the diplomatic interactions between China and other claimants in the SCS disputes and suggests a pattern in a series of negotiations and agreements. This chapter neither overpraises the inception of interstate agreements nor opposes the China threat theory. Relationships change, negotiations break down, and agreements do not endure; however, China's diplomatic goals were achieved throughout each interaction and negotiation with claimants. The Chinese principles of indisputable sovereignty and pragmatism in diplomacy do not seem to be able to coexist and even oppose each other but they appeared consistently in interstate interactions to protect Chinese national interests.

In the twenty years before the Cold War ended, when China maintained favorable relations with the US but not with the Soviet Union, Southeast Asian countries were cautious about both the Soviet Union and China. One of the concerns of Southeast Asian states, in addition to the spread of communism, was China's policy and aggression in the SCS. In 1980, an Indonesian admiral in the Analysis Department of the Indonesian Navy's General Staff stated that "Beijing's design in the South China Sea poses a serious threat to Southeast Asian countries, including Indonesia." The admiral further warned that Southeast Asian countries "should consider the question of the increase of China's military strength in the framework of its long-term strategic plan."[2]

This chapter elucidates the patterns of China's negotiations by asking, first, When does China enter a negotiation with claimants in the South China Sea? Second, Do China's negotiations have any commonalities and are they significant? Chapter 3 discussed the continuity of Chinese expectations for diplomacy and official claims in the SCS throughout negotiations; so, third, Do China's negotiations with different claimants exhibit divergent patterns depending on the claimants' economic and military capabilities, and does the number of negotiating countries affect Chinese negotiation patterns? Fourth, do China's negotiations with certain claimants address specific agendas while the agendas regarding other claimants present abstract principles and imprecise plans? Last, how do we know which Chinese negotiations were successful?

This chapter demonstrates that China's expectations of diplomacy and claims in the SCS are consistently presented through various negotiation patterns. These patterns are defined by the various configurations of the negotiating parties and the factors consistently affecting China's stance in various negotiating steps. Understanding China's negotiation patterns in the context of the constant elements over time is helpful in forecasting its behavior in various negotiations.

Size and Specificity Matters in Negotiations

How did China engage in negotiations regarding the SCS disputes with its neighbors? This chapter considers the negotiation size and analyzes three different sizes of negotiation: bilateral, trilateral, and multilateral. William Zartman and Guy Faure, along with other scholars, define negotiation as "a process by which the parties combine their divergent positions into a single agreed outcome."[3] Along with this definition, the following analysis reveals the "divergent positions" from the Chinese point of view and the "agreed outcome" of Chinese negotiation with other claimants. This chapter also balances the analysis of the process of negotiation and the relevant outcomes as mentioned by Zartman and Faure.[4]

China has maintained diplomatic relations with other claimants in the SCS disputes in bilateral, trilateral, and multilateral forms. China's respective bilateral relations and related negotiations with other claimants are examined in the following sections. The analysis of bilateral negotiations uses primary data, including the Joint Statement between the Republic of the Philippines–People's Republic of China Consultations on the South China Sea and on other Areas of Cooperation (signed in 1995) and the Agreement on the Delimitation of the Territorial Seas, Exclusive Economic Zones and Continental Shelves in the Beibu Gulf between the People's Republic of China and the Socialist Republic of Vietnam (signed in 2000). The Beibu Gulf is better known in English as the Tonkin Gulf. There are few officially and jointly signed bilateral agreements involving China and explicitly addressing the SCS issue; however, these selected agreements have been publicly released and repeatedly mentioned by the signing parties because they have imposed meaningful long-term effects on the signatories' bilateral relations since they were agreed upon.

The China–Vietnam–Philippines trilateral agreement on joint exploration is also analyzed. The primary data available for analysis is the Tripartite Agreement for Joint Marine Scientific Research in Certain Areas in the South China Sea by and Among China National Offshore Oil Corporation, Vietnam Oil and Gas Corporation, and Philippine National Oil Company (signed in 2005). China–ASEAN relations will be examined as a prominent case in multilateral negotiation of the SCS dispute. The Declaration on the Conduct of the Parties in the South China Sea (signed in 2002) is discussed. There are eleven participants in the declaration: ten members of ASEAN (Brunei, Cambodia, Indonesia, Laos, Malaysia, Myanmar, the Philippines, Singapore, Thailand, and Vietnam) and China.

The patterns of each size of negotiation are analyzed with a focus on the key features of negotiation: responsiveness, specificity, and compliance. Responsiveness in negotiation refers to the extent to which negotiators respond to each other and whether their response is escalatory or de-escalatory. Specificity is assessed on a spectrum from a general to a detailed discussion of the issues, including maritime delimitation, joint development, and seeking the status quo in island occupation. Compliance with the provisions of the agreements is assessed against breaches that occurred after the agreement was signed.

Objectively comparing the above negotiations is challenging. For example, how can the goals of the various negotiations and whether these agreements were complied with be analyzed together? Were these negotiations prepared for and conducted similarly? One reasonable comparison point is *specificity*. Specificity is pertinent to the following criteria: Does the article of the agreement contain the aim and objective of the agreed action in specific detail? If the agreement contains the aim and objective as an abstract principle or idea, then its specificity is low. The aims and objectives of each negotiation are key to assessing its specificity.

For example, Article 7 of the China–Philippines Code of Conduct (signed in 1995) is *specific* because the parties agreed to cooperate (action) "in the protection and conservation of the marine resources of the South China Sea" (aim and objective). In contrast, Article 2 of the Declaration on the Conduct between ASEAN and China (signed in 2002) deals with principles that are *not specific* because the participants agreed to explore (action) ways to "[build] trust and confidence" (aim and objective) in accordance with certain principles. The specificity of China's agreements is assessed in the following section.

Bilateral Interactions: Small and Specific

Bilateral negotiation has become a practical and effective method by which China pursues sensitive issues directly relevant to territorial and delimitation issues in the disputed waters. Wu Shicun, the president of the National Institute for South China Sea Studies, states that bilateral negotiation is the solution for the SCS dispute because not all member countries of ASEAN have maritime disputes with China. Among the direct claimants, each of them has different claims and positions toward negotiations.[5] China insisted that the SCS dispute could be resolved only through direct talks after the Philippines filed a case with the Permanent Court of Arbitration in 2013. According to the Chinese perspective, international judicial mechanisms would not help mediate or resolve the tension.[6] A broader context, however, could be found in the argument that the SCS conflict is confined to one part of the Sino–Southeast Asian relationship. Therefore, the relevant countries can strengthen relations with China in other sectors, such as the economic and cultural sectors, without being constantly overwhelmed by the looming threat of a worsening maritime dispute with China.[7]

China's neighboring countries are wary of its efforts to build a modern navy and shift the regional balance of power in China's favor. The SCS disputes have strained China's relations with ASEAN and prompted China to pursue multiple foreign policy objectives to maintain the status quo in its relations with each member of ASEAN. In other words, China seeks to separate the SCS disputes from its overall relations with the claimant countries.[8] This tendency to separate issues becomes more pronounced, especially when bilateral relations deteriorate overall. The following sections explore how China has negotiated the SCS issues through bilateral diplomacy with key disputants.

China and Vietnam

> The demarcation of the Beibu Bay left over by history has been resolved.
> —Ministry of Foreign Affairs of the People's Republic of China, July 19, 2005

> China and Vietnam "adhere to pushing forward bilateral negotiations . . . so as to avoid the issue becoming internationalized."
> —Ministry of Foreign Affairs of the People's Republic of China, June 13, 2013

China and Vietnam normalized their diplomatic relations in November 1991. The China–Vietnam relationship is an exemplary case of variability and stability among China's bilateral relations. China and Vietnam quickly restored their relationship through direct communication between high-level officials right after nationalism and tensions arose in the two countries due to a Chinese maritime surveillance vessel cutting the cable of a Vietnamese seismic vessel in May 2011.[9] They agreed to continue the "long-term and steady growth of bilateral relations" and strive for a peaceful resolution to the SCS dispute even after China's oil rig installation in the Paracel Islands in 2014, which affirms the deepened understanding achieved in their bilateral relationship.[10]

The Sino–Vietnamese Agreement on Maritime Boundary Delimitation in the Gulf of Tonkin was the first maritime delimitation China agreed to in the SCS. On December 25, 2000, the respective foreign ministers from

China and Vietnam met in Beijing and signed "The Agreement on the Delimitation of the Territorial Seas, Exclusive Economic Zones and Continental Shelves in the Beibu Gulf between the People's Republic of China and the Socialist Republic of Vietnam."[11] The Beibu Gulf is located between the coast of northern Vietnam, China's Hainan Island, and the southernmost coast of mainland China. The agreement came into effect four years later.[12] Historically, China dealt with foreign negotiators in Tonkin Bay during the 1884–85 Sino–French War. An agreement between China and France was drawn while Chinese influence over its periphery diminished.[13]

The history of negotiation leading to the Sino–Vietnamese agreement on the Gulf of Tonkin goes back to 1974. Vietnam initiated the discussion that led to the 2000 agreement after the normalization of bilateral relations between the two parties in 1991. The negotiations started in 1974, the same year that China forcefully occupied the Paracels and expelled Vietnam from the islands. A series of bilateral discussions ensued between October 1977 and June 1978 and between 1992 and 2000. Seven total rounds of negotiation (three summit meetings between 1992 and 2000), eighteen rounds of negotiation at the working level, and forty-nine meetings of the Joint Working Team and the Mapping Team were held.[14]

In a summit meeting between China and Vietnam in 2000, the leaders signed the agreement to demarcate the Beibu Gulf and establish fishery cooperation. The agreement consists of eleven articles that warrant further analysis to discover how much of the agreement deals with specific and nonspecific issues. Article 1 defines the area of the Gulf of Tonkin to delimit the territorial seas, exclusive economic zones, and continental shelves of the two countries. Article 2 sets out the twenty-one geographic points that define the maritime boundary of the Gulf of Tonkin.

The specificity of the maritime delimitation agreement between China and Vietnam is shown in table 5. Table 5 records how many articles of the agreement (out of a total of eleven articles) address the aim and objective of the agreed action in specific detail, meeting the analytical standards for specificity. Nine articles satisfy this criterion and only two articles in the agreement contain nonspecific aims and objectives, that is, abstract principles or ideas.

The leaders of China and Vietnam maintained frequent exchanges before and after the delimitation agreement. As a state-level meeting, Jiang Zemin and his Vietnamese counterpart Tran Duc Luong met in Beijing on April 19, 2001. They published a joint statement and signed several important agreements, including the agreement on the demarcation in the Beibu Gulf and

Table 5. Agreement on the Delimitation in the Beibu Gulf between China and Vietnam, 2000

Year:	2000
Parties involved:	China, Vietnam
Negotiation size:	Bilateral
Official document name:	Agreement on the Delimitation of the Territorial Seas, Exclusive Economic Zones and Continental Shelves in the Beibu Gulf between the People's Republic of China and the Socialist Republic of Vietnam
Total articles (*N*)	11
Specific articles (*N*)	9
Nonspecific articles (*N*)	2

the agreement on fishery cooperation, which outlined directions and tasks to strengthen and expand bilateral cooperation in various fields.[15] One day later, Hu Jintao, then Vice President, also met Vietnamese President Tran Duc Luong. They agreed to facilitate the process of defining land borderlines, promote oil and gas exploration and exploitation and fisheries cooperation in the Beibu Gulf, and jointly tap the SCS so both sides could make active progress in these fields.[16]

On November 19, 2004, the Sino–Vietnam summit meeting between Hu Jintao and Tran Duc Luong in Santiago, Chile (at the tenth Asia-Pacific Economic Cooperation, or APEC, summit) confirmed that "the two agreements concerning the Beibu Gulf are under implementation."[17] The two agreements referred to are the demarcation agreement and fishery cooperation agreement. Hu and Tran further asserted the importance of "the guidance of the 16-word principle defined by the leaders of the two countries" and agreed that "China–Vietnam ties are generally developing well." China confirmed that "the Chinese government persistently supports Vietnam to accede to the World Trade Organization (WTO)."[18]

In the 2005 summit meeting, China and Vietnam confirmed that "the demarcation of the Beibu Bay left over by history has been *resolved*" (emphasis added).[19] During Hu Jintao's visit to Vietnam, the China–Vietnam Joint Declaration was issued.[20] They agreed to hold a joint working group in the 12th China–Vietnam Government-Level Border Negotiation one month after the Joint Declaration. Therefore, the joint working group held four rounds of talks in January 2006, September 2006, April 2007, and January 2008.[21] In the fourth round of joint working group meetings, Chinese and

Vietnamese negotiators discussed possible joint field research beyond the mouth of Beibu Bay.[22]

On March 21, 2006, Jia Qinglin, the chairman of Chinese People's Political Consultative Conference, met Vietnamese President Tran Duc Long. Jia suggested that the two countries "promote oil and gas exploration and fisheries cooperation in the Beibu Gulf, and joint tapping of the South China Sea so that the two sides will make active progress on the fields."[23] The subsequent expert-level exchanges between China and Vietnam were made through the eleventh round of the China–Vietnam Experts Meeting on Maritime Affairs on 10–12 July 2006, in Vietnam. During this meeting, China and Vietnam discussed maritime cooperation "in the fields of low sensitivity."[24] The expert group was one of China's preferred and "highly appreciated" types of dialogue.[25] In *2007–9 China's Foreign Affairs*, published by the Ministry of Foreign Affairs, China was described as steadily advancing negotiations with Vietnam on maritime delimitation and joint development in an area *beyond* the mouth of Beibu Bay.[26] In December 2006, the second joint patrol of the navies of China and Vietnam was also held in the Beibu Gulf.[27]

As of 2007, there were three streams of dialogue between China and Vietnam regarding maritime cooperation in the Beibu Gulf: government-level boundary talks (thirteen rounds), talks on maritime demarcation outside the mouth of the Beibu Gulf (three rounds), and the joint committee on Beibu Gulf fishery cooperation (four rounds).[28] In 2008 and 2009, China and Vietnam continued to hold the fourth and fifth rounds of negotiations on the demarcation and joint development of territorial waters outside the mouth of the Beibu Gulf. They also held the fifth and sixth annual meetings of the Joint Committee on Fishing Cooperation in the Beibu Gulf.[29]

On May 30, 2008, in Beijing, Hu Jintao and his Vietnamese counterpart Nong Duc Manh, general secretary of the Communist Party of Vietnam Central Committee, met and agreed that they "should make joint efforts to develop China–Vietnam comprehensive strategic cooperative partnership under the guidance of the 16-word principle."[30] They positively assessed their general relationships by stating that "the issues left over from history (referring to the Tonkin Bay demarcation) between the two countries have also been gradually resolved in a proper manner." Hu Jintao urged that they "maintain the fine tradition of frequent exchange of visits and contact" "in a timely manner," and properly handle problems with bilateral ties by strengthening "bilateral consultations . . . under . . . multilateral frameworks." Regarding the land border as well, both leaders noted that "both sides should intensify their efforts . . . erecting markers along their land border and sign new documents on regulating the border by year end." During the meeting, Nong Duc Manh pledged to grant additional aid of US$200,000 for Wenchuan earthquake recovery in addition to Vietnam's previous aid.

On October 11, 2011, Vietnamese Communist Party chief Nguyen Phu Trong visited Beijing. The delegations from China and Vietnam signed an agreement on the basic principles guiding the settlement of sea-related matters between the Socialist Republic of Viet Nam and the People's Republic of China.[31] Two months later, on December 21, 2011, Vice President Xi Jinping met Vietnamese president Truong Tan Sang and congratulated him on the twentieth anniversary of the normalization of China–Vietnam relations.[32] The two states defined their historical relations as "both countries' joint responsibility to carry on the friendship from generation to generation." Xi pointed out that "the Communist Party of China and Chinese government have always viewed China–Vietnam relations from a strategic and long-term perspective." More specifically, Xi "called for more efforts to develop and deliver the joint action plan on a comprehensive strategic partnership of cooperation." A year after, in 2012, Xi Jinping met with Da Ba Ty, chief of the general staff of the Vietnamese army, and strengthened the "16-word principle" and the "spirit" (*jingshen*) of "good neighbors, good friends, good comrades, and good partners" (*haolinju, haopengyou, haotongzhi, haohuoban*) between two states.[33] The *spirit* aligns with China's 16-word principle in defining the overall relationship between China and Vietnam.

On March 21, 2013, during a phone conversation between Chinese president Xi Jinping and Nguyen Phu Trong, general secretary of the Communist Party of Vietnam Central Committee, China's view of China–Vietnam relations was articulated:

> "The Communist Party of China and the Chinese government view *inter-party* and inter-governmental ties with Vietnam from a strategic height and long-term perspective and will maintain high-level exchanges and deepen *inter-party* cooperation."[34] (emphasis added)

Interparty cooperation makes Sino–Vietnam relations unique compared with other Chinese bilateral relations. On June 19, 2013, during a meeting between Xi Jinping and Truong Tan Sang, Xi mentioned that "China and Vietnam are important neighbours and cooperative partners" and "both sides should unswervingly march along the path of friendly cooperation no matter what problems and distractions occurred."[35] Xi further defined China's interest in forming better relations with Vietnam by stating that "China is now striving for the goals and tasks set by the 18th National Congress of the Communist Party of China and therefore requires peaceful and stable surroundings." Furthermore, China and Vietnam exchanged practical ways to improve their relationship, such as exchanging views in a "timely manner for major issues regarding bilateral relations." The economic benefits of bilateral China–Vietnam relations were also mentioned: "Both sides need to . . . realize in advance the goal of $60 billion in bilateral trade for the year 2015. The Vietnamese side welcomes investments from Chinese businesses."

More importantly, in the summit meeting on June 19, 2013, there was a discussion directly concerning the SCS disputes. Both state leaders agreed to "prevent it [SCS issue] from disturbing the bilateral relations. The key lies in maintaining stability and promoting cooperation."[36] The two parties agreed to "adhere to pushing forward bilateral negotiations . . . so as to avoid the issue becoming *internationalized*" (emphasis added). Therefore, negotiations would be throughout "the working groups for sea waters out of the mouth of Beibu Bay, striving to conduct joint development and *demarcation* concurrently" (emphasis added). This invites the interpretation that China planned to negotiate with Vietnam beyond Tonkin Bay and make deals regarding demarcation—as long as Vietnam cooperated with China.

On April 7, 2015, a summit meeting between Xi Jinping and Nguyen Phu Trong confirmed that two countries maintained the 16 words, 4 spirits, and traditional China–Vietnam friendship. Their relations were described as "a comprehensive strategic partnership of cooperation." China welcomed Vietnam's participation in the construction of the Maritime Silk Road from China through the South China Sea and then the Indian Ocean, which was suggested by Xi two years before. In the meeting, the SCS issue again arose. Both sides agreed that they "should abide by the important consensus reached by the leaders of the two parties and countries to jointly manage and control maritime disputes and maintain the overall China-Vietnam relations and peace and stability on the South China Sea."

These findings and implications are derived from the chronological records of bilateral interactions between China and Vietnam. One of the anomalies found in the relations between China and Vietnam is that while summit-level dialogues and high-level officials' exchanges maintained a certain level of friendliness, ministerial-level policies and public emotions ran counter to each other. The negotiation with China did not stop Vietnam's military buildup in the region. According to market research conducted by a private body, in 2016, Vietnam was planning to deploy six kilo-class sonobuoys with an expendable sonar system that conducts antisubmarine missions and underwater research into the SCS to deter China's maritime assertiveness.[37]

What lessons does the Beibu Gulf agreement case, the only maritime delimitation case in the SCS, offer for negotiators in the SCS disputes? It is important to understand the background circumstances, including international and regional developments, which made the delimitation agreement between China and Vietnam possible. China's global strategy was to settle its growth within the liberal order around the time of its WTO accession in 2001. This strategy influenced its regional approach, seeking ASEAN's support for China's accession to the WTO, which reflected its bilateral ties with Vietnam and were strengthened by the territorial delimitation. The diplomatic willingness of both countries was evident before and after the maritime delimitation, marked by the Accord on the Basic Principles for the Resolution of the Boundary Territory Question in 1993, the Treaty on Land Boundary in 1999, and the Agreement on Joint Patrols by the Navies of China and Vietnam in the Beibu Gulf in 2005.

However, the international, regional, and bilateral conditions did not automatically lead to the agreement. As table 5 shows, the presence of specific, exchangeable agendas between China and Vietnam was as important as the favorable conditions. It is unlikely that the exact same conditions that made the maritime delimitation agreement possible will reoccur, and even if any similar circumstances occur, it would still be impossible to advance delimitation discussion in the SCS beyond the Beibu Gulf without the identification and development of a concrete, specific, and exchangeable agenda.

China and the Philippines

The normalization of diplomatic relations between China and the Philippines occurred on June 9, 1975, much earlier than with Vietnam. The Philippines is the only country among the other SCS claimants that signed the bilateral Code of Conduct with China regarding SCS disputes. In 1995, the two parties pledged to solve their dispute by peaceful means through the Code of Conduct.[38] The bilateral Code of Conduct between China and the Philippines is significant because it demonstrates how the Philippines tends to respond to and deal with China and reveals how the internalization of the SCS disputes began. The Philippines preferred to internationalize to solve the dispute—that is, it tried to involve actors beyond the bilateral interaction, such as ASEAN and the Permanent Court of Arbitration. The Sino–Philippines clash over the Scarborough Shoal in the EEZ of the Philippines during April–June 2012 was the direct cause of the Philippines initiating third party arbitration.

The Code of Conduct agreed between the two parties in 1995 is an important source of information on variables of the China–Philippines bilateral negotiations. The Code of Conduct was made between the two parties during the meetings of their respective delegations in August 1995 in Manila. These meetings were held after an incident in Mischief Reef, located within the boundary of the Philippines' EEZ. In January 1995, a fishing vessel and its crew from the Philippines were reported to have been detained for several days by Chinese troops on the reef. In the following month, the Philippines discovered that the Chinese had built four clusters of octagonal buildings supported on stilts with the Chinese flag on the reef. The Philippines strove for a commitment from China that it would not advance into the Philippines' EEZ again, as in the Mischief Reef incident.

The Code of Conduct was signed on August 9–10, 1995, in the form of a Joint Statement after bilateral consultations concluded. Before the signing, two rounds of bilateral talks were conducted in Hangzhou, China, and Manila, the Philippines. Along with the broad outline of a code of conduct, the two sides also agreed to further discuss confidence-building measures .[39] However, during the talks, China rejected the Philippines' demand that China leave Mischief Reef.[40] Ultimately, the Philippines signed the Code of Conduct to avoid another incident rather than force China to withdraw from Mischief Reef. A Philippines official described the objective of negotiations:

> Wang Yingfan, then Assistant Foreign Minister in Charge of Asian Affairs, and I [the Philippines official] negotiated, in August 1995, a bilateral code of conduct for the South China Sea, the Philippines objective being to obtain a Chinese commitment *not to pull another Mischief Reef*.[41] (emphasis added)

There was backlash after the 1995 Mischief Reef incident and ASEAN members expressed their concern over China's behavior, which intimidated the existing regime in the SCS established by the ASEAN Declaration on the South China Sea that was signed in 1992 by ASEAN members.[42]

The Code of Conduct consists of eight articles. The specificity of the Code of Conduct agreement between China and the Philippines is shown

Table 6. Code of Conduct between China and the Philippines, 1995

Year:	1995
Parties involved:	China, Philippines
Negotiation size:	Bilateral
Official document name:	Joint Statement, Republic of the Philippines–PRC Consultations on the South China Sea and on other Areas of Cooperation
Total articles (*N*)	8
Specific articles (*N*)	4
Nonspecific articles (*N*)	4

in table 6. Out of the agreement's eight articles, four contain specific aims and objectives of the agreed action and the remaining four articles contain abstract aims and objectives in the form of principles or ideas.

The April–June 2012 Scarborough Shoal clash between China and the Philippines is similar to the 1995 Mischief Reef incident for two reasons: first, China again occupied reefs within the Philippines' EEZ, and second, the Philippines sought a nonbilateral solution—the regionalization and internationalization of the problem. In 1995, the Mischief Reef incident led the Philippines to seek a declaration among ASEAN states that efforts would be made to refrain from tension in the SCS. The Scarborough Shoal clash and China's subsequent occupation of the shoal in 2012 led the Philippines to submit this case to the International Tribunal for the Law of the Sea. The Philippines Foreign Ministry stated that it was impossible to continue bilateral discussions due to China's hardline position, and thus the Philippines had been forced to resort to international arbitration.[43] Historically, the Philippines had attempted to resolve the dispute with China in various ASEAN forums and regional and international platforms.[44]

In both 1995 and 2012, the Philippines achieved part of its goal. Due to the Philippines' activity, ASEAN and China discussed drafts of the multilateral Code of Conduct in 1999 and eventually released the China–ASEAN Declaration on the Conduct of Parties in the South China Sea in 2002. Again, due to the Philippines' proactive defense during arbitration, the Permanent Court of Arbitration made an award in 2016 that denied China's historical claims in the SCS. Another similarity between the Mischief Reef incident in 1995 and the Scarborough Shoal incident in 2012 is that the subsequent international support did not materially stop China's behavior.

Relations between China and the Philippines were at their most cordial under Philippine president Gloria Macapagal-Arroyo's administration from

2001 to 2010. The dialogue on cooperation in the SCS was lively during this time. However, according to *China's Foreign Affairs*, China–Philippines cooperation in the SCS was not reviewed in bilateral interactions between the two states but rather was mostly addressed in the context of trilateral cooperation among China, the Philippines, and Vietnam. Arroyo visited Nanning, China, in October 2006 to attend the Summit Meeting of China–ASEAN Dialogue. In the meeting with Premier Wen Jiabao, China and the Philippines agreed to "push forward the joint development of the South China Sea by China, the Philippines and Vietnam," referring to the Joint Marine Seismic Undertaking (JMSU).[45] In 2008, *China's Foreign Affairs* reported on China–Philippines relations in the context of an assessment that "the tripartite cooperation on the South China Sea among China, the Philippines, and Vietnam continued to move forward."[46] Nevertheless, from the year 2009 onwards, subsequent volumes of *China's Foreign Affairs* neither reported maritime cooperation with the Philippines in the SCS nor the progress of the JMSU.[47] This is primarily due to the suspended trilateral JMSU, and because of that, the bilateral maritime cooperation between China and the Philippines was also suspended.

According to a 2015 statement by the US Department of State, "The United States has designated the Philippines as a Major Non-NATO Ally, and there are close and abiding security ties between the two nations."[48] The Manila Declaration signed in 2011 reaffirmed the 1951 US–Philippines Mutual Defense Treaty as the foundation for a responsive security partnership. The 1951 Mutual Defense Treaty followed previous pacts between the Philippines and the US: the Military Bases Agreement and the Military Assistance Pact, both in 1947. Richard Heydarian argues that "the Philippines effectively outsourced its territorial integrity-related concerns to the US," thereby making the US into the Philippines' "de facto guarantor" of survival.[49]

The Philippines was the only state among the SCS claimants with a formal defense treaty with the US; nevertheless, how the defense treaty supports the Philippines' stance in SCS disputes is unclear. First, the behavior of the US regarding the SCS dispute in the 1990s is different from its current behavior. In 1995, the US did not attempt to accord special meaning to the treaty between the US and the Philippines with regard to the maritime disputes in the SCS. According to the US State Department spokesperson in 1995, "We [the US] do have the defense treaty, and of course the United States honors its treaty commitments. But I don't have anything beyond that related to the possible relationship of that to the maritime issues."[50] In 2014, there was an enhanced defense cooperation agreement between the US and the Philippines. In sum, although US–Philippines defense relations have existed historically, how the US utilizes this relationship depends on changing US interests in the region.

A comparison of China–Vietnam and China–Philippines bilateral relations is possible during a short period in 2011 when these relations diverged. On June 26, 2011, Chinese state councilor Dai Bingguo met Vietnamese vice foreign minister Ho Xuan Son, the special envoy of the Vietnamese leader, and both sides agreed to solve the maritime disputes between China and Vietnam through negotiations and friendly consultations. At the same time, the BBC reported that the Philippines and the United States would begin an eleven-day joint naval drill in disputed waters in the SCS on June 28. The comparable situation justified China's belief that it tried to solve territorial disputes peacefully with diplomacy, while the US used its military alliances in the region to promote fear and insecurity in regional actors. China further criticized the US for promoting the US defense industry and maintaining regional hegemony.[51] A quantitative study in 2016 on China's view of Vietnam and the Philippines further supports the observation that China maintains bilateral relations with Vietnam and the Philippines with different expectations. According to Pascal Abb, who delved into 1,500 pieces of written commentary by Chinese public commentators, Chinese experts are "optimistic about a future partnership with Vietnam," while "they have increasingly come to identify the Philippines as an opponent."[52]

In relations with the Philippines, China used economic interdependence as leverage. When the Scarborough Shoal incident increased tension between China and the Philippines in April 2012, Chinese people canceled their trips to the Philippines—because China is the third-largest source of tourists in the Philippines, this was troublesome for the Philippines. China also cut banana imports from the Philippines. Bananas are the Philippines' second-largest agricultural export and China imports one-quarter of the crop.[53] Economic interdependence is often considered supportive of regional stability, but it can also be used as a weapon by the stronger side in interdependent relationships.

ASEAN Countries: Direct Criticism or Disengagement

Malaysia and Brunei are claimants in the SCS disputes in addition to China, Vietnam, the Philippines, and Taiwan. China's diplomacy with Malaysia and Brunei is comparable to its diplomacy with the other three claimants. The talks on SCS disputes between China and Vietnam have developed based on

Table 7. ASEAN States' Attitudes toward China in the SCS Disputes, with Direct Claimants in Bold

Direct criticism	Diplomatic middle ground	Disengagement
Philippines	**Malaysia**	Cambodia
Vietnam	Indonesia	Myanmar
	Thailand	

Source: Marc Lanteigne, "The South China Sea in China's Developing Maritime Strategy," in *Power Politics in Asia's Contested Waters: Territorial Disputes in the South China Sea*, ed. Enrico Fels and Truong-Minh Vu (Cham, Switzerland: Springer International, 2016), 102.

the relationships between two communist parties, and China and the Philippines have clashed over issues of asymmetric capabilities and the internalization of SCS disputes. However, Malaysia "disassociates itself from both Vietnam and the Philippines and pursues its own bandwagoning policy towards China."[54] Except for a visit of Malaysia's prime minister to Swallow Reef in 2009 and Malaysia's joint submission to the Commission on the Limits of the Continental Shelf with Vietnam, "Malaysia has proved to be a 'quiet claimant'" in the SCS disputes.[55] Rather than politically confronting Beijing, Malaysia prefers to maintain trade and economic relations with China. Malaysia is an example of an ASEAN member state pursuing self-interest rather than collective interest.[56]

Christopher Roberts further argues that an assertive China has divided ASEAN states into pro-China states and a few SCS claimants that are unfavorable to China.[57] In other words, China has used diplomatic flexibility to form bilateral, trilateral, multilateral, and international connections while increasing its bargaining power by creating an environment that protects China's interests in the SCS. Through bilateral interactions with claimants and nonclaimants in the SCS disputes, China has been able to divide ASEAN into manageable individual relationships.[58]

Indonesia is not a direct claimant in the SCS disputes; however, it has commented on the disputes and maintained its position in dispute resolution as a middle power in the region.[59] Although not claiming contested features in the SCS, Indonesia became concerned over Chinese fishing boats' intrusion into Indonesia's EEZ around the Natuna Islands off the northwestern coast of Borneo. On March 26, 2013, the Indonesian vessel *Hiu Macan 001* of the Ministry of Maritime Affairs and Fisheries encountered a Chinese fishing boat operating illegally in the SCS, roughly 107 nm northeast of Natuna Island, in the Indonesian EEZ. The Chinese ship (number

58081) was subsequently boarded and all nine Chinese fishermen on board were arrested, but the Indonesian captain was later forced to release his prisoners by the Chinese maritime law enforcement vessel *Yuzheng 310*'s threats and harassment.[60]

Nevertheless, Indonesia benefits by pursuing neutrality in its diplomatic relations with China. Indonesia is free of severe maritime disputes with China and anti-Chinese sentiment, allowing Indonesia to be an amiable neighbor to China and other regional powers. For instance, Indonesia welcomed both the Asian Infrastructure Investment Bank and the Asian Development Bank. Indonesian president Joko Widodo requested that Xi assist Chinese state companies in developing Indonesia's infrastructure, which is urgently needed for Indonesia to increase its economic growth, and even suggested that the Asian Infrastructure Investment Bank be headquartered in Indonesia. Meanwhile, the (Japan-backed) Asian Development Bank is the third-largest source of financing for Indonesian development, providing 15.2 percent of total financing. Indonesia sees participation in the Asian Infrastructure Investment Bank as an opportunity to expand its infrastructure development funding options.[61] Indonesia has adopted the position of regional mediator and power broker.[62] Its most substantial concern in dealing with China is the Indonesian economic situation rather than maritime disputes, which are not a direct or prioritized issue between China and Indonesia.

China has insisted that the South China Sea dispute can only be resolved through direct talks. China believes that international judicial mechanisms will not necessarily help mediate or resolve the tension. While the UNCLOS has played an important role in promoting maritime cooperation in the past, it may not be able to solve this territorial dispute.[63]

Trilateral Interactions: Viable and Vulnerable

As a trilateral cooperative agreement involving China, the Joint Marine Seismic Undertaking is the most prominent example of trilateral interaction in the SCS dispute. JMSU is the tripartite agreement between China, the Philippines, and Vietnam that promoted the joint exploration of marine resources in the SCS while putting aside the signatories' sovereignty disputes. What is the value and uniqueness of the JMSU as the sole case of trilateral cooperation? The JMSU represented a cooperative effort over natural resources, which are often regarded as the source of conflict that claimants compete over in the SCS. This case set a precedent that cooperation over energy resources is possible in the SCS. It suggests that access to energy resources is negotiable rather than an absolute bottom line or red line in China's negotiations. This implies that it is possible to identify cooperation agendas that do not overlap with multiple claimants' bottom lines in the SCS, including China.

Nevertheless, the background and rationale for this unusual cooperation among three major competitors in the disputed waters have been analyzed in only a few works.[64] The text of the agreement signed in 2004 between China and the Philippines is unavailable to the public.[65]

On September 1, 2004, China and the Philippines reached an agreement to conduct pre-exploration studies in the Spratly Islands to identify oil and gas exploration areas. Both governments granted approval and their heads witnessed the signing of the agreement between the China National Offshore Oil Corporation and the Philippines National Oil Corporation. Vietnam initially opposed the plan but later cooperated with it, sending representatives to the talks from the Vietnam Oil and Gas Corporation (Petrol Vietnam). On March 14, 2005, China, the Philippines, and Vietnam signed the JMSU in Manila. The official name of the agreement is "The Tripartite Agreement for Joint Marine Seismic Undertaking in the Agreement Area in the South China Sea."

Barry Wain and Richard Heydarian analyze key individuals related to the JMSU[66] and view it as a unique case in the SCS of three competitors (China, Vietnam, and the Philippines) agreeing to joint exploration. Along with President Arroyo's visit to Beijing in 2004, China signed a memorandum of understanding on defense cooperation with the Philippines and offered US$1.2 million in military assistance as well. China's economic statecraft permeated the Philippine economy through transportation, telecommunication, infrastructure, and overall bilateral trade investment.[67] The JMSU was initially planned in cooperation between China and the Philippines, and Vietnam later joined the joint maritime exploration scheme, making it trilateral.

According to the 2007 edition of *China's Foreign Affairs*, in 2006 China "continued to promote the Joint Marine Seismic Undertaking and cooperation in other fields of low sensitivity with Vietnam and the Philippines."[68] The first phase of the JMSU was successfully completed in 2006.[69] In the 2008 edition of *China's Foreign Affairs*, the names of corporations were mentioned rather than those of participating governments and there was an indication that China was expanding cooperation with Vietnam and the Philippines to "other fields of low sensitivity."[70] The second phase of the JMSU

Table 8. A Tripartite Agreement for Joint Marine Scientific Research among China, Vietnam, and the Philippines, 2005

Year:	2005
Parties involved:	China, Philippines, Vietnam
Negotiation size:	Trilateral
Official document name:	A Tripartite Agreement for Joint Marine Scientific Research in Certain Areas in the South China Sea by and among China National Offshore Oil Corporation Vietnam Oil and Gas Corporation Philippine National Oil Company
Total articles (*N*)	29
Specific articles (*N*)	26
Nonspecific articles (*N*)	3

was also reported to have been successfully launched.[71] However, by 2009 there was no progress in cooperation and the 2009 edition of *China's Foreign Affairs* did not report any JMSU-related activities.

The tripartite agreement on joint development between China, Vietnam, and the Philippines is analyzed in table 8 according to the specificity criteria. Table 8 shows twenty-nine articles in the agreement with twenty-six containing specific aims and objectives in detail. Only three articles involve abstract aims and objectives through principles or ideas. These statistics demonstrate that the JMSU was designed for specific outcomes of the trilateral agreement. Though nonstate corporate actors led the JMSU from the three countries, it deserves further attention because, first, it is an exemplary case of trilateral cooperation in the SCS, and second, all participants in the JMSU are state-owned corporations that were commissioned by their respective governments.

In terms of compliance, the JMSU did not lead to any tangible results and was suspended after the completion of the first stage. Why did this trilateral project not really go the way the three parties had hoped for? For a joint development to succeed, two conditions are essential: good relations among the relevant parties and the political will to make potentially controversial decisions within their countries.[72] These conditions ae closely interrelated, and the JMSU heavily depended on them, particularly the latter. The political will of the pro-Chinese leadership in the Philippines was a crucial initial driver for the JMSU. However, the agreement lost momentum when the leadership changed. As an article criticizing the Philippines' pro-China president at the time noted, "by the time the foreign ministry heard about it [the then president's agreement with China] and objected, it was too late, the officials say."[73]

When the regime changed in the Philippines in 2010 from the pro-Chinese President Arroyo to the anti-Chinese president Benigno Aquino, bilateral relations between China and the Philippines as well as the trilateral cooperation failed to continue. The JMSU, as the only example of trilateral cooperation, shows that China's stated intent to shelve disputes and seek joint development was once executed but was ultimately unsuccessful. As Huaigao Qi from Fudan University suggests, positive overall relations with other claimant countries and political will from each party are crucial initial drivers for joint development.[74] Additionally, public support and bipartisan (if democratic) interest in such agreements is essential to make the joint development plan sustainable.

Multilateral Interactions: Normative and Contested

China has consistently argued that the sovereignty disputes in the SCS should be solved bilaterally, rather than through multilaterally or international mechanisms.[75] For issues other than sovereignty, one of China's diplomatic strategies is the use of "two hands" (*liangshou*), aimed at addressing the pressure and criticism regarding its reluctance to prioritize a multilateral approach to the SCS disputes.[76] The two hands strategy involves using both bilateral and multilateral diplomacy to pursue different purposes. China used the cooperative framework of the China–ASEAN interaction to address nontraditional issues in the SCS. Nontraditional security issues include marine environmental protection, marine scientific research, the safety of navigation and communication at sea, search and rescue operations, and combating transnational crime.

On November 13, 2014, Premier Li Keqiang clarified China's stance on the SCS dispute with an explanation of its "dual-track approach." Before Li's speech, in August 2014, Foreign Minister Wang Yi also mentioned the dual-track approach. Xue Li believes that the dual-track approach sent "the message that China agreed to handle the South China Sea disputes under a multilateral framework" in which China and ASEAN stand on either side of the conversation.[77] He continued to explain that the dual-track approach demonstrated China's more flexible policy in the SCS and that China willingly accepted "regionalization" of the SCS issues instead of seeking solely bilateral solutions.[78]

On December 14–15, 2011, an international seminar was held at Haikou, China, with the theme of China–ASEAN cooperation in implementing the Declaration on the Conduct of Parties in the South China Sea.[79] In the seminar, Liu Zhenmin, then the assistant foreign minister, stated that "China expects friendly cooperation with the Association of Southeast Asian Nations (ASEAN) to make the South China Sea safe." He positively assessed the development in China–ASEAN relations overall, stating that "politically mutual trust and pragmatic cooperation have been strengthened between China and ASEAN countries." The DOC has been acclaimed and criticized simultaneously by many sources as the "most remarkable document ever signed between China and ASEAN countries,"[80] and also as an empty paper. Sam Bateman considers the DOC a "soft law" and a regime that coordinates the littoral countries to cooperate on specific activities that preserve the SCS as a shared resource.[81]

One of the implications of the seminar held in Haikou was that China and ASEAN members recognized the effectiveness of the DOC and discussed the cooperation required to promote SCS security within its framework. For example, China and ASEAN participants agreed that cooperation and technological means of crime detection remained weak before the threat of piracy and transnational crime. They further agreed that the engineering maintenance of shipping channels should be improved. An Indonesian ambassador said that the seminar reflected the determination of China and ASEAN to increase mutual understanding and cooperation. He especially endorsed the importance of the DOC as a cooperative framework.[82]

China–ASEAN relations are centered in multilateral diplomacy in the SCS. China and ASEAN appeared to embrace their relationship in the context of community spirit. Chinese foreign minister Wang Yi, in the China–ASEAN Foreign Ministers' Meeting held in 2014, stated that "China and ASEAN share a common destiny," and ASEAN foreign ministers agreed that "ASEAN and China have built a high level of mutual trust and deepened their partnership" in the past decade.[83] One scholar even asserts that the ASEAN countries in direct dispute with China are pathologically patient despite China's prolongation of talks on a maritime code of conduct.[84] If ASEAN states are showing exceptional patience, as Rory Medcalf argues, an examination of the source of that patience, China's diplomatic skills, and the power structures of the region is necessary. Money, power, and diplomacy are all involved in China's maneuverings in the region and this book focuses on the diplomatic principles and practices that affect China's negotiations.

Chinese multilateral cooperation in SCS disputes can be found in various cases, although since the late 2000s it has been limited to maintaining the regional status quo. The most prominent case was the Declaration on the Conduct of Parties in the South China Sea signed in 2002.

Why did China and the ASEAN countries agree to sign the DOC? Certain factors led to the DOC in the multilateral negotiations of the SCS disputes. First, the DOC was China's response to the China threat theory promulgated after the 1995 Mischief Reef incident. ASEAN members expressed their "serious concern" over China's behavior, which undermined the dispute management regime in the SCS agreed among ASEAN members—the ASEAN Declaration on the South China Sea signed in 1992.[85] In these unfavorable circumstances, Chinese foreign minister Qian Qichen declared that China was prepared to hold multilateral discussions on the Spratly Islands and would not limit its diplomacy to bilateral talks.[86]

The Asian Financial Crisis in the late 1990s was an opportunity for China to create a good image as a regional white knight. China helped Thailand, South Korea, and Indonesia by offering US$4 billion in bailout packages. Japan, the leading Asian country in technology and economy, was less effective at combating the regional crisis. Beijing was thus encouraged to advocate greater economic interdependence in the region, which largely shaped its foreign policy. For example, China has been increasingly proactive in its stance on emerging markets since joining the WTO in December 2001 and pursuing the ASEAN–China Free Trade Agreement that came into effect in 2010. Despite US concerns that China would disrupt the WTO process after gaining membership, China's relationship with the organization has been largely nonconfrontational.[87]

China signed the DOC in 2002 and has maintained its engagement with ASEAN in line with the Code of Conduct negotiations to prevent isolation from the SCS community and accept multilateral crisis management.[88] Leszek Buszynski and Christopher Roberts suggest three possible reasons China signed this multilateral agreement. First, China intended to demonstrate its moderation and willingness to accept norms of behavior in the SCS. Second, China wanted to constrain ASEAN states from fortifying islands or features in the disputed waters. Third, the DOC was "a diplomatic device to forestall US involvement" in the SCS, especially after China learned that the Philippines sought support from the US following the Mischief Reef incident in 1995.[89]

Another circumstance that enabled the DOC to be signed between ASEAN and China was China's perception of ASEAN. Until the early 2000s, China treated ASEAN as an effective regional grouping. However, this perception was not entirely institution-driven and did not come from China's advocacy of further integration of Southeast Asia for regional benefit; instead, it derived from China's practical requirements. In 2001, Foreign Minister Tang Jiaxuan's implied that the background of the good neighbor policy was that China and ASEAN were facing "challenges of globalization" *together* and that "China has to deal with a series of challenges after its accession to the WTO."[90] He argued that China and ASEAN "need to further strengthen unity and cooperation for the long-term common development."[91] His remarks can be viewed as a starting point for the discourse of the "common destiny of China and ASEAN" that Foreign Minister Wang Yi and Defense Minister Chang Wanquan later promoted in 2014 and 2015.[92]

How Can Norms Be Negotiated?

China, in general, does not oppose the concept of dealing with ASEAN as a group. Tang Jiaxuan mentioned, "I am glad to see that more and more ASEAN countries have come to realize that China's accession to the WTO will bring more development opportunities to ASEAN."[93] One of the short-term purposes of China treating ASEAN as a group was to seek ASEAN's support for China joining the WTO. In 2014, Chinese foreign minister Wang Yi stated in the China–ASEAN Foreign Ministers' Meeting that "China and ASEAN share a common destiny," and ASEAN foreign ministers replied that "ASEAN and China have built a high level of mutual trust and deepened their partnership" in the past decade.[94] Wang added that China hoped to see a "united" ASEAN:

> China hopes to see a still more *united*, stable and prosperous ASEAN and will do all it can to support ASEAN in its endeavor to quicken the integration process and narrow the gap of development among its members. It will also support ASEAN in playing a bigger role in both regional and international affairs.[95] (emphasis added)

Why was it important for China to treat ASEAN as a single player? In the early 2000s, the role of ASEAN as a group of individual states was significant in endorsing China's status in the region for the sake of China's rise to power. This economic motivation allowed China to form a positive relationship with ASEAN as a single player. In the 2010s, China attempted to group ASEAN states again to support its One Belt One Road initiative—later called the Belt and Road Initiative—and new Maritime Silk Road as part of the initiative.[96] The One Belt One Road was sought for strategic, diplomatic, and economic goals; however, one of its goals was to address China's concerns regarding limited maritime shipping routes that mostly relied on the Strait of Malacca. Hu Jintao expressed his concerns over this issue and the "Malacca Dilemma" (*Maliujia kunju*) appeared in political discourse under Hu Jintao, followed by Xi Jinping's One Belt One Road initiative offering one way to address China's sea route vulnerability.[97]

Finally, China had to address the China threat theory in the region in the early 2000s. Starting in 1995, China had associated multilateral negotiations with nontraditional and environmental security. For example, in the Joint Statement on consultations between China and the Philippines held in 1995, China and the Philippines agreed:

> 6. The two sides agree to promote cooperation in fields such as protection of the marine environment, safety of navigation, prevention of piracy, marine scientific research, disaster mitigation and control, search and rescue operations, meteorology, and maritime pollution control. They also agree that on some of the above-mentioned issues, *multilateral cooperation* could *eventually* be conducted.[98] (emphasis added)

Multilateral cooperation was mentioned in relation to nontraditional security cooperation, such as the "protection of the marine environment" and the "safety of navigation." However, bilateral interaction was the preferred method to resolve territorial disputes. China further implied that the role of international laws was to guarantee a sovereign state the right to pursue the style of diplomacy it prefers. In other words, international laws were not considered appropriate authorities to order or intervene in territorial disputes. The Joint Statement between China and the Philippines also states:

> 2. Efforts (to settle territorial disputes) must be undertaken to build confidence and trust *between the two parties.*

and

> 8. Disputes shall be settled by the countries *directly concerned* without prejudice to the freedom of navigation in the South China Sea.[99] (emphasis added)

The DOC was created from the increased cooperation between China and ASEAN in the late 1990s. As the cooperation between China and ASEAN was expected to increase, possible conflicts among parties were deliberated in a favorable atmosphere and with a positive outlook. Chinese foreign minister Tang Jiaxuan indicated that China had a positive view of its relationship with ASEAN at the beginning of the 2000s, noting top leaders' frequent visits between China and ASEAN member states and increasing numbers in economic cooperation statistics.[100]

What specific needs drove the DOC in the early 2000s, amid expanding economic and regional cooperation between China and ASEAN? What trade-offs did China and ASEAN make through the DOC? China's negotiating strategy in the SCS at the time needs to be understood in line with its ASEAN strategy, regional strategy, and global strategy. China's economic growth has occurred within the framework of the US-led liberal economic order. According to G. John Ikenberry, the liberal international order, based on US-led institutions, incentivized China to further integrate into the existing system.[101] A key event cementing China's position in the US-centered liberal order was its accession to the WTO in 2001. As China became more embedded in the liberal order internationally, its regional diplomatic strategy also aligned largely with this order.

When China signed the DOC with ASEAN, the greater regional cooperation between China and ASEAN included negotiating a free trade area, regional projects like Mekong River Basin development, and addressing transnational crime and public health issues. Tang Jiaxuan's speech highlights the prioritization of China-ASEAN cooperation from the Chinese perspective, which was gaining significant momentum at the time.[102] He described the DOC negotiations within the broader context of a normative task to bring successful cooperation across various sectors.

Buszynski explains that China aimed to establish regional norms for the SCS to prevent extraregional powers, particularly the US, from intervening in the disputes and to stop the disputes from being internationalized by ASEAN countries or offshore states.[103] Especially after events such as the Philippines signing the Visiting Forces Agreement with the US in 1998, "China realized the value of norms of behavior in terms of constraining external powers."[104] Buszynski's analysis highlights China's strategy for negotiating the SCS disputes that did not conflict with its international, regional, and ASEAN strategies, which is evident in the normative nature of the DOC.

What are the specific trade-offs for norms? How can norms be negotiated? The DOC achieved China's objectives (securing the balance of power by isolating the SCS in a regional dispute and obtaining ASEAN's support for China's regional and international diplomatic agenda) while offering

ASEAN the possibility of engaging with China through diplomatic interaction and pursuing a peaceful resolution of the disputes. The DOC was a deal of norms versus norms, a negotiation of norms. The DOC carries significance as historical data in two different aspects. First, it serves as a historic example of norm bargaining in the region. Second, the negotiating documents reveal China's bottom line at that time. Both implications are crucial for understanding the ongoing negotiations of the Code of Conduct, which continue more than two decades after the DOC was agreed upon. Multilateral negotiations between China and ASEAN have remained within the *normative* bargaining framework established by the DOC.

Since 2002, the DOC has maintained its status as a common agreement on SCS-related issues. On July 20, 2012, the foreign ministers of ASEAN member states agreed on six principles *without* China that reaffirmed the effectiveness of the DOC. The "Six-Point Principles" confirmed that the parties intended to implement the DOC. The Six-Point Principles were promulgated four months after China and the Philippines clashed over the Scarborough Shoal in April 2012.[105] China's response to the Six-Point Principles included statements on its agreements and disagreements with ASEAN partners (see table 9).[106] In the statement, China argued that it had abided by the DOC and intended to complete COC negotiation, therefore agreeing with ASEAN. China further asserted its respect for the UNCLOS in concert with other ASEAN members: however, it did not agree that the UNCLOS is a dispute resolution mechanism.

China presented this view in response to the sixth principle of the Six-Point Principles agreed among the ASEAN foreign ministers, as table 9 shows. The sixth principle addresses "the peaceful resolution of disputes, in accordance with . . . International Law, including the 1982 UNCLOS." Thus, the sixth principle suggests that the ASEAN foreign ministers view international law, such as UNCLOS, as a universally applicable and feasible mechanism for the peaceful resolution of SCS disputes.

In opposition to this belief, the Chinese spokesperson Hong Lei quoted the UNCLOS Preamble:

> The States Parties to this Convention (UNCLOS) . . . with due regard for the sovereignty of all States, [recognize] *a legal order* for the seas and oceans which will facilitate international communication.[107] (emphasis added)

China views UNCLOS as "recognized principles of international law," but does not deem it the only source of "the peaceful resolution of disputes,

Table 9. China's Responses to ASEAN's Six-Point Principles

Issue	Six-Point Principles Agreed among ASEAN Foreign Ministers (July 20, 2012)	China's Responses to Six-Point Principles (July 21, 2012)
DOC	1. The full implementation of the Declaration on the Conduct of Parties in the South China Sea (2002). 2. The Guidelines for the Implementation of the Declaration on the Conduct of Parties in the South China Sea (2011).	"China is ready to work with ASEAN countries to fully and effectively implement the Declaration on the Conduct of Parties in the South China Sea (DOC)."
COC	3. The early conclusion of a Regional Code of Conduct in the South China Sea.	"China is open to discussions with ASEAN countries on working out a Code of Conduct in the South China Sea (COC)."
UNCLOS	4. The full respect of the universally recognized principles of international law, including the 1982 United Nations Convention on the Law of the Sea (UNCLOS).	"As a signatory to the UN Convention on the Law of the Sea (UNCLOS), China attaches great importance to upholding the principles and purposes of the UNCLOS."
Action	5. The continued exercise of self-restraint and nonuse of force by all parties.	[*No comment*]
Principle	6. The peaceful resolution of disputes, in accordance with universally recognized principles of International Law, including the 1982 United Nations Convention on the Law of the Sea (UNCLOS).	"The Convention (UNCLOS) is not an international treaty to regulate disputes of territorial sovereignty between states, nor can it serve as the basis to arbitrate such disputes."

Source: "Foreign Ministry Spokesperson Hong Lei's Remarks on ASEAN Foreign Ministers' Statement on the Six-Point Principles on the South China Sea Issue," Ministry of Foreign Affairs of the People's Republic of China, July 21, 2012, https://www.mfa.gov.cn/mfa_eng/xw/fyrbt/fyrbt/202405/t20240530_11349140.html

in accordance with universally recognized principles of International Law, including the 1982 UNCLOS."[108]

Further, China did not comment on the fifth principle of ASEAN's Six-Point Principles about the "non-use of force" and maintaining the status quo in the SCS through self-restraint. The difference between ASEAN's and China's positions on the use of force in the SCS implies that China might have intended to remove its legal liability in maintaining the status quo in disputed waters.

DOC to COC

The DOC and the COC may be confused with each other. The DOC is the Declaration on Conduct of the Parties in the South China Sea, signed between China and ASEAN in 2002. The COC refers to the code of conduct that is expected to impose compliance. ASEAN states had pursued a COC with China to treat issues in the SCS more effectively before signing the DOC in 2002.[109] Efforts to establish the code of conduct between ASEAN and China have been made since 2002. In the tenth clause of the DOC, the upcoming COC negotiation was mentioned:

> 10. The Parties concerned reaffirm that the adoption of a *code of conduct* in the South China Sea would further promote peace and stability in the region and agree to work, on the basis of consensus, towards the eventual attainment of this objective.[110] (emphasis added)

The critiques of the DOC's effectiveness in maintaining stability in disputed waters vary. First, the DOC has provided a bedrock for further negotiation between China and ASEAN countries regarding issues in the SCS. China tends to endow each step of achievement with rhetorical significance. In the 2014 China–ASEAN Summit, the parties agreed that they had achieved initial steps in implementing the DOC, including practical activities dubbed "early harvest measures."[111] These measures include adopting the first list of common views on COC consultation, establishing hotlines for search and rescue agencies and among foreign ministries for maritime emergencies, and a tabletop exercise on search and rescue.[112]

Within China, there was also motivation to prioritize the stability of neighboring regions by practicing a more pragmatic and friendly foreign policy.[113] China's participation in multilateral cooperation in the SCS appeared on successive platforms after the DOC; for example, the Joint Declaration of ASEAN and China on Cooperation in the Field of Non-traditional Security Issues (November 2002), the Treaty of Amity and Cooperation (October 2003), and the Memorandum of Understanding between ASEAN and China on Cooperation in the Field of Non-traditional Security Issues (January 2004). This participation supports the assertion in China's white paper that China has made a constructive proposal to "shelve disputes and seek joint development" and uphold stability in the SCS and other surrounding areas.[114]

Doubt about the effectiveness of these platforms remains, however. The DOC, for example, is a political document without any legally binding force and, thus, its effectiveness in practice is in question.[115] Some scholars, even from China, treat the DOC as an empty paper. Counterintuitively, Qin Yaqing stresses the lesser-known Chinese ways of achieving regional integration or cooperation: informal relations, processes, and nonbinding consensus. China and ASEAN might be regarded as having reduced the binding force to increase flexible cooperation.[116]

Nevertheless, the benefits that China could gain from the DOC are tangible. China publicly hosted a Joint Working Group on implementing the DOC and steadily pushed forward consultations on a COC. The eleventh joint working group meeting between China and ASEAN on the implementation of the DOC was held June 24–25, 2014, in Bali, Indonesia. The DOC is more relevant to nontraditional security issues. In a recent international seminar on the DOC, delegations from each country discussed what specific cooperation should be implemented in the SCS, such as technological devices against piracy and transnational crime threats and the engineering maintenance of the shipping channel.[117]

Not all countries in ASEAN are SCS claimants and the DOC indicates this. Article 4 of the DOC states:

> The Parties concerned undertake to resolve their territorial and jurisdictional disputes . . . through friendly consultations and negotiations by *sovereign states directly concerned*, in accordance with universally recognized principles of international law, including the 1982 UN Convention on the Law of the Sea.[118] (emphasis added)

This article essentially prevents two unfavorable actions against China: first, collective activities of ASEAN against China and, second, third-party inter-

Table 10. The Specificity of the Declaration on Conduct of Parties in the South China Sea

Year:	2002
Parties involved:	China, ASEAN
Negotiation size:	Medium Multilateral
Official document name:	Declaration on the Conduct of Parties in the South China Sea
Total articles (*N*)	10
Specific articles (*N*)	3
Nonspecific articles (*N*)	7

vention such as arbitration. Three months before the results of the arbitration initiated by the Philippines emerged, Chinese foreign minister Wang Yi traveled to Brunei, Cambodia, and Laos, which were favorable to China. One of his intentions was to reaffirm China's legal position and Article 4 of the DOC. During the trip, Wang agreed with these ASEAN countries that "the disputes over territorial and maritime rights and interests should be resolved through dialogues and consultations by parties directly concerned under Article 4" of the DOC.[119]

The specificity of the DOC is shown in table 10 according to the specificity criteria. Of ten total articles, only three articles contain concrete aims and objectives. Seven articles address abstract aims and objectives that are related to principles or ideas. These numbers imply that the DOC is a principle-focused and abstract agreement rather than a specific future roadmap.

The formation of the ASEAN–China Joint Working Group on the Implementation of the DOC was agreed in the ASEAN–China Senior Officials' Meeting on the implementation of the DOC convened in Kuala Lumpur on December 7, 2004. According to the "Terms of Reference," the Joint Working Group's main task is to recommend measures to realize the DOC provisions for consideration by the Senior Officials' Meeting. The Joint Working Group is tasked to suggest specific recommendations primarily addressing action plans for the implementation of the DOC and nontraditional security issues.[120]

Another type of China–ASEAN dialogue was the Workshop on Managing Potential Conflicts in the South China Sea. The Sixteenth Workshop was held in Indonesia November 22–24, 2006. This workshop included Taiwan as Chinese Taipei. The workshop was unofficial and requested donations from participants to the Special Fund for the Workshop.[121] The Seventeenth and Eighteenth Workshops were also held in Indonesia in 2007 and 2008,

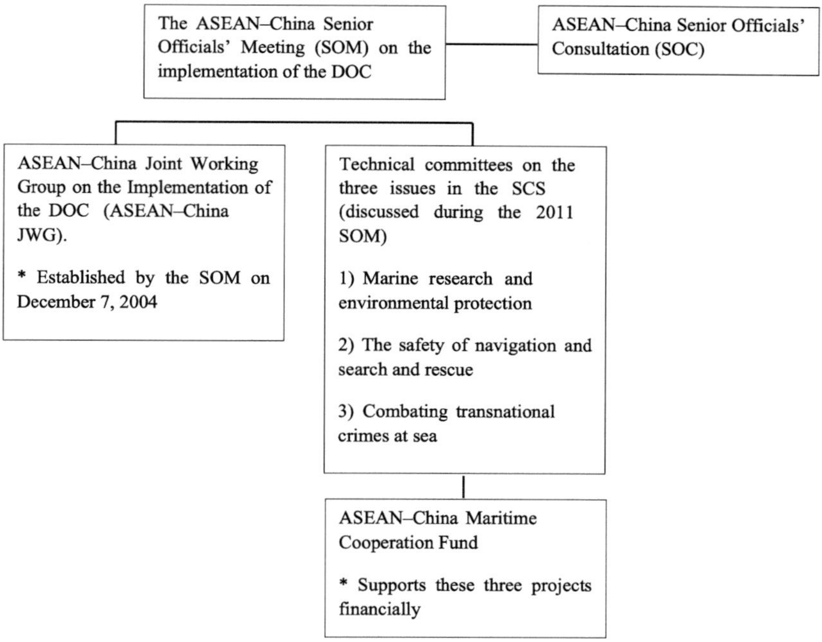

Fig. 1. The organizational system of joint working groups in ASEAN

and participants attended "in their private capacities," including Taiwan. During the Seventeenth and Eighteenth Workshops, China expressed a positive attitude toward financially supporting the workshop (17th) and willingness to provide "additional financial support to the Workshop" (18th).[122]

Table 11 compares two bilateral agreements, a trilateral agreement, and a multilateral agreement in terms of the specificity of the agreements. The China–Philippines agreement shows a balance of specificity and nonspecificity, but the agreement was not complied with in several subsequent incidents. The China–Vietnam agreement on delimitation had an overwhelming level of specificity and compliance has been well maintained. The trilateral agreement also offered noteworthy specificity; however, it lost force as the Philippine regime changed and the new leadership denied this trilateral agreement with China. The DOC is the only case of more nonspecific than specific articles and its effectiveness remains in question.

China has connected regional organizations in which it has core membership or vital interest. In 2005, ASEAN and the Shanghai Cooperation Organization signed the first memorandum of understanding. In 2017,

Table 11. Specificity in Chinese Negotiations with SCS Claimants

Year:	1995	2000	2005	2002
Parties involved:	China, the Philippines	China, Vietnam	China, the Philippines, Vietnam	China, ASEAN
Negotiation size:	Bilateral	Bilateral	Trilateral	Medium Multilateral
Official document name:	Joint Statement, Republic of the Philippines–PRC Consultations on the South China Sea and on Other Areas of Cooperation	Agreement on the Delimitation of the Territorial Seas, Exclusive Economic Zones and Continental Shelves in the Beibu Gulf between the People's Republic of China and the Socialist Republic of Vietnam	A Tripartite Agreement for Joint Marine Scientific Research in Certain Areas in the South China Sea by and among China National Offshore Oil Corporation, Vietnam Oil and Gas Corporation, Philippine National Oil Company	Declaration on the Conduct of Parties in the South China Sea
Total articles (*N*)	8	11	29	10
Specific articles (*N*)	4	9	26	3
Nonspecific articles (*N*)	4	2	3	7

the two organizations are expected to conclude the updated memorandum of understanding. According to Xi, China's "global economic integration is accelerating . . . By intensifying cooperation between the SCO and the EAEC [Eurasian Economic Community], we will create further space for development."[123] By connecting existing regional organizations, China could extend the boundaries of the regional security block and create more interdependent economic dynamics around its territory. Because one of China's diplomatic goals is to maintain a peaceful and stable region, strengthening the interdependent security interests of regional institutions surrounding China makes the security environment too complex to engage in conflicts.

In its contemporary bilateral, trilateral, multilateral, and international legal diplomacy, China's principles are intended to attract others' support and bilateral and international diplomatic platforms serve as tools to realize its practical interests. This chapter examined the hypothesis that principles of indisputability and pragmatism in China's diplomacy have increased China's bargaining capacity and flexibility in SCS disputes. In this chapter, flexibility in China's diplomacy refers to its diversified diplomatic channels: bilateral, trilateral, multilateral, and international diplomacy. This chapter argues that China's diplomatic goals were realized in each interaction and negotiation; therefore, the Chinese principles of indisputability and pragmatism coexist with various diplomatic platforms.

FIVE

Norms and Power

Why China Joined UNCLOS

On September 7, 2014, State Councilor and Foreign Minister Wang Yi was visiting Sydney, Australia, at the invitation of the Australian foreign minister, Julie Bishop. The two foreign ministers held their second round of the China–Australia Diplomatic and Strategic Dialogue, during which Wang introduced China's so-called Four Respects doctrine regarding the SCS disputes. At that time, the Australian government had not yet demonstrated any particular position on the SCS disputes, nor did Wang's Four Respects receive much attention from Australian media. The Four Respects referred to the following four issues: first, the dispute over the sovereignty of the Spratly Islands is a problem left over from history; second, China insists on upholding the international laws on territorial disputes and the UN Convention on the Law of the Sea; third, direct dialogue between countries involved should be respected; and fourth, relevant countries should respect efforts that China and ASEAN have made to maintain peace and stability.

China's participation in international regimes has attracted observers' curiosity as to China's intentions in being a party to the United Nations Convention on the Law of the Sea system. This question is usually marginalized while most criticisms focus on China's disrespect toward UNCLOS. David Shambaugh and Lai-Ha Chan provide the patterns of China's engagement in the international regimes and the practical reasons behind them.[1] However, in regard to the UNCLOS case, there are unanswered questions. China has been hammered by the international community, which blames China for ignoring international rules and norms; however, China has been a signatory of UNCLOS since 1982, ratified it in 1996, and insists that it abides by UNCLOS provisions. China consistently responds to any international-law-related criticisms by stating that it respects and observes UNCLOS—the country does not defy or degrade UNCLOS. What made China choose to be a party to UNCLOS and to remain in this system?

This section delves into the relations between China's diplomatic principles discussed in chapter 3 and China's diplomatic practices observed in international-level interactions. Shambaugh studies China and its participation in global governance, and he questions whether China is a "free rider" or a selective contributor to global governance.[2] Shambaugh suggests three chronological phases that describe China's participation in global governance: a passive position during the 1980s and 1990s, a selective and active position during the early 2000s, and a moderately revisionist posture since 2008.

China's motivations for participating in international regimes are varied. One explanation is based on the economic driving force and China's capability. Chan argues that China seeks to minimize any intrusion into its sovereignty and place conditions on state-centric engagement in international regimes while enjoying benefits like international grants.[3] Her primary case study is focused on health governance, and she points out that China indeed needed international assistance given its lack of capability to deal with the spread of infectious diseases such as HIV/AIDS. She defines China's behavior as "regional utilitarian calculations."[4]

China's utilitarian view of international laws is also found in the development of Chinese domestic laws on maritime affairs according to the development of international laws. Table 12 presents China's domestic laws on maritime affairs responding to international laws. Two major international laws have prevailed in maritime affairs since 1958—the Geneva Convention on the Territorial Sea and the Contiguous Zone and UNCLOS.[5] The Geneva Convention was introduced in 1958 and was replaced by UNCLOS, which was concluded in 1982. The Geneva Convention provided the conceptual consensus on territorial sea and contiguous zone, and UNCLOS developed the Geneva Convention by incorporating a new maritime zone—the exclusive economic zone. When the new definition in the maritime legal regime was agreed upon, China did not hesitate to incorporate the new concept into its domestic laws. Table 12 shows how China reacted domestically with its law promulgation and declarations as norms developed internationally.[6] China incorporated a new concept of maritime jurisdictional zones such as territorial sea, contiguous zone, EEZ, and continental shelf as these zones were conceptually defined, established, and concurred with in international legal regimes.

Table 12. China's Domestic Laws on Maritime Affairs in Relation to International Laws

	International Laws	China's Domestic Laws/Declarations
1958	Geneva Convention on the Territorial Sea and the Contiguous Zone (April 29)	Declaration on Territorial Sea (4 September)
1982	UNCLOS concluded (replaced 1958 treaties)	n/a
1992	n/a	Law on the Territorial Sea and the Contiguous Zone
1994	UNCLOS came into force	n/a
1996	n/a	Decision of the Standing Committee of the National People's Congress on the Ratification of the United Nations Convention on the Law of the Sea
1998	n/a	Law of the Exclusive Economic Zone and the Continental Shelf
2006	n/a	Declaration under UNCLOS Article 298

Source: Jiye Kim and Daniel Druckman, "Shelved Sovereignty or Invalid Sovereignty? The South China Sea Negotiations, 1992–2016," *The Pacific Review* 33, no. 1 (2020): 45.

Before UNCLOS, with UNCLOS, beyond UNCLOS

The United Nations Convention on the Law of the Sea was concluded on December 10, 1982, and came into force in 1994. It is currently a leading international legal regime and a norm provider regarding maritime affairs. UNCLOS is regarded as "a 'constitution' for the peaceful use of the seas and oceans" and has led to a "comprehensive global legal order for the maritime sphere."[7] UNCLOS is treated as both conventional and customary law because it has a conventional basis while being inspired by practices followed by states and adopted by states over time.[8] For example, the concept of the EEZ is an original creation of UNCLOS; however, the International Court of Justice has affirmed that the concept of the EEZ had customary existence well before the advent of the convention.

UNCLOS provides its signatories with the *rights* and *responsibilities* of coastal states over the maritime jurisdictional zones such as the territorial sea and the EEZ.[9] However, two years after UNCLOS came to effect, a report from the *Economist* complained that UNCLOS had instead made maritime disputes more complicated with the new rule of the EEZ. EEZs stretch up to 200 nautical miles—far beyond the twelve nautical miles of the territorial sea, and as a result, "the number of overlapping claims has multiplied."[10]

The issue of overlapping claims, as the consequence of EEZs reaching up to 200 nautical miles, has been further exacerbated by the increasing technological and defense capabilities of coastal states. A comparable example is the Outer Space Treaty of 1967, which declared that outer space is not subject to national appropriation. However, the treaty does not fully address modern challenges, such as when a national government "grants sovereignty in the form of property rights to private companies,"[11] which have emerged as major players in outer space due to the rapid expansion of the space industry. This regulatory gap underscores the importance of direct negotiation among stakeholders. For maritime disputes, this involves national governments primarily, while in outer space both governments and private companies are involved.

Numerous scholars have discussed the role of, and expectations for, UNCLOS in the SCS disputes.[12] One of the controversial issues in the literature is a relatively neutral and even mundane question. Does the international regime need to protect weak or nonaggressive sovereign states from others first (that is, advocate equal rights), or is a sovereign right given ultimate autonomy to choose how to solve disputes beyond the international regime?

In 2013 the Philippines instituted arbitration under UNCLOS against China over China's territorial claims in the SCS. Questions about the result of this legal case have followed—will an award from the tribunal be a game changer in the SCS, or will the award at least affect the involved actors' policies? If so, to what extent? The first question might be answered by observing the pattern of cooperation and conflict in the SCS, while the second is answered by assessing changes in the interactions among actors. The final award, released in July 2016, roundly rejected China's historic rights and claims as well as the lawfulness of Chinese actions; however, these questions remain unanswered.

Each word in the tribunal's award issued in July 2016 may have dealt severe blows to the Chinese, who hold dear their ancestors and national history, by ruling in favor of the Philippines and determining that China's key claims in the SCS were unlawful. While China officially denied and rejected the tribunal from the beginning of the Philippines' initiation of arbitration until the release of the ruling outcome, some records made by Chinese sources "recognised the legal weakness of the U-shaped line" to some extent even before the award.[13] Within China, debates and public opinion on the arbitration engagement and response to its outcome were complex. A study dealing with primary data collated in China reveals that some in China believed participation in the arbitration was necessary, while others, including the Ministry of Foreign Affairs, expressed strong opposition against participation.[14] An interview with a ministry official indicated that although China expected the ruling to favor the Philippines, the outcome was still a surprising and humiliating defeat for Beijing.[15] However, despite the humiliating content of the award, it had no meaningful impact on China. Ironically, the reason lies in "the sweeping nature of the award."[16] The breadth of the ruling made it difficult for other countries to demand China's compliance, providing China with an opportunity to maintain its claims. Thus, the worst outcome for China, as suggested by the content of the award, did not materialize.

China's decades-long claim to conduct direct negotiations between claimant countries was not nullified either after the tribunal's award. Historical rights certainly constitute a significant part of China' claims in the SCS; however, as far as *how* to proceed with conflict resolution, China's advocacy towards concerned countries conducting direct negotiations also abides by the inviolable norm of sovereignty. An anarchical system and the loopholes in the US offshore balancing in the Asia-Pacific have bought China time to reach the current balance of power in the SCS. This balance is more unfavorable than before toward Southeast Asian claimant countries with China successfully moving southward in the SCS since the 1970s.

Questions on the relations between UNCLOS and the sovereignty of individual states evoke different answers from countries in different power relations. For example, the Philippines would say yes to the question of whether the international regime needs to protect weak or nonaggressive sovereign states from other states. On the other hand, China would avoid answering this question, but it would say yes if asked whether a sovereign right should be given ultimate autonomy. The power of autonomy includes decisions on whether a state participates in a particular regime, to what extent the state wants to follow norms provided by the regime, and whether the state exits from the regime when necessary.

Hasjim Djalal, a former Indonesian diplomat and a law-of-the-sea expert, phrases the question differently. He finds the sovereignty issue to be a problem of finding a balance between the sovereignty and rights of the coastal states and the interests of other foreign states. In his view, in norms related to maritime affairs, sovereign actors have different geographical conditions; thus, their rights to pursue dispute resolution are different. Not only is power involved in state relations, but states' geographic conditions matter as well, and UNCLOS regulates these rights depending on the "coastal states" and "non-coastal neighbors." The collision often occurs between the sovereignty of coastal states and the foreign countries' military activities in the EEZ, including surveillance and reconnaissance actions. Djalal points out that the collision of interests between coastal states and foreign states has been addressed in UNCLOS with a remark on "due regard."

> Therefore it could be concluded that the "due regard provisions" attempt to secure a good balance between the various interests of all parties involved, in the sense that neither sovereignty or sovereign rights of the coastal states, nor the freedoms of navigation and over-flight of other states, could be exercised with "absoluteness," but should always be exercised with responsibility and by taking into account the interests of others. Otherwise, it may result in some kind of state responsibility and liability.[17]

According to his interpretation of the related UNCLOS articles to "due regard provisions," including Article 27 (4), Article 39, paragraph 3 (a), Article 56 (2), Article 58 (3), Article 60 (3), Article 66, paragraph 3 (a), Article 79 (5), Article 161 (4), and Article 267, UNCLOS impairs neither the sovereignty of signatory countries—especially coastal states—nor the freedom of navigation of noncoastal states. Djalal further argues that the rights of neither party—coastal or noncoastal countries—are *absolute*. His liberal view on UNCLOS further justifies his argument that "the states should also pay attention to the rights of others."[18]

Djalal's interpretation on clauses regarding "due regard" is apparently not compatible with China's interpretation of the sovereign rights of signatory states to UNCLOS. His view is in a stream of idealism; however, Buszynski and Roberts indicate a competing idea against idealists that "power can shape law," and nothing can prevent the littoral states from insisting on their claims.[19] Ryan Griffiths delivers the enduring role of power within a normative domain, arguing that "norms are not simply epiphenomenal to power; actors need to prevail in the contest of ideas."[20]

Yet UNCLOS and state practice cannot be treated as the same. Norms are changing, and the interpretation of the meaning of terms in UNCLOS has been evolving. UNCLOS itself is an evolving and flexible body of law rather than one that provides fixed interpretations. For example, the uncertainties of UNCLOS provisions are repeatedly raised with cases including various types of baselines from which the territorial sea, contiguous zone, and EEZ are measured.[21] In the context of the SCS disputes, UNCLOS has been idealized by commentators with an overall image of jurisdictional authority that decides which country is "guilty" and "not guilty." However, UNCLOS has a burden that consists of controversial and ambiguous provisions. One clear case that shows UNCLOS is an "open law" is that UNCLOS allows one party to seek arbitration over a dispute unilaterally; however, UNCLOS also allows another party to choose not to participate in that arbitration. This has been proved by the case of the arbitration initiated by the Philippines in 2013 against China over the issues regarding China's claim of the nine-dash line. The Philippines initiated this legal "showdown" with China under Article 287 of UNCLOS. And what happened next? China chose to opt out of compulsory arbitration, as Article 298 of UNCLOS delineates.[22]

China's Perception of UNCLOS

China advocates the shared perception on UNCLOS that it provides the parties with conditions for claiming maritime rights. Nevertheless, China's priority in terms of internalizing UNCLOS in its policymaking is different from that of other signatories, including the US.[23] The US did not ratify UNCLOS in Congress, although the US functionally follows UNCLOS.

China's intention to be a party to UNCLOS is indicated in its statement made upon its ratification of UNCLOS. This statement was released when China ratified UNCLOS in 1996, and the full text is provided by the UN Division for Ocean Affairs and the Law of the Sea. China ratified UNCLOS with the decision of the Standing Committee of the Eighth National People's Congress at its nineteenth session. China's statement on UNCLOS ratification consisted of the following four numbered points:

1. In accordance with the provisions of the United Nations Convention on the Law of the Sea, the People's Republic of China shall enjoy sovereign rights and jurisdiction over an *exclusive economic zone* of 200 nautical miles and the continental shelf.
2. The People's Republic of China will effect, *through consultations*, the delimitation of the boundary of the maritime jurisdiction *with the States* with coasts opposite or adjacent to China respectively on the basis of international law and in accordance with the principle of equitability.

3. The People's Republic of China reaffirms its *sovereignty* over all its archipelagos and islands as listed in article 2 of the Law of the People's Republic of China on the territorial sea and the contiguous zone, which was promulgated on 25 February 1992.
4. The People's Republic of China reaffirms that the provisions of the United Nations Convention on the Law of the Sea concerning innocent passage through the territorial sea shall not prejudice the right of a coastal State to request, in accordance with its laws and regulations, a foreign State to obtain advance approval from or give prior notification to the coastal State for the passage of its warships through the territorial sea of the coastal State.[24]

The first point expresses the most significant legal benefit that China seeks to obtain by joining UNCLOS: 200 nautical miles of EEZ and the continental shelf. As a coastal state, for China to secure the EEZ and continental shelf was consistent with its national interests, particularly when other coastal states in the South and East China Seas also would take these rights. The second point is about the delimitation issue. Maritime delimitation may be subject to a different level of maritime rights: sovereignty, sovereign rights, and jurisdiction. China indicates that it would initiate dialogue on an overlapped maritime area with maritime neighbors when the case concerns the maritime jurisdiction.

Today, virtually all travel through the South China Sea passes through one or more EEZs of its coastal countries. One of China's background motivations is found in the advantages that the EEZ brings. Joseph Nye complains that "if China claimed such a zone (EEZ) for each of the sites it occupies, it could close off most of the South China Sea."[25] In map 2, the central part of the map shows the name of the maritime area, "South China Sea," and the convex lines around this area represent the limits of the 200 nm (EEZs) of the surrounding countries involved in maritime disputes.[26] The space within these lines, where the EEZs do not overlap, designates the high seas, which are not under the jurisdiction of any one nation.

Within the high seas, key features are located including Thitu Island (occupied by the Philippines since 1971), Itu Aba Island (Taiwan since 1956), and Fiery Cross Reef (occupied by China since 1988). If the hypothetical 200 nm EEZs are drawn from these features, i.e., if the respective occupant country were to declare EEZs, then there would be no high sea in the SCS.[27] In other words, the legal and effective EEZ of islands in the South China Sea is the key to controlling the troubled waters enclosed by six claimant countries.

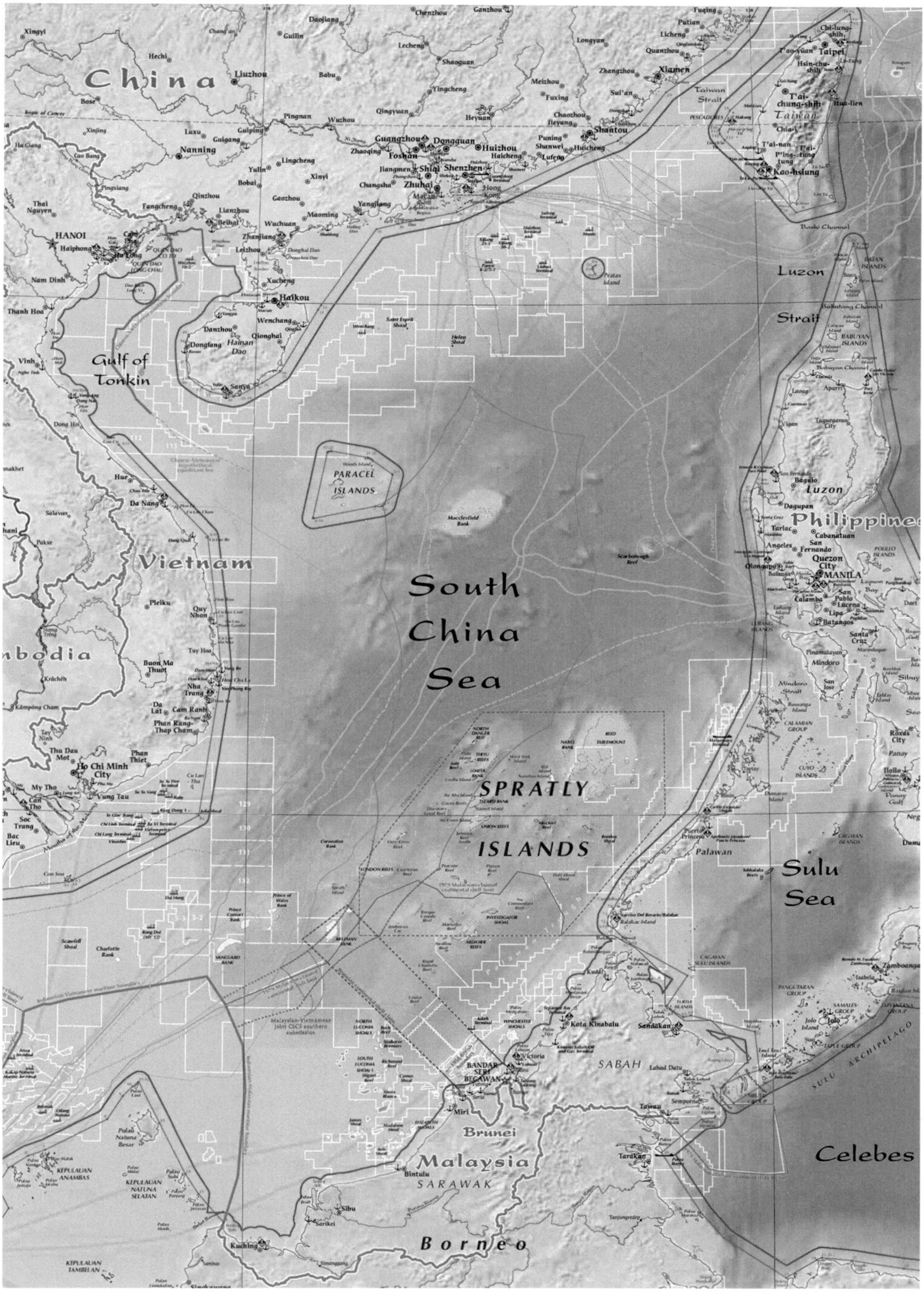

Map 2. High seas in the South China Sea

In addition to the islands appearing on the map, there are three strategic outposts of China in the high seas that should be pointed out. Fiery Cross Reef, Cuarteron Reef, and Subi Reef are situated between Thitu Island and Spratly Island on the high seas. China occupied these three features in 1988, along with three other features in the Spratly Islands. As of 2020, China's largest collection of radar and communications arrays in the South China Sea is deployed at Fiery Cross Reef. If EEZs drawn from Fiery Cross Reef, Cuarteron Reef, and Subi Reef are effective, then the occupant—China—economically controls the activities occurring at the mouth of these troubled waters. Likewise, if Vietnam's EEZ from Spratly Island is legally effective, or if the Philippines' EEZ from Thitu Island is effective, one of the countries will enjoy the economic benefits. China signed UNCLOS in 1982, and occupied seven islands and reefs in the Spratly Islands between 1988 and 1995.

UNCLOS and Its Complexity

UNCLOS Article 86 defines the high seas as "all parts of the sea that are not included in the exclusive economic zone, in the territorial sea or in the internal waters of a State, or in the archipelagic waters of an archipelagic State." However, the concept of "international waters" is practically applied by the US to refer to broader maritime zones, including EEZ and high seas. For example, the United States holds the position that "all waters seaward of the territorial sea are international waters where the ships and aircraft of all States enjoy the high seas freedom of navigation and overflight"[28] and "the international respect for freedom of the seas guarantees legal access up to the territorial waters of all coastal countries of the world."[29]

The third point of China's 1996 declaration on UNCLOS, that China "reaffirms its sovereignty over all its archipelagos and islands as listed in Article 2 of the Law of the People's Republic of China," indicates from which maritime features in the SCS China claims its EEZ and the continental shelf. The Law of the People's Republic of China on the Territorial Sea and the Contiguous Zone was promulgated in 1992. Article 2 of the Law states:

> The *land territory* of the People's Republic of China includes the mainland of the People's Republic of China and its coastal islands; Taiwan and all islands appertaining thereto including the Diaoyu Islands; the Penghu Islands; the *Dongsha Islands*; the *Xisha Islands*; the *Zhongsha Islands* and the *Nansha Islands*; as well as all the other islands belonging to the People's Republic of China. (emphasis added)

According to the 1992 Law, all island features in the Paracel, Pratas, Macclesfield, and Spratly Islands are China's "land territory." Therefore, the Chinese statement upon the ratification of UNCLOS implies that the Chinese EEZ and the continental shelf are measured from the baseline of the mainland and the baseline of "land territory," including the Paracel, Pratas, Macclesfield, and Spratly Island features. A question arises here because the second point of China's declaration states that China will seek the delimitation of the maritime jurisdiction boundary in accordance with the principle of equitability. It is possible that the equitability principle that appeared in the second point was purposedly added before stating a "land territory" claim in the following point of the declaration in order to moderate the overall declaration. In the 1992 Law, there is no statement on historical entitlement or any line circumscribing areas in the SCS. The historic rights and the nine-dash line are the "non-legal" rationale beyond the legal claim of China.

In the ASEAN Regional Forum Foreign Ministers Meeting in 2012, Chinese foreign minister Yang Jiechi clearly stated how China perceived UNCLOS:

> China is a party to the United Nations Convention on the Law of the Sea (UNCLOS) and places importance on upholding the principles and purposes of the Convention. The Convention states at the very outset the desirability of "establishing, with due regard for the sovereignty of all States, a legal order for the seas and oceans." This means that the Convention has *not given itself the authority to change the territory of countries* and that it *cannot be cited as the basis for arbitration* in territorial disputes between countries.[30] (emphasis added)

After China's ratification of UNCLOS in 1996, China made another declaration in 2006. The 1996 declaration provides evidence of what China sought to obtain by signing UNCLOS—in other words, the practical benefits that China wants to secure: effective territorial sea and EEZ. On the other hand, the 2006 declaration reveals what China considered problematic about UNCLOS, potential diplomatic barriers, and which particular clauses of UNCLOS may intrude on China's national interests. The ten-year gap between the first declaration in 1996 and the second declaration in 2006 indicates that China gained more experience in international interaction around UNCLOS over the course of a decade. The 2006 declaration asserts the following:

> Declaration under Article 298: The Government of the People's Republic of China does *not* accept any of the procedures provided for

> in Section 2 of Part XV of the Convention with respect to all the categories of disputes referred to in paragraph 1 (a) (b) and (c) of Article 298 of the Convention.[31] (emphasis added)

This declaration means that, according to Article 298, a member state does not accept specific *compulsory* dispute resolution procedures, including disputes with respect to (a) territorial sea, (b) EEZ, (c) continental shelf, and further historic bays or titles. In addition to China, thirty-six other members of UNCLOS, including major powers, also declared under Article 298 that they do not accept compulsory dispute resolution procedures.[32] Interestingly, the Philippines also made a declaration under Article 298 with a different context:

> The Philippines Declaration under Article 298: "The agreement of the Republic of the Philippines to the submission for peaceful resolution, under any of the procedures provided in the Convention, of disputes under *article 298* shall *not be considered* as a derogation of Philippines *sovereignty*." [33] (emphasis added)

China's argument on the invalidity of the arbitration initiated by the Philippines in 2013 was based on China's perception of the UNCLOS, stating that "the essence of the subject-matter of the arbitration is the territorial sovereignty"; China further argued that "territorial sovereignty" is "beyond the scope of the Convention [UNCLOS]."[34] Moreover, China further argued that "China and the Philippines have agreed . . . to settle their relevant disputes through negotiations" in their agreements in the past. Therefore, according to China, "the Philippines has breached its obligation under international law."

Table 13 shows the pattern of China's changing views on UNCLOS and related activities regarding the International Tribunal for the Law of the Sea and Commission on the Limits of the Continental Shelf (CLCS).[35] According to *China's Foreign Affairs* (the official report published by the Chinese Ministry of Foreign Affairs), until 2009 China expressed its positive expectations of the UNCLOS. From 2007 to 2009, China stated that issues "should be settled through friendly consultations on the basis of international law including the UNCLOS." However, despite China's trust in the legal process based on UNCLOS, China further pointed out its preferred order, or method, of dispute settlement. *China's Foreign Affairs* stated similarly in 2007, 2008 and 2009, "before the final solution of the issues, countries concerned may strive to reach a *de facto* provisional arrangement," indicating that China preferred an in-advance discussion and creating a de facto solution before initiating processes relying on UNCLOS. However, the word "de facto" appeared in 2007 and 2008 in *China's Foreign Affairs* but was eventually removed in 2009. This change implies that China may have been growing convinced that a de facto agreement between directly concerned parties before consulting UNCLOS was not realistic.

Another pattern found in those primary sources is the progressively increasing urgency of China's attitude regarding the submission of the delimitation of the continental shelf to the Commission on the Limits of the Continental Shelf, especially extending the submission deadline. In 2007, China showed no urgency in postponing the submission deadline and merely "highlighted the important significance of the Commission on the Limits of the Continental Shelf's work for coastal states and the international community."[36] However, in 2008, the report stated that "serious consideration should be given to the provisions regarding the deadline of the submission."[37] The report demonstrated still more urgency in 2009 by expressing that China "supported the request of developing countries for extended time limits for the submission on the outer limits of the continental shelves."[38]

In 2010, China presented another strategy by suggesting a "common heritage of mankind" on the international seabed area. It therefore attempted to delay other states' submission on their outer limits of the continental shelves. China found a handful of countries that supported this idea: Cote d'Ivoire, Pakistan (which jointly proposed the common heritage of mankind along with China), Argentina, Russia, and Germany (which endorsed the proposal at the UNCLOS meeting).[39] China, however, was eventually unable to prevent Malaysia and Vietnam from jointly filing a submission to the Commission on the Limits of the Continental Shelf in May 2009that proposed outer limits of the continental shelf beyond 200 nautical miles in the SCS.

Sovereignty, *sovereign rights*, and *jurisdiction* are defined differently. China has made a maritime delimitation agreement with Vietnam that extends the delimitation of maritime zones and sovereignty. The agreement between Vietnam and China ensures the two countries "respective sovereignty over, sovereign rights to and jurisdiction in the territorial sea, exclusive economic zones and continental shelves" in the agreed maritime zone in the Beibu Gulf.

Some analyses from non-Chinese commentators potentially support China's perception of UNCLOS. John Kemp, an energy analyst from Reuters,

Table 13. China's Expectations and Activities regarding UNCLOS, ITLOS, and CLCS Appearing in *China's Foreign Affairs*

	China's expectation of UNCLOS	China's activities regarding ITLOS and CLCS in the UNCLOS meetings[a]
2007	• "China always believes that the relevant issues should be settled through friendly consultations on the basis of international law including the UNCLOS." • "Before the final solution of the issues, countries concerned may strive to reach a de facto provisional arrangement, including 'seeking joint development while shelving differences' and conducting cooperation in other fields, so as to maintain peace and tranquility in the relevant sea area."	• The Chinese participants listened to the 2005 annual reports of the ITLOS and CLCS. • The Chinese participants examined and adopted the 2007–8 annual budget of the International Tribunal for the Law of the Sea. • The Chinese participants highlighted the important significance of the Commission on the Limits of the Continental Shelf's work for coastal states and the international community.
2008	• "China stands for the settlement of maritime disputes with neighboring countries on the basis of international law, including the UNCLOS." • "Pending the final settlement of the disputes, countries concerned may strive to reach a de facto provisional arrangement by 'seeking joint development while shelving differences' and conducting cooperation in other fields, so as to maintain peace and stability in the relevant sea area."	• The Chinese participants listened to the annual reports of the ITLOS and CLCS. • The Chinese participants suggest that "to increase the Commission's working time indiscriminately would damage the quality of its work . . . Serious consideration should be given to the provisions regarding the deadline of the submission of delimitation proposals as set in Annex II of the UNCLOS and appropriate measures should be taken to ensure smooth progress in the work of the Commission."
2009	• "China stands for the settlement of maritime disputes with neighboring countries on the basis of international law, including the UNCLOS." • "Pending the final settlement of the disputes, countries concerned may strive to reach a provisional arrangement of *a practical nature* by 'seeking joint development while shelving differences' and conducting cooperation in other fields, so as to maintain peace and stability in the relevant sea area." (emphasis added on newly appearing words)	• The Chinese participants focused on "the time limit for the submission on the outer limits of the continental shelves beyond 200 nautical miles, the work of the Commission on the Limits of the Continental Shelf and . . . the International Tribunal for the Law of the Sea." • "The Chinese delegation supported the request of developing countries for extended time limits for the submission on the outer limits of the continental shelves. The meeting agreed upon consultation that coastal states would meet the time limits of the UNCLOS if they submit before the end of 2009 preliminary information indicative of the outer limit of its continental shelf beyond 200 nautical miles."

2010	The relevant part was deleted.	"China, Cote d'Ivoire and Pakistan proposed a supplementary item entitled 'International Seabed Area as the Common Heritage of the Mankind and Article 121 of the Convention' in the provisional agenda of the Meeting. The proposal won endorsement of more than a dozen countries including Argentina, Russia and Germany. The Meeting agreed to defer the consideration on the inclusion of the proposed agenda item to a future Meeting. It was also agreed that an exchange of views would be conducted under relevant existing items."
2014	The relevant part was deleted.	The Chinese participants "elaborated on China's proposition of building and maintaining a harmonious maritime order, and called on the members of the international community to adopt a coordinated approach to . . . balance the interests of the coastal states and the overall interests of international community, take in to proper consideration the right and freedom of all countries to the lawful utilization of oceans and seas and resolve maritime disputes through peaceful means."

Source: Ministry of Foreign Affairs of the People's Republic of China, Department of Policy Planning *China's Foreign Affairs* (Beijing: World Affairs Press, 2007); Ministry of Foreign Affairs of the People's Republic of China, Department of Policy Planning, *China's Foreign Affairs* (Beijing: World Affairs Press, 2008); Ministry of Foreign Affairs of the People's Republic of China, Department of Policy Planning, *China's Foreign Affairs* (Beijing: World Affairs Press, 2009); Ministry of Foreign Affairs of the People's Republic of China, Department of Policy Planning, *China's Foreign Affairs* (Beijing: World Affairs Press, 2010); Ministry of Foreign Affairs of the People's Republic of China, Department of Policy Planning, *China's Foreign Affairs* (Beijing: World Affairs Press, 2014).

[a]UNCLOS meeting refers to the Meeting of States Parties to the United Nations Convention on the Law of the Sea. The meeting is regularly held at UN headquarters in New York and China sends its delegation, which consists of the Ministry of Foreign Affairs, the State Oceanic Administration, and the Permanent Mission to the United Nations.

says that UNCLOS is not entirely about maritime disputes because the core of the disagreement concerns ownership and sovereignty over the islands and other outcrops. Once sovereignty has been established and agreed upon by claimants, UNCLOS can help assign economic rights and responsibilities to all the parties, including control of shipping, fishing, and oil and gas drilling. Nevertheless, UNCLOS cannot resolve the underlying disputes about sovereignty.[40] Gregory Poling also argued that "there is nothing in the UNCLOS to resolve sovereignty disputes over land (islands)," concluding that "UNCLOS has nothing to say on the territorial disputes."[41]

China and other states have different interpretations of key concepts of UNCLOS, such as EEZ and freedom of navigation (FON). For example, FON can be interpreted as a principle, a practice, or both. Practically, "FON is a term of art that means sailing or flying within 12 nautical miles of disputed territory to demonstrate that you don't accept the claim."[42] However, the US does not always refer to flying and sailing within twelve nautical miles when conducting FON operations. FON in the SCS, according to the official US position and historical practice, has been maintained for a long time. But the US has only recently added flying within twelve nautical miles to its FON operations.

Interpretations and applications of EEZ are diverse as well. China takes the position that islands sustaining economic life can have EEZ. "As calculated, an island that cannot sustain human life can have a territorial sea of 1,550 km^2, while a big island that can maintain economic life or human habitation can obtain an EEZ of about 420,000 km^2."[43] This argument indicates that China (and other states) compete for small islands for maritime zones and resources legally attached to them, not for the islands' land territory itself. An increase in claims on small islets, including even small rocks, has provoked disputes among countries because "the rocks are not so important per se—but there are vital resources within the maritime zones around them."[44] The location of the islands in the SCS is highly strategic due to the sea lines upon them, which link East Asia to other parts of Eurasian shores. Hence, Choon-ho Park, judge of the International Tribunal for the Law of the Sea for twelve years as an inaugural member, attested that "to the countries of the region and the major powers of the world alike, it is a matter of vital importance into whose hands the islands will ultimately fall, whether into the hands of a small country without global ambitions or those of a major power."[45]

The EEZ and the continental shelf are not part of the high seas or the territorial sea. The EEZ is a maritime zone sui generis.[46] On April 1, 2001, there was a collision between a US surveillance plane and a Chinese jet fighter over a Chinese EEZ near Hainan Island. China argued that the US plane was flying inside China's EEZ and was therefore subject to Chinese laws and regulations.

In essence, UNCLOS provides to its signatories the *rights* and *responsibilities* of coastal states over the maritime jurisdictional zones such as the territorial sea and EEZ.[47] According to Article 56:

> In the exclusive economic zone, the coastal State has (a) *sovereign rights* for the purpose of exploring and exploiting, conserving and managing *the natural resources*, whether living or non-living, of the waters superjacent to the seabed and of the seabed and its subsoil, and with regard to other activities for the economic exploitation and exploration of the zone, such as the production of energy from the water, currents and winds; (b) *jurisdiction* as provided for in the relevant provisions of this Convention with regard to: (i) the establishment and use of artificial islands, installations and structures; (ii) marine scientific research; (iii) the protection and preservation of the marine environment. (emphasis added)

Ji You argues that the conflicting interests of the coastal state and noncoastal maritime powers are implied in the UNCLOS definition of EEZ. In accordance with a sovereign state's interpretation and application of UNCLOS, he sees that some states may pursue "territorialization" whereas others pursue "internationalization" of EEZ. The challenge is to find a balanced relationship among the vital interests involved in the issue.[48]

Military activities in EEZs also have brought different interpretations from China and other states. The Law of the People's Republic of China on the Territorial Sea and the Contiguous Zone, promulgated in 1992, and the Survey and Mapping Law of the People's Republic of China, enacted in 2002, include articles on China's objection to foreign vessels' military activities in China's territorial and "other sea areas under the jurisdiction of the People's Republic of China."[49] On the other hand, few states have domestic laws with specific objections against military activities by other states; the exceptions are China, Brazil, and India.[50]

China's point of view in adopting UNCLOS suggests that it has priorities in internalizing UNCLOS in its domestic law and policymaking. One clear example of this set of priorities was seen in the Four Respects announced by Chinese foreign minister Wang Yi during his 2014 visit to Australia. In these, China claimed that it respects international law and therefore abides by UNCLOS; however, Wang also implied that for China, other important considerations supersede UNCLOS, especially Chinese domestic law. Therefore, China eventually pursued UNCLOS membership to legitimize its "uncontested" maritime features and its sovereignty over them.[51]

Historical analysis suggests that China has a diplomatic "habit" of establishing its own principles and making them standard in forming relations with external actors. For China, these principles work as a starting point of any negotiation. Feng Zhang points out three components of China's exceptionalism in the era of China rising: great-power reformism, benevolent pacifism, and harmonious inclusionism. He argues that exceptionalism is in part a product of the ideological discourse to facilitate China's rise—and an example of the use of history and culture to discursively counter structural pressures from the international system, and ultimately "support for China's re-emergence as a great power in the modern world."[52]

Feng Zhang describes Chinese exceptionalism as an essential part of China's worldview. He suggests three distinctive sets of Chinese literature examining China's unique worldview: neo-Tianxiaism, the project on China's pre-Qin thoughts of international relations, and "China model" literature, respectively refer to a reinterpretation of the Chinese concept of *tianxia* (all under heaven), an initiative of reconstructing ancient Chinese political thought, and a body of work discussing China's unique modernization path. He pointed out the importance of historical thinking in the core of the approach of Chinese policy-making circle, and the SCS is no exception—China uses historical arguments before any others in its official claims, and its arguments toward the SCS dispute are another example of Chinese exceptionalism.

How Does Power Matter?

For the realists, comprehensive national power is the independent variable that determines international relations. Xuetong Yan lists the components of comprehensive national power as military power, economic power, cultural power, and political power.[53] Generally, the former two components are considered *hard power*, and the latter two components are typically labeled as *soft power*. The novelty of his theory is that he puts the last component, political power, into the category of *operating power*. In his equation, this operating power is a multiplier (*chengshu*) that largely affects comprehensive national power as a significant independent variable. Yan's equation reminds us of three resources that consist of the soft power as defined by Joseph Nye. According to Nye, a country's soft power rests primarily on three resources: its culture (in places where it is attractive to others), its political values (when it lives up to them at home and abroad), and its foreign policies (when they are seen as legitimate and as having moral authority).[54] Nevertheless, agreeing with the Confucian philosopher Xunzi, Yan considers political power as the most significant component in comprehensive national power.[55]

Between 2002 and 2012, China underwent a process of naval modernization that began under the leadership of President Hu Jintao. The naval modernization was called "Far Sea Operations" (*yuanhai zuozhan*) and extended beyond the so-called first island chain and reached the second island chain, including the Kurile Islands, the Marianas, the Caroline Islands of Micronesia, and Papua New Guinea.[56]

China's coercive behavior can also be viewed as an investment in its energy security. Andrew Cheon and Johannes Urpelainen have developed a theory of when and how states invest in energy security. They find two important variables that are decisive factors driving states' policies in energy security: perceiving a risk from a militarized dispute and a small number of oil producers.[57] Clashes between China and the US have continued since the early 2000s in the SCS, and other claimants' growing capabilities have certainly increased the risk of militarized disputes, Cheon and Urpelainen argue. For examples, they point to Vietnam's military buildup and the Philippines strengthening its alliance with the US—and even Indonesia, which is not a direct claimant in the SCS disputes, is deploying more policing resources near the disputed area in the SCS.[58]

Concerns about China's increasing assertiveness in the later 2000s have been highlighted in various studies conducted by both Chinese and non-Chinese scholars. In the late 2000s, expectations of amicable diplomacy in the SCS drastically decreased, and China began to firmly associate its core interest with the SCS. This change suggested a growing pattern of assertiveness as observed by Western scholars.[59] This observation comes not only from Western scholars; a leading Chinese scholar, Yan Xuetong, also argues that China strengthened its position in the SCS in the later 2000s. However, his explanation of this shift mainly derives from his critical analysis of the unfavorable security environment in the Asia-Pacific against China, which coincided with the declaration by Secretary of State Hillary Clinton, that the US was returning to a focus on Asia, in the 2009 ASEAN Regional Forum.[60]

Chinese scholars and analysts from other claimants in the SCS disputes agree that China's assertiveness in the later 2000s was not caused entirely by China's domestically driven security concerns or policy but was instead catalyzed by external factors, especially actions of the US. In the Asian Regional Forum in July 2010—chaired by Vietnam—Secretary of State Clinton affirmed the US position that freedom of navigation in international waters constituted the US "national interest." The US strategic pivot to Asia led to China's response in well-known remarks at the meeting with ASEAN countries by Chinese foreign minister Yang Jiechi: "China is a big country and other countries are small countries, and that's just a fact."[61] Heydarian writes that "America's entry into the disputes . . . encouraged further belligerence on China's side."[62]

In the early days of the country's history following its establishment in 1949, China's claim in the SCS was focused on the Paracels and a group of reefs near the mainland. China had insufficient capability to reach the southern part of the waters (the Spratly Islands) and China recognized that its limited military and economic capability would not permit it to reach islands at more significant physical distances. This assumption makes sense, according to Tommy T. B. Koh, Singapore's ambassador to the United States and president of the Third United Nations Conference on the Law of the Sea from 1981 to 1982: "It is not enough for a coastal State to adopt conservation and management measures. The coastal State must also develop a capacity to ensure compliance with its conservation and management laws and regulations."[63] Indeed, China occupied the Paracel Islands in the 1970s and the Spratly Islands later in the 1980s and the 1990s.

Map 3 was issued by the Republic of China in December 1946 and showed the eleven dashed lines.[64] The circled numbers on the map track China's coercive moves in the SCS since 1974 chronologically.

(1) In January 1974, China attacked western Paracel and occupied five uninhabited islands. Vietnam military resistance collapsed within two days (casualties: Vietnam 123, China 67). This naval skirmish in the Paracels was the first naval clash in the SCS. China has controlled all of the Paracel Islands since then.
(2) In March 1988, China and Vietnam again clashed on Johnson Reef in the Spratly Islands. People's Liberation Army marines occupied six reefs in the Spratlys, territorializing them, including the Johnson islets previously held by Vietnam.[65] China sank three Vietnamese transport ships and killed 72 seamen in a brief naval battle. Liu Huaqing, the commander of the People's

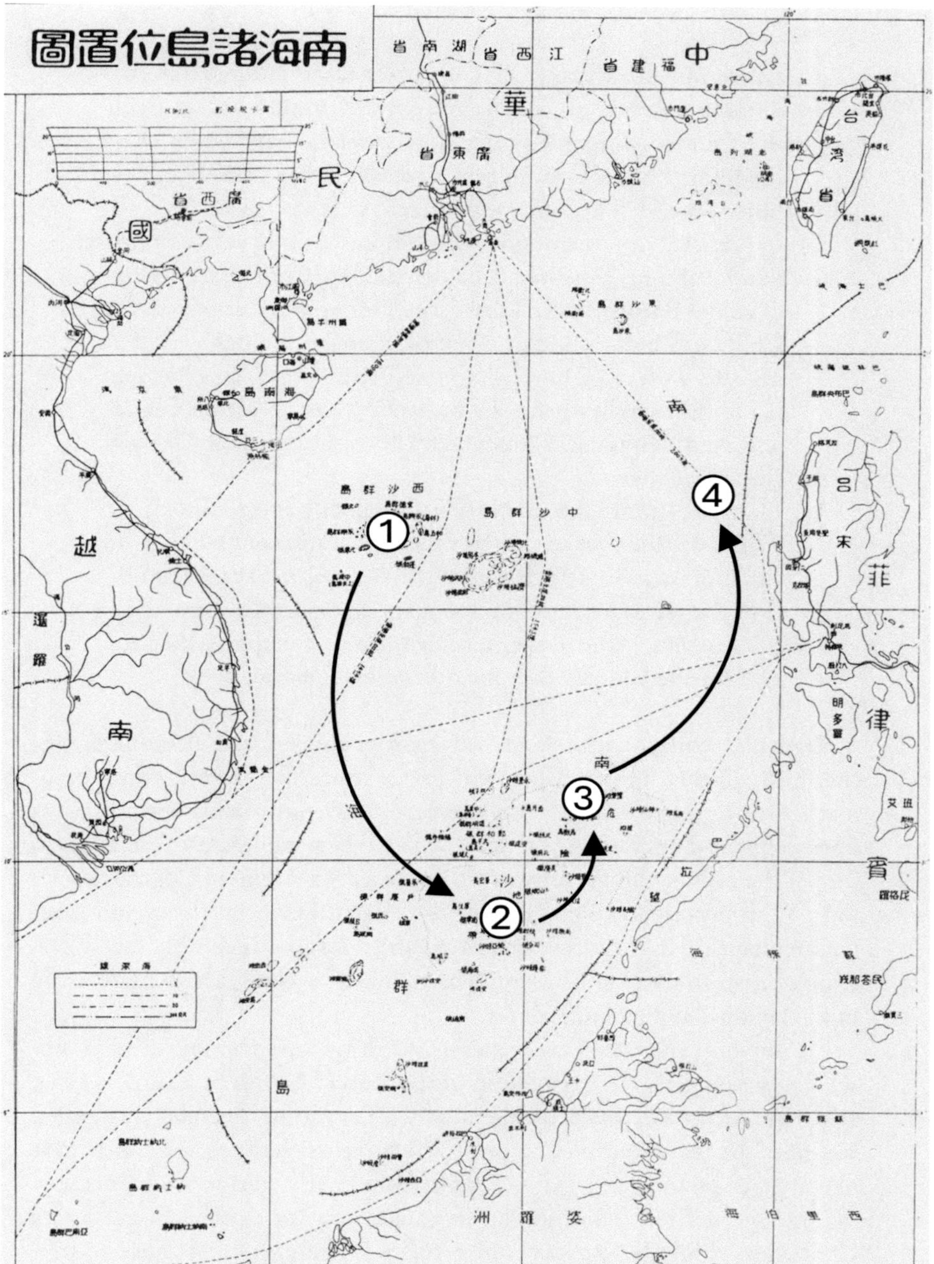

Map 3. China's strategic moves to restore maritime presence in the South China Sea

Liberation Army Navy (PLAN), wrote in his autobiography that the action to take six reefs in the Spratlys in 1988 was an exclusive Central Military Commission decision approved by Deng Xiaoping.[66] Such a centralized direction in the PLAN's operation in the SCS had not been present in earlier cases.[67]

(3) In January 1995, the captain of a Filipino fishing vessel reported that he and his crew had been detained by Chinese troops on Mischief Reef for several days. The Philippines discovered that China had built four clusters of octagonal buildings supported on stilts with the Chinese flag on Mischief Reef. This incident led to the establishment of a code of conduct between China and the Philippines. Chinese have been stationed on Mischief Reef since then.

(4) In April 2012, a Filipino Navy surveillance plane found eight Chinese fishing vessels at the waters of Scarborough Shoal. The Philippines promptly deployed the *Gregorio del Pilar*, the nation's largest warship. China sent two surveillance ships (*Zhonggou Haijian 75* and *Zhonggou Haijian 84*) that approached to prevent the Chinese fishermen from being arrested.

In the last thirty years, China's self-identity has clearly undergone significant changes that have had practical implications for its policy and diplomacy. One sign that China was becoming more comfortable with its rising status appeared in November 2006 when the documentary series *Daguo Jueqi* (The rise of the great powers) was aired on Chinese Central Television. With experiences from the 1997–98 Asian Financial Crisis and gaining membership in various international organizations including the WTO, China began to develop its identity as a "joiner" seeking active partnership in the regional and global realms.

Meanwhile, criticism was leveled against China in 1974, 1995, and in subsequent years. After the occupation of the Paracel Islands by China in 1974, an article in the *Guardian* condemned China, stating that the occupation was not "the behaviour of a country which insists that it will never behave like a super power," and in 1995, China was criticized due to its "occupying of Mischief reef, renewing anxieties and fears of conflict in the South China Sea."[68] Similar criticisms of perceived Chinese actions have continued since then, focusing on the two main factors that allegedly motivated China to start building installations on Mischief Reef. First, China planned "the greater integration of Chinese coastal regions into the global economy";

Table 14. Comparing Sizes of South China Sea Maritime Features

	Fiery Cross Reef	Taiping Island	Thitu Island	Swallow Reef	Spratly Island	Johnson South Reef
Occupation	PRC	ROC	Philippines	Malaysia	Vietnam	PRC
Reclaimed Size (km^2)	2.74	0.51	0.37	0.35	0.15	0.1
Airstrip (km)	3	1.195	1	1.368	0.55	n/a

Note: Data sources from Ministry of Foreign Affairs of People's Republic of China and Asia Maritime Transparency Initiative.

second, the US military base in the Philippines had closed two years before China began the installations, thereby reducing the risk of direct conflict between the two powers.[69] Table 14 lists reefs and islands occupied by various claimants and provides details on the size of the claimed territory and airstrip length.[70]

China's diplomacy is supported and strengthened by its economic and physical power in the region. One occasion when China utilized its economic leverage in the SCS resulted in damaging relations with the Philippines. The Philippines suffered a drastic financial loss due to decreased tourism and export volume when the conflict with China surrounding the Scarborough Shoal worsened in 2012.[71] China is willing to show its military power against the small forces of littoral states, and even against the US as evidenced by its confrontation with a US survey ship in 2001, an EP-3 surveillance plane incident in the same year, and the Impeccable incident in 2009, an incident in which a US Navy ship was confronted by Chinese navy ships. In order to nullify China's island reclamation and support the freedom of navigation principle, US naval ships have regularly entered the 12 nm of territorial sea of Chinese-claimed islands in the SCS. The spiral of troubles has further increased the risk of a dangerous face-off with Chinese forces in the disputed waters.[72]

However, a careful diplomatic decision is required before China exerts any sort of physical leverage, and a study of China's "one-plus strategy" suggests that China's principles are considered before it exerts aggressive behavior. The one-plus strategy, according to Ji You, refers to an approach in which China takes assertive actions in response to perceived provocations by other claimants.[73] You Ji holds the view that China has been conducting a one-plus strategy as an effective crisis management strategy in the East China Sea and SCS since Xi Jinping came to power. He further argues that the one-plus strategy limits China's physical power to a reactive and passive one and allows limited military power that would not cause further armed conflict.[74]

The interdependent economy of Southeast Asia also faces the danger of violent behavior, as Assistant Secretary of State Daniel Russel pointed out in 2014, because the regional economy is too important and too fragile for any country, or any claimant, to use the threat of military force or paramilitary force in retaliation, for intimidation, or as a coercive effort. This statement was made in a news briefing ahead of Russel's trip to the ASEAN Regional Forum.[75] Interestingly, in 2014 Singapore prime minister Lee Hsien Loong expressed his belief in China as a peaceful power avoiding the use of military might.[76] However, Singapore prime minister Goh Chok Tong stated in 1995, immediately after the Mischief Reef incident, that it was important to express an underlying sense of discomfort, even insecurity, about the political and military ambitions of China.[77] This difference in view twenty years apart underscores the shift in regional perceptions of China, shaped initially by the Hu Jintao era in the early 2000s, which promoted a narrative of peaceful development and a vision of a harmonious world. The Xi Jinping era in late 2012, marked by Chinese dream and national rejuvenation, followed a decade of relatively favorable relations between China and Southeast Asia. These relations had developed prior to Xi's rise to power and accompanied expectations that the peaceful development agenda would continue to guide China's regional approach.

China continues to pursue a long-term, comprehensive military modernization program; meanwhile, it remains committed to stable relationships with neighbors to strengthen a favorable external environment for China.[78] For example, China held its annual military training of the People's Liberation Army Navy (PLAN), the Maneuver 5 exercise, to test open-sea mobile combat tactics, command and control capabilities, and the combat effectiveness of equipment. Three major fleets of the PLAN participated in this exercise in the West Pacific.[79] According to the US Department of Defense Annual Report, the exercise conducted in the Philippine Sea was the largest PLAN open-ocean exercise seen to date. Further, China conducted the three-part Mission Action series of joint military exercises in 2013. These exercises combined PLA ground, navy, and air forces in large-scale maneuvers along China's southern and southeastern coasts.[80]

Chinese submarines, among other weapon systems, are expected to soon be a larger undersea force than that of the US, and their diesel design could be used to create mobile minefields in the SCS. The SCS has uneven depths, high levels of background noise, strong currents and shifting thermal layers, which make detecting Chinese submarines very difficult.[81] An interesting war simulation written by a US officer presupposed that PLAN used its submarine capability to defeat the US forces in a hypothetical battle that occurred in the SCS.[82] Vietnam is also upgrading its submarine capability at the Cam Ranh Bay base and sending its officers to Russia and India for training.[83] China's all-out effort to expand its resources and supplies in defense of the SCS was evident when Xi Jinping visited a fishing village in Hainan to assure fishers that the government would do more to protect them when they were in disputed waters.[84] An integrated strategy has key elements of diplomacy and psychological warfare, and throughout its history of communist victories, Chinese political thought internalized those elements.[85]

Does the Malacca Dilemma push China toward a stronger stance in the SCS, eventually elevating Malacca Strait security to one of China's core interests? Analysts generally suggest a passive response to this question. The Malacca Dilemma stems from the strategic importance of the Malacca Strait as a maritime chokepoint and the potential threat of a naval blockade. However, Andrew Erickson and Gabriel Collins challenge this view, arguing that China can mitigate its heavy reliance on the Malacca Strait by rerouting energy imports at a manageable cost.[86] Moreover, the US, the only naval power capable of enforcing such a blockade, is unlikely to do so, given its commitment to freedom of navigation.[87]

Coerciveness for Effective Diplomacy

When China did not have the capability to exercise sufficient force, the country had two choices: first, to avoid initiating a war; second, if forced to participate in a war, to find a winning strategy. This dilemma arose prominently when the KMT fled to Taiwan in 1949 and when the US was about to reach China's border in 1950 during the Korean War. However, in the case of the SCS, China's interests have always been present in the form of territorial interests. Although China took decades to increase its capability, the SCS waters and features have been under a vacuum of power status for the time being; the threats from outside capable of changing the status quo were limited. It is noticeable that China's territorial interests in the SCS as a whole remain the same, although specific interests over the waters—or its features or resources—in the SCS have been differently prioritized over time. Initially, China had a strong desire to restore its historic dominance after having been colonized by Westerners and Japanese; however, the SCS took on economic value as international surveys emerged, and the Communist Party of China must now present a stronger nation's power to not disappoint strong nationalist sentiments among domestic public opinion in order to ensure the party's legitimacy. Both the constant and changing interests are equally as important as China's increasing capability. China's increasingly multifaceted *interests* in the SCS can provide it with reasons to initiate militarized disputes—more than the favorable *balance of power* to China does.

Diplomacy does have a role in restraining military conflicts by exchanging negotiable options between actors. Diplomatic flexibility is required to establish pluralistic order (between states, and between a state and its people), and bargaining capability is required to achieve effective negotiation. The important point is that bargaining capability requires a state to possess not only military or hard power but also economic statecraft, diplomatic strategies, and the ability to take advantage of others' needs. Therefore, even when a state's interests are very urgent and it has reasonable capability to fight and win, this does not mean that the state will always initiate a war—because diplomatic flexibility and capability are still capable of securing the state's interests.

But if the external threat against the country's self-help intervenes, then the country's choice can be shifted. In the case of the 1974 Battle of the Paracel Islands, as table 15 shows, there was undoubtedly a concern regarding the tensions along the Sino–Soviet border and improving relations between the USSR and North Vietnam. Deng Xiaoping, the chief of the PLA general staff at the time, used the battle "to send a political signal to North Vietnam, showing Beijing's displeasure with Hanoi's relations with Moscow."[88] The distances between mainland China and the Paracel Islands, and the rapidity with which China deployed the PLAN ships to the area, sent a signal to North Vietnam. Mao Zedong attempted to use China's consolidated control over the Paracel Islands as leverage to make North Vietnam turn against the USSR.[89] However, China did not initiate the battle entirely because of the USSR's direct threat; therefore, the USSR is flagged in table 15.

US intervention in the SCS, which led to clashes between China and US aircraft and surveillance ships, has been done as part of the operation to ensure freedom of navigation. The US has not attempted to occupy any islands in the SCS or directly supported Vietnam or the Philippines' further occupation of other islands in the SCS. US intervention is therefore limited to ensuring freedom of navigation, and appears devoid of territorial interests; thus, China's response was reactive in principle. This situation permits observers to assume that as long as the US does not attempt to change the status quo of territorial occupancy in the SCS, China will maintain that reactive position—at least toward US freedom of navigation operations.

The new trend with freedom of navigation operations under the first Trump administration was the increased frequency, which led to more severe reactions from China. In 2020, US secretary of defense Mark Esper stated, "In 2019 we conducted the greatest number of freedom of navigation operations, FONOPs, in the South China Sea in the 40-year history of FONOPs program, and we will keep up the pace this year."[90] But freedom of navigation operations and China's reaction to them were relatively restrained so far because they have been a long-standing practice, and the data on both countries' activities are publicly available, albeit involuntarily. Transparency, although mutually enforced, plays a crucial role in preventing unexpected spirals of conflict between two major powers and serves as a public diplomacy channel for each country.

The action-reaction dynamic between the US and China is evident in the data collected by think tanks from each country: the Asia Maritime Transparency Initiative from the US and the South China Sea Strategic Situation Probing Initiative from China. the Asia Maritime Transparency Initiative, launched by the Center for Strategic and International Studies in 2014, serves as a database of maritime conflict data, including artificial reclamation of maritime features and militarization, documenting China's aggression in the region. Similarly, the South China Sea Strategic Situation Probing Initiative, established in 2019, provides data on US freedom of navigation operations, indicating US intervention in the region and actions of its allies and partners. The South China Sea Strategic Situation Probing Initiative is led by experts and advisors from Chinese government-affiliated institutes and major Chinese universities.

The more serious problem directly associated with the cause of violence is, as table 15 shows, the external threat toward the status quo that could even cause China to consider initiating a war. In this regard, Rex Li convincingly argues for the presence of a causal relationship between China's sea power aspirations and Chinese leaders' apprehensions of potential US military intervention in the SCS.[91] Pascal Abb further presents quantitative research on 1,500 pieces by Chinese public commentators,[92] indicating that the SCS disputes have been viewed by those commentators as a strategic contention with the US, and that local actors such as Vietnam and the Philippines are also viewed by those Chinese experts in relation to their closeness to the US rather than from a bilateral point of view.

Table 15. Causes in China's Use of Force and Coercive Actions

Year	State	Area or region under militarized disputes or increased tension	Interests (territorial)	Threats	Capability
1949	China	Taiwan Strait	O	X	No
1950	China	Korean Peninsula	X	O (US)	No
1974	China	Paracels	O	O (USSR)*	Yes
1988	China	Spratlys (Johnson South Reef)	O	X	Yes
1995	China	Spratlys (Mischief Reef)	O	X	Yes
2012	China	Scarborough Shoal	O	X	Yes
2013	China	Senkaku*	O	X	No

In table 15, Senkaku is asterisked because it has been included for comparison, although the particular tension raised over the Senkaku Islands in 2013 did not incur casualties and there was no militarized dispute per se—nor is it part of the SCS. The 2013 case has been included in the table because China announced an air defense identification zone (ADIZ) over the East China Sea at that time. The Taiwan Strait and the Korean Peninsula are not part of the SCS disputes; however, these historical cases are closely related to China's use of force and coerciveness analysis, and they have been included in this table. In table 15, the column labeled "Interests" strictly refers to a territorial interest, and "Threats" indicate threats that may change the territorial status quo. "Capability" means the relative capability of China compared to its competitors, that is, whether the balance of power is favorable to China or not.

It is important to understand China's multifaceted interests, threat perceptions, and the balance of power together to accurately analyze the pattern of causes behind China's use of force and coercion. In the context of the SCS, China's territorial interests have been a constant variable, although they have become multifaceted alongside the diversification of specific concerns over time. Therefore, analysis of interests, diplomatic flexibility, and diplomatic capability in the context of China and the SCS could add meaning to the approach this book pursues. Meanwhile, China's military capability has already trumped that of the ASEAN countries and even Taiwan since the 2000s—and it is scarcely necessary even to mention China's nuclear capability, which has further increased China's diplomatic capability. Studies on diplomatic flexibility and capability may also bolster strategic studies by suggesting what it is that China is willing to fight for.

SIX

The Traces of Negotiations

The People's Republic of China aims to celebrate its 100th anniversary in 2049, marking the completion of its two centenary goals: becoming a great modern socialist country in all respects and achieving the rejuvenation of the Chinese nation. What is the view that looks beyond 2049? The rationale behind this book is to emphasize the importance of understanding the past to gain insight into the future. By examining the records of the past seventy years, we can find signposts to navigate the troubled waters ahead. The history of the South China Sea disputes is marked by irregular but persistent changes to the status quo, sometimes accompanied by violence. China's occupation of the Paracel Islands in the 1970s caused hundreds of casualties for Chinese and Vietnamese combined. In the 1980s, dozens of casualties were caused in the naval skirmish when China took reefs from Vietnam in the Spratly Islands. Filipino sailors were detained when Chinese troops began stationing in the Mischief Reef in the Spratlys in the 1990s. The Philippines deployed warplanes and warships when Chinese vessels approached the Philippines-claimed features between 2011 and 2013. Before another violent conflict could erupt, US freedom of navigation operations intensified in the SCS in the mid-2010s. Changes to the status quo in the SCS are violent, visible, and measurable—whether through casualties, military deployments, or the occupation of reefs. These developments inevitably draw the attention of policymakers, their constituents, and the media.

Despite the record of violence, the history of the SCS is equally marked by efforts at negotiation and diplomacy, though these records often reflect a more complex and nonlinear progression. For example, the first and only delimitation agreement between China and Vietnam in the SCS, signed in 2000, did not pave the way for subsequent delimitation talks between China and Vietnam or any other claimants in the region. Similarly, the 2005 joint development initiative between China, Vietnam, and the Philippines—the first of its kind—collapsed due to domestic regime change in the Philippines. In 2018, China and the Philippines signed a Memorandum of Understanding on Cooperation on Oil and Gas Development, which led to the ground-breaking of a joint LNG hub project in 2019. However, this initiative too stalled without further progress. The Declaration on the Conduct of the Parties in the South China Sea, China's first multilateral agreement on the SCS, was signed in 2002, followed by the adoption of implementation guidelines in 2011 and a single-draft Code of Conduct negotiation text in 2018. Yet, the COVID-19 pandemic severely disrupted these negotiations in 2020 and 2021. These traces of China's negotiations in the SCS, however, reveal much about the country's underlying interests, a central theme explored in this book. While the path of diplomacy in the region has been fraught with setbacks and interruptions, these records offer critical insights into China's strategic priorities and approaches. Negotiations in the SCS are conducted within the interplay of these changing priorities, underlying interests, and bottom lines. This fluidity makes the diplomatic landscape complex.

While China's interests have seemed incompatible with those of other claimants, the records of its diplomacy and China's negotiating patterns have been observed in various ways since the 1980s. The role of diplomacy and negotiation has been ever increasing in the evolving security environment in the Indo-Pacific region.[1] Due to the complex background of the SCS disputes, China constructed various platforms of diplomacy for negotiations. China has principles or equivalent guidelines in its diplomacy regarding the SCS disputes. Through the bilateral and multilateral dialogues involving China over decades, the tradition upon which China's principled diplomacy is based has emerged: indisputable sovereignty, peaceful coexistence, and pragmatism. These principles affected China's negotiations for the SCS disputes and transformed the SCS disputes into a dynamic entity of conflict and cooperation. China's interests were deemed to be incompatible with other claimants' interests. Yet the records of China's diplomacy and negotiations reveal the exchangeable and compatible nature of these interests, although they at points culminated in a zero-sum outcome.

China's diplomacy featured two characteristics—principled and pragmatic—which were shaped by Deng Xiaoping's axiom, "shelving dispute and seeking joint development," in the 1970s. The two pillars of China's diplomacy in the SCS disputes were the indisputable sovereignty principle and pragmatism; they continued to influence China's relations with the claimants as well as external actors beyond the SCS. However,

China's sovereignty claim has been further specified by what the claim is over time in accordance with the development of international norms on maritime affairs. The features of diversification and capability define China's bargaining practices. Diversification in China's diplomacy refers to its ever-branching out diplomatic channels with the SCS claimants. Bargaining capability is assessed by observing whether China obtains what it wants—its interests—through these interactions.

The question remains regarding what China really claims in the SCS. Wang Yi, China's state councilor and foreign minister, attended the East Asia Summit Foreign Ministers' Meeting on August 4, 2021, remarking that "the allegation that China claims *all* waters within the dotted line as its internal waters and territorial sea is a deliberate *distortion* of China's position" (emphasis added).[2] This statement was not random, and similar remarks were made earlier. In 1994, Chinese president Jiang Zemin also stated that China only claimed the islets and their adjacent waters.[3]

How will China's underlying interests change as the SCS is becoming a flashpoint for the worsening US-China rivalry? Hu Bo, the director of South China Sea Strategic Situation Probing Initiative (SCSPI), commented in August 2020 that "in recent years, the US has been paying increasingly less attention to safe distance, and a crisis would very easily take place."[4] However, the US was not always interested in the SCS disputes. For example, when the Philippines promulgated its sovereignty over the islands and islets in the SCS within the Kalayaan Island Group in 1978, US officials indicated that the US was not obligated to protect the Philippines' claim.[5] Similarly, in 1995 the US State Department spokesperson also insinuated that the defense treaty with the Philippines did not include provisions related to these maritime issues.[6] However, as the tension between the US and China grew, US involvement in the SCS has also escalated. Secretary of State Hillary Clinton declared at an ASEAN Regional Forum held in Vietnam in 2010 that freedom of navigation operations are in the US national interest. In 2011, the US joined the East Asia Summit—the ASEAN-centered meeting consisting of ASEAN and eight major powers—six years after the formation of the summit.

The US positions in the SCS disputes have toughened under the Trump administration. Since the beginning of the Trump presidency in 2017, the US has shifted from relatively nominal intervention in the SCS, advocating the principle of freedom of navigation, to firmly supporting claimants opposed to China. Official US government documents that illustrate this shift include the Pentagon's *National Defense Strategy*, *Indo-Pacific Strategy Report*, and *Defense Space Strategy*, all published between 2018 and 2020.

These documents express a clear anti-China approach, stating that "China is a strategic competitor using predatory economics," "it [China] seeks Indo-Pacific regional hegemony in the near-term and, ultimately, global preeminence in the long-term," and "China and Russia present the most immediate and serious threats to U.S. space operations."[7]

In 2020, on the anniversary of the Permanent Court of Arbitration's Arbitral Tribunal Ruling on the SCS, the US State Department harshly criticized Beijing for "using intimidation to undermine the sovereign rights of Southeast Asian coastal states in the South China Sea, bully them out of offshore resources, assert unilateral dominance, and replace international law with 'might makes right,'" and stated that "the world will not allow Beijing to treat the South China Sea as its maritime *empire*" (emphasis added).[8] This marks a turn from the Obama administration's intervention approach, which was based on the principle of freedom of navigation. The Trump administration's stance on the SCS reflects the overall shift in its strategy for dealing with China.

The Trump administration's position did not change in Biden's administration but continued and strengthened. The Biden administration has continued the "tradition" of commemorating the anniversary of the Arbitral Tribunal Ruling on the SCS. Since 2021, the administration has issued press statements annually to mark the fifth, sixth, seventh, and eighth anniversaries of the ruling, with the most recent statement released in 2024. The statement on the fifth anniversary of the Arbitral Tribunal Ruling on the SCS reaffirmed Secretary Pompeo's statement and further provided security guarantees to the Philippines by declaring that "an armed attack on the Philippines . . . in the South China Sea would invoke U.S. mutual defense commitments under Article IV of the 1951 U.S.-Philippines Mutual Defense Treaty."[9] This commitment was reiterated when the Chinese Coast Guard used water cannons against Philippine supply ships in the SCS in November 2021. The US Department of State issued a press statement noting that "an armed attack on Philippine public vessels in the South China Sea would invoke U.S. mutual defense commitments under Article IV of the 1951 U.S. Philippines Mutual Defense Treaty." The Biden administration's security commitments to the Philippines are notably absent in the 2023 and 2024 press statements on the Anniversary of the Arbitral Tribunal Ruling on the SCS. This omission may reflect a shift in the US strategy in the SCS and its approach to US-China relations, so it is worth closely monitoring these annual statements.

An overarching query is what the fierce competition between the US and

China implies for China's underlying interests in the SCS. As competition between the US and China is on the rise, it is likely that China's interests in the future will be to exclude US influence in the SCS. China's quantitative and qualitative advancement in military power cannot be stopped. The balance of power will change on a zero-sum basis, and when China slows down its military modernization for any internal or external reasons, US power will remain dominant. If China grows faster, US power will diminish faster. Nevertheless, unlike the US-China power game, the zero-sum logic in the SCS does not always prevail in diplomacy and negotiations between China and other claimants. These mixed results derive from the perspectives of Southeast Asian claimants in the SCS disputes. There are benefits being gained from expanding US influence in the SCS at the price of paying for the costs caused by the US-China power game.

An example is the Southeast Asian countries' immediate response when Australia, the US, and the UK announced an enhanced trilateral security partnership—AUKUS—in September 2021. The immediate response from individual Southeast Asian countries and ASEAN as a group was not welcoming or objecting to this new arrangement that could potentially curb China's maritime ambitions. In July 2020, Philippine president Rodrigo Duterte reiterated during his State of the Nation Address the destructive risk potentially caused by the power competition and subsequent conflict between the US and China.[10] For the Southeast Asian claimants in the SCS, deterring China's advancement in the SCS is necessary, but the SCS as a new battlefield of the US and China does not benefit them either. Considering the dual fear of Southeast Asian claimants, namely China's aggressiveness and insecurity in the region caused by US-China competition, China would likely choose to continue the power game. China could use the dual fear to isolate its negotiation with the claimants from the US-China power game to maximize its interests. These interests would include in the short term decreasing US influence on the Southeast Asian claimants. Ultimately, China desires acknowledgment from regional claimants of China's historical rights to create appropriate agreements on other practical and specific issues such as resources, delimitations, and nontraditional security issues.

The diplomatic interactions between China and other claimants in the SCS disputes suggest a pattern in a series of negotiations and agreements. The principles of indisputable sovereignty and pragmatism in diplomacy consistently appeared in interstate interactions to protect Chinese national interests. However, on the surface they do not coexist and even resist each other. Furthermore, China's expectations on diplomacy and claims in the

SCS are reflected in various patterns of China's negotiation. The size of negotiation is the key to dissecting the patterns. Bilateral negotiation is the smallest but most effective form of diplomacy and China's preferred format to address disputes with the claimants. For instance, China signed a maritime delimitation agreement in Beibu Bay in the SCS with Vietnam and a Code of Conduct in the SCS with the Philippines. Maritime delimitation and signing a Code of Conduct are the two most desirable and effective ways to reduce conflicts in the SCS. Trilateral negotiation was the most vulnerable form because it could not be sustained for long. However, it was a viable method in the past and produced the most practical and specific agreements between China and other claimants on joint development of resources in the SCS.

China's engagement in multilateral diplomacy began far later than bilateral negotiations in the SCS, which started in the 1970s. ASEAN initiated a multilateral declaration on the SCS disputes in the 1990s, and essentially, China joined the platform later in the 2000s and agreed on a declaration between China and ASEAN, that is, the Declaration on the Conduct of Parties in the South China Sea. Therefore, China's multilateral negotiations in the SCS encompass nonclaimants in the SCS in ASEAN. Subsequent negotiations on the Code of Conduct between China and ASEAN also involved nonclaimants as parties. By joining the multilateral platform, China unofficially accepted *regionalization* of the SCS issues and treated ASEAN as a group instead of solely relying on a bilateral solution, that is, China adopted a "dual track" approach. Compared to bilateral and trilateral negotiations, multilateral negotiations of China are normative, developing regional norms and initiatives to address local disputes of regional actors. Therefore, the agreed outcome is also abstract and ideational. Articles in the DOC articulate specific cooperation between China and ASEAN in detail, for example, articles about exercising self-restraint, maintaining the status quo in occupation, and cooperating in nontraditional security issues. However, unlike bilateral and trilateral negotiations, these articles are not expected to develop into tangible outcomes. The subsequent multilateral Code of Conduct negotiations between China and ASEAN will also likely have the DOC's limitations of multilateral diplomacy.

As a signatory to the United Nations Convention on the Law of the Sea, China's engagement with UNCLOS illustrates the country's SCS diplomacy on an international platform. As for China's position on UNCLOS, the interpretation is drastically polarized between China and other countries in the region. Since its ratification of UNCLOS, China has repeatedly claimed that it has respected and followed UNCLOS, but other countries have blamed China for rejecting and violating the UNCLOS. What is the truth? China's track record in UNCLOS-related activities leads to the conclusion in chapter 5 that the answer to this question is not straightforward. An individual country's internalization of UNCLOS is different from others. For example, China signed UNCLOS in 1982 and ratified it along with dozens of other signatories in 1996, while the US has not ratified UNCLOS in Congress, though the US effectively follows UNCLOS.

China's intentions as a party to the UNCLOS system is a marginalized topic among scholars though it is related to China's normative development that shapes its narrative and provides grounds for its claims. First, it is evident that China advocates the shared perception on UNCLOS with other signatories that it provides the parties with conditions for claiming the maritime rights of coastal states. By analyzing China's declaration on UNCLOS in 1996 and 2006, chapter 5 argues that what China wanted to obtain by signing UNCLOS on the one hand was practical benefits such as effective territorial seas and an exclusive economic zone. On the other hand, China diplomatically removed potential barriers that might intrude on China's interests by submitting another declaration in 2006. China's position paper published right after the 2016 arbitration award recalled the 2006 declaration, stating that the maritime delimitation dispute "has been excluded from the UNCLOS dispute settlement procedures" by China's 2006 declaration submitted to UNCLOS.[11]

China's "Four Respects" introduced in 2014 are self-explanatory regarding China's positions on international law, covering (1) disputes left over by history, (2) China upholding UNCLOS, (3) direct dialogues between claimants, and (4) the significance of China–ASEAN relations. That is, China's historical rights and UNCLOS do not negate each other, and China's bilateral talks with claimants coexist with regionalized efforts to address the SCS issues. China's perception of UNCLOS stands on the country's own portrayal of it—ideal, harmonious, and utilitarian. The approach is ideal because China's domestic law and international law do not invalidate each other. It is harmonious because China's historical rights can coexist with international law. The view is also utilitarian because China can legally protect resources by virtue of being a coastal state through the UNCLOS regime, such as territorial seas, EEZ, and the continental shelf. China can expand its resources beyond these territorial waters using the UNCLOS terms. Based upon this approach, China refuted the 2016 arbitration award, asserting that the territorial issue is "not subject to" UNCLOS, and that the Philippines "abused" the UNCLOS dispute settlement procedures.[12] China's domestic laws on declaring territorial seas, the contiguous zone, EEZ, and the continental shelf were also formulated in accordance with developments in international law, such as the Geneva Convention in 1958 and UNCLOS in 1982. Thus far, China has not indicated any interest in leaving the UNCLOS system.

How does China create rules? Beyond currently existing international norms, China has begun to organize international conferences in the 2000s and will continue to empower them. These events are Track 1.5 or Track 2 diplomacy for their face value. They invite government officials, military officers, diplomats, scholars, and journalists from all around the world. The impact of these conferences cannot be ignored because China attempts to spread its own norms and values through these events. China's proactive construction of regional dialogue platforms implies important changes to Chinese diplomacy. First, the spread of the diplomatic version of the Beijing Consensus (also known as the Chinese Economic Model). Second, a strategy of *hexiao kongda*—cooperate with the small countries to counter the big. The South Asian Association for Regional Cooperation is a good example for China in this regard. The ancient strategy of China, *hexiao kongda*, had been implemented in South Asia throughout China's proactive approach toward the South Asian Association for Regional Cooperation.[13] Also, China attempts to prevent a "China threat" perception from its rising influence in the region.

One of the examples is the Xiangshan Forum, which began in 2006 and has been organized biennially by the China Association of Military Science as a Track 1.5 platform between 2006 and 2014. In 2014, the forum was upgraded to a 2.0 platform, hence inviting wider participation from outside government, and started to hold forums annually. The forum's structure offers an expectation that the discussions in the forum are geared toward specific themes that China initiates, and the forum is more receptive and broader than other regional dialogues, as the host country claims. The Xiangshan Forum provides another example of China's regional diplomacy in the realm of security and defense. Compared to the Shangri-La Dialogue organized by the International Institute for Strategic Studies based in the UK, which invites government officials from twenty-eight countries, the Xiangshan Forum includes forty countries in addition to four international organizations. China also attends the Conference on Interaction and Confidence Building Measures in Asia, which consists of participants from Eurasian countries as the core group of the meeting. In 2014, the conference was held in Shanghai, and Xi Jinping delivered a famous speech introducing the

New Asian Security Concept. He stated that "we all live in the same Asian family. With our interests and security so closely intertwined, we will swim or sink together."[14]

The Asian Infrastructure Investment Bank (AIIB) is an example of a China-proposed intergovernmental regional development institution in the realm of finance. The AIIB was introduced for the first time during Xi Jinping's visit to Indonesia in 2013 where he proposed the Maritime Silk Road—the second pillar of his Belt and Road Initiative. In his speech in Indonesia, Xi proposed the establishment of the AIIB "that would give priority to ASEAN countries' needs."[15] Twenty-one Asian countries, including China, signed the memorandum of understanding establishing the AIIB in October 2014, and the AIIB was officially formed in January 2016.[16] From the Chinese perspective, it is frustrating that the country's voting share is fairly limited in other international organizations, for example, 3.8 percent of the International Monetary Fund and 5.5 percent of the Asian Development Bank. However, China will be the largest shareholder of the AIIB, with a stake of up to 50 percent, and it has administrative initiatives such as the headquarters location and presidency. This institutional peculiarity, namely China's overwhelming voting share and the lack of large economies other than China in the region, raises concerns that the AIIB would serve China's interests, including primarily supporting its new Silk Road project.[17] On the contrary, as a former chief economist of the Asian Development Bank, Jong Wha Lee, objectively points out, regional developing Asian countries would find necessary infrastructure investment from the AIIB to support their long-term economic growth.[18]

Youngkwuan Yoon, the former minister of foreign affairs and trade of the Republic of Korea and professor at Seoul National University, writes that China has weakened the motivation of Southeast Asian countries to confront China in a coalition by offering them economic benefits. He contends that a nuanced change in China's diplomacy is observed as China has been shifting its diplomatic orientation from hard power to soft power. China's efforts are evident in its initiatives in the AIIB, the Maritime Silk Road Bank, and the New Development Bank, while the US is suffering from the remaining problems from the global economic crisis and is deemed to have a reduced regional role. As Wang commented, "The South China Sea was the main route of what may be called the Asian East-West trade in commodities and ideas. It was the second Silk Route."[19]

The entire development surrounding the SCS bestows a strong analytical inclination to the realist idea that comprehensive national power determines international relations. In particular, the concerns regarding China's increasing assertiveness in the later 2000s were real. Nevertheless, China's enhanced power does not squarely determine the focus of underlying interests or the agenda-setting for negotiations per se. It is important to understand China's multifaceted interests, threats, and the balance of power altogether to accurately analyze the pattern of causes of China's use of force and coerciveness.[20] China's physical capability is a useful tool to enhance its bargaining power, but it only partially determines the negotiation focus and agenda. When the People's Republic of China was established in 1949, China had an urgent task to retake historical dominance by Westerners and Japanese. However, the SCS obtained economic value as international natural resource surveys were conducted. Now, the Communist Party of China needs to project a stronger nation's power to avoid disappointing nationalists among domestic public opinion and to bolster the party's legitimacy. China's consistent territorial interests and its changing objectives are equally as important as China's increasing capabilities. The diverse and multifaceted interests of China in the SCS could instigate militarized disputes more than the favorable balance of power does to China and can motivate it to fight.

This book reveals how China's principled approach was adopted in the course of diplomacy with the claimants in the SCS disputes. China's bilateral, trilateral, and multilateral diplomacy has had a variety of influences on the SCS disputes, depending on the counterparts to the negotiations and the agenda. Bilateral diplomacy is the form that China has consistently claimed as the only way to resolve disputes. Trilateral diplomacy was the rarest form of diplomacy in the history of the SCS negotiations, and demonstrated the most vulnerable continuity, but it was simultaneously the most detailed form of negotiation on the agenda. China's multilateral diplomacy began in the early 2000s when the country was confident enough to manage multiple parties. Regardless of the debate on the symbolic multilateral agreement—the DOC—the China-ASEAN multilateral platform has been a framework for regional dispute management in the SCS that China most closely employed over the past twenty years.

The China-ASEAN Code of Conduct negotiations were delayed when the world was fighting against the pandemic in 2020 and 2021. Previously, in 2018, China and ASEAN reached a Single Draft Code of Conduct negotiation Text, which constitutes the framework of the Code of Conduct. At the time of reaching the Single Draft, the initial completion timeline of the Code of Conduct negotiation was targeted for 2021. However, in August 2021, at a China-ASEAN Ministerial Meeting via video format, the parties agreed to resume the COC text consultations and virtually hold joint working group meetings.[21] In the ongoing negotiations, Southeast Asian claimants wanted to use the Code of Conduct to engage with China diplomatically, yet China wanted the code to include a mutual agreement that no external party would intervene in the SCS, which refers to the US, its allies, and partners.

The objective of cutting out the external influence in the region has gained more significance in negotiations for China. The US freedom of navigation program has continued over more than forty years worldwide to exercise US navigation and overflight rights; however, the frequency of China-US encounters and the US freedom of navigation operations in the SCS have increased. In 2019, China launched the SCSPI to counter the security posture narrative led by US-based institutions. According to the SCSPI, US reconnaissance aircraft operating over the South China Sea notably increased when the People's Liberation Army Navy was conducting military exercises around the Paracel Islands. Furthermore, according to SCSPI, the US conducted more than 150 reconnaissance aircraft activities in the SCS between May and July 2020.[22] China's argument was indirectly affirmed by US secretary of defense Mark Esper, who noted that the US conducted a record number of freedom of navigation operations in 2019 and intended to continue them in the years ahead.[23]

Based on the analysis of China's negotiations, the end game China aims to accomplish in the SCS is not a monolithic or immutable goal. China insists on its absolute sovereignty over the SCS for the past seventy years and has been negotiating with the SCS claimants for forty years; meanwhile, China's official claims and bottom-line policies have become disjointed. China's underlying interests in the SCS have varied in content and urgency from time to time, depending on economic, historical, domestic, and international concerns and nontraditional security issues. Based on this analysis, SCS disputes are likely to involve compatible interests, as illustrated by Fisher and Ury's orange quarrel metaphor, where two people arguing over an orange for different objectives can move to interest-based negotiation over positional bargaining.

Notwithstanding the findings above, this book does not argue that China approaches the SCS disputes with diplomatic maneuvers only. China's use of force has occurred and will occur again in the future. As this chapter elaborated in the beginning, the historical change of status quo in the SCS has been accompanied by violence from China. China's use of force demonstrates that China is comparatively superior to its counterparts in military power and has the means to enforce China's interests without relying on diplomatic measures. Diplomacy by force appears in the following situations: a situation in which compatible interests do not exist at all, or even if such compatibility exists, the parties are not aware of them due to diplomatic limitations. Finally, force occurs even if parties are aware of such underlying interests through competent intelligence or back-channel negotiations, but a situation occurs in which a compromise could not be made for internal and external reasons. Chapter 5 examines the history of China's pursuit of the use of power and in what cases China has excluded diplomatic options for what specific interests.

China, as a key party in the SCS disputes, has engaged in negotiations with other claimants that have oscillated between principle-oriented and pragmatic approaches. Over the past seventy years, China has walked a line between these two bargaining strategies. However, beneath the surface of these disputes lie interests—both Chinese and those of other claimants—that, while not identical, are compatible and negotiable. What once seemed irreconcilable can be aligned in a specific and mutually beneficial way. Successful negotiation requires uncovering the underlying interests hidden behind official claims, recognizing that these interests, while not always the same as those of other claimants, can be traded to find common ground. This task is challenging at any level, let alone in state-level diplomacy, but it is crucial for avoiding unnecessary actions that could destabilize the region. China's narrative of *indisputable sovereignty* evolves as its national interests shift, but the core lesson remains: the traces of past negotiations offer vital clues for advancing peaceful resolution in the SCS.

Notes

CHAPTER 1

1. Seokwoo Lee, "Territorial Disputes among Japan, China and Taiwan concerning the Senkaku Islands," *Boundary & Territory Briefing*, International Boundaries Research Unit (2002); Junwu Pan, *Toward a New Framework for Peaceful Settlement of China's Territorial and Boundary Disputes* (Leiden: Martinus Nijhoff, 2009).

2. Asia Maritime Transparency Initiative, "Island Features Occupation Status in the South China Sea" (2020), https://amti.csis.org/scs-features-map

3. Yi Yang, "Modernizations of China's National Defense," in *Transformation of Foreign Affairs and International Relations in China, 1978–2008*, ed. Yizhou Wang (Leiden: Brill, 2011).

4. Leszek Buszynski, "ASEAN, the Declaration of Conduct, and the South China Sea," *Contemporary Southeast Asia* 25, no. 3 (2003).

5. Jianwei Wang, "China's Multilateral Diplomacy in the New Millennium," in *China Rising: Power and Motivation in Chinese Foreign Policy*, ed. Yong Deng and Feiling Wang (Lanham, MD: Rowman and Littlefield, 2005).

6. Declaration On the Conduct of Parties in the South China Sea, "Declaration on the Conduct of Parties in the South China Sea, the Governments of the Member States of ASEAN and the Government of the People's Republic of China, done on November 4, 2002, Phnom Penh, the Kingdom of Cambodia," 2002, http://www.asean.org/asean/external-relations/china/item/declaration-on-the-conduct-of-parties-in-the-south-china-sea; Wang, "China's Multilateral Diplomacy."

7. Information Office of the State Council, *White Paper: China's Peaceful Development* (Beijing, 2011).

8. Michael Hsiao and Alan Yang, "Soft Power Politics in the Asia Pacific: Chinese and Japanese Quests for Regional Leadership," *Asia-Pacific Journal* 8 (2009).

9. David L. Shambaugh, *China Goes Global: The Partial Power* (Oxford: Oxford University Press, 2013); Toshi Yoshihara and James R. Holmes, "Can China Defend a 'Core Interest' in the South China Sea?," *Washington Quarterly* 34, no. 2 (2011).

10. Information Office of the State Council, *White Paper: China's Peaceful Development*.

11. Chi-kin Lo, *China's Policy towards Territorial Disputes: The Case of the South China Sea Islands*, ed. Michael Leifer (London: Routledge, 1989), 2.

12. John W. Garver, "China's Push through the South China Sea: The Interaction of Bureaucratic and National Interests," *China Quarterly* (1992): 999.

13. Clarence J. Bouchat, *The Paracel Islands and U.S. Interests and Approaches in the South China Sea* (Carlisle Barracks, PA: Strategic Studies Institute and U.S. Army War College Press, 2014).

14. Bouchat, *Paracel Islands and U.S. Interests.*

15. Erica Strecker Downs and Phillip C. Saunders, "Legitimacy and the Limits of Nationalism: China and the Diaoyu Islands," *International Security* 23, no. 3 (1998): 117.

16. Ji You, "A Test Case for China's Defence and Foreign Policies," *Contemporary Southeast Asia* 16, no. 4 (1995).

17. Taylor M. Fravel, *Strong Borders, Secure Nation: Cooperation and Conflict in China's Territorial Disputes* (Princeton: Princeton University Press, 2008); Ryan D. Griffiths, "States, Nations, and Territorial Stability: Why Chinese Hegemony Would Be Better for International Order," *Security Studies* 25, no. 3 (2016): 537.

18. Jiye Kim, "Disputed Waters, Contested Norms: Framing Discourses on the South China Sea Disputes," *Pacific Affairs* 90, no. 2 (2017), https://doi.org/10.5509/2017902297

19. Thucydides, *The Peloponnesian War*, trans. Martin Hammond (Oxford: Oxford University Press, 2009).

20. Hans J. Morgenthau, *Politics among Nations: The Struggle for Power and Peace* (New York: Knopf, 1961); Kenneth Waltz, *Theory of International Politics* (Reading, MA: Addison-Wesley, 1979); Robert Gilpin, *War and Change in World Politics* (Cambridge: Cambridge University Press, 1981); John J. Mearsheimer, *The Tragedy of Great Power Politics* (New York: Norton, 2001).

21. Feng Zhang, "The Rise of Chinese Exceptionalism in International Relations," *European Journal of International Relations* 19, no. 2 (2013): 307.

22. Yves Heng Lim and Jiye Kim, "Determining the Determinants: Factors of Change in China's South China Sea Strategy, 1995–2015," *Pacific Focus* 35, no. 2 (2020), https://doi.org/https://doi.org/10.1111/pafo.12167

23. Shambaugh, *China Goes Global.*

24. Xuetong Yan, *Analysis of China's National Interests*, trans. East Asia Nonproliferation Program, James Martin Center for Nonproliferation Studies (Monterey Institute of International Studies, 2002).

25. Yan, *Analysis of China's National Interests.*

26. Shambaugh, *China Goes Global*; Xuetong Yan et al., *Ancient Chinese Thought, Modern Chinese Power* (Princeton: Princeton University Press, 2013).

27. Zemin Zheng, "Asia and the Pacific under the South China Sea Dispute Pattern," PhD diss., Central Party School, 2004.

28. Bernard D. Cole, *The Great Wall at Sea: China's Navy in the Twenty-First Century* (Annapolis, MD: Naval Institute Press, 2010).

29. Huaqing Liu, *Liu Huaqing Huiyilu* [Memoirs of Liu Huaqing] (Beijing: Jiefangjun Chubanshe, 2004).

30. Caiyun Chen and Zhouping Deng, "Lun Nanhaifenzheng De Zhongguo

Duice" [Discussion on China's response to the South China Sea disputes], *Jiangsu Kejidaxue Xuebao* 11, no. 3 (2011); Nong Hong, *UNCLOS and Ocean Dispute Settlement: Law and Politics in the South China Sea* (Abingdon, UK: Routledge, 2012); Keyuan Zou, "China's U-Shaped Line in the South China Sea Revisited," *Ocean Development & International Law* 43, no. 1 (2012); Keyuan Zou, *Law of the Sea in East Asia: Issues and Prospects* (London: Routledge, 2005).

31. Jingdong Yuan, "Emerging Maritime Rivalry in the South China Sea: Territorial Disputes, Sea-lane Security, and the Pursuit of Power," paper prepared for the International Security Research and Outreach Programme, 2012, accessed June 2, 2013, http://www.international.gc.ca/arms-armes/isrop-prisi/research-recherche/intl_security-securite_int/Report-South_China_Sea.aspx

32. Sam Bateman, "Cooperation or Trust: What Comes First in the South China Sea?," *RSIS Commentary*, no. 167 (Singapore: S. Rajaratnam School of International Studies, 2013), accessed September 17, 2013, http://www.rsis.edu.sg/publications/Perspective/RSIS1672013.pdf

33. Joseph S. Nye and David Welch, *Understanding Global Conflict and Cooperation: An Introduction to Theory and History*, 10th ed. (London: Pearson, 2017).

34. Xiaofeng Yu, "The Emergence of Non-Traditional Security Issues in China and Corresponding Strategies," in *Transformation of Foreign Affairs and International Relations in China, 1978–2008*, ed. Yizhou Wang (Leiden: Brill, 2011).

35. Hailong Ju, "Heping Jiejue Nanhai Wentide Xianshi Sikao" [Realistic thought of peaceful settlement of the South China Sea issue], *Dongnanya Yanjiu* 5 (2006).

36. Keyuan Zou, "Can China Respect the Law of the Seas? An Assessment of Maritime Agreements between China and Its Neighbors," *Harvard Asia Quarterly* 12, no. 3 (2010).

37. Wang, "China's Multilateral Diplomacy."

38. Shicun Wu and Huaifeng Ren, "More Than a Declaration: A Commentary on the Background and the Significance of the Declaration on the Conduct of the Parties in the South China Sea," *Chinese Journal of International Law* 2, no. 1 (2003).

39. Guoqiang Luo, "Duobian Lujing Zai Jiejue Nanhai Zhengduan Zhong De Zuoyong Jiqi Goujian Jian Ping—Nanhai Gefang Xingwei Xuanyan" [Multilateral approach in the South China Sea dispute settlement: Effects and its constructions—with respect to the Declaration on the Conduct of Parties in the South China Sea), *Faxue Luntan* 4, no. 25 (2010).

40. Buszynski, "ASEAN, the Declaration of Conduct."

41. Scott Snyder, Brad Glosserman, and Ralph A. Cossa, "Confidence Building Measures in the South China Sea," *Issues & Insights*, nos. 2–01 (Honolulu: Pacific Forum, Center for Strategic and International Studies, 2001), https://csis-website-prod.s3.amazonaws.com/s3fs-public/legacy_files/files/publication/issuesinsightsv01n02.pdf

42. Tao Xiong, "Nanhai Gefang Xingwei Xuanyande qiyuan, kunjing Yu Chulu" [The Declaration on the Conduct of Parties in the South China Sea: Origin, plight, future], master's thesis, Jinan University, 2012.

43. Yan Yu, "Bridge over Troubled Water," *Beijing Review* 54, no. 31 (2011).

44. Alexander E. Wendt, "The Agent–Structure Problem in International Relations Theory," *International Organisation* 41, no. 3 (1987).

45. Yaqing Qin, "Zhongguo Guoji Guanxi Lilun" [The Chinese theory of international relations], in *Zhongguo Duiwai Guanxi Zhuanxing 30 Nian* [Thirty years of transformation in Chinese foreign relations], ed. Yizhou Wang (Beijing: Shehui Kexue Wenxian Chubanshe, 2008), 322.

46. Li Xue and Huanrong Xiao, "Zhongguo de Jiangou Zhuyi Guojiguanxi Yanjiu (1998–2004): Chengjiu yu Buzu" [Research on constructivist international relations theory in China], *Shijie Jingji yu Zhengzhi* 8 (2006): 44.

47. Marc Lanteigne, *Chinese Foreign Policy: An Introduction* (Abingdon, UK: Routledge, 2009).

48. Zhang, "Rise of Chinese Exceptionalism," 307.

49. Yaqing Qin, "Development of International Relations Theory in China: Progress through Debates," *International Relations of the Asia-Pacific* 11, no. 2 (2011).

50. Yaqing Qin, "Relationality and Processual Construction: Bringing Chinese Ideas into International Relations Theory," *Social Sciences in China* 30, no. 4 (2009).

51. Waltz, *Theory of International Politics*; Robert Keohane, "Neoliberal Institutionalism," in *After Hegemony: Cooperation and Discord in the World Political Economy*, ed. Robert Keohane (Princeton: Princeton University Press, 1984); Alexander E. Wendt, *Social Theory of International Politics* (Cambridge: Cambridge University Press, 1999).

52. Qin, "Relationality and Processual Construction."

53. B. Creutzfeldt, "Theory Talk #45: Qin Yaqing on Rules vs. Relations, Drinking Coffee and Tea, and a Chinese Approach to Global Governance," *Theory Talks*, November 30, 2011, https://www.files.ethz.ch/isn/155106/Theory%20Talk45_Yaqing.pdf

54. Lanteigne, *Chinese Foreign Policy.*

55. Lanteigne, *Chinese Foreign Policy.*

56. Lai-Ha Chan, *China Engages Global Health Governance: Responsible Stakeholder or System-Transformer?* (New York: Palgrave Macmillan, 2010).

57. Xuetong Yan, *Lishide Guanxing: Weilai Shiniande Zhongguo Yu Shijie* [Inertia of history: China and the world in the next years] (Beijing: Zhongxin Chubanshe, 2013).

58. Yan, *Lishide Guanxing.*

59. Andrew J. Nathan and Andrew Scobell, *China's Search for Security* (New York: Columbia University Press, 2012).

60. Marwyn S. Samuels, *Contest for the South China Sea* (New York: Methuen, 1982); Lo, *China's Policy.*

61. Nathan and Scobell, *China's Search for Security.*

62. Liu, *Liu Huaqing Huiyilu.*

63. Nathan and Scobell, *China's Search for Security.*

64. Ji You, "Deciphering Beijing's Maritime Security Policy and Strategy in Managing Sovereignty Disputes in the China Seas," *Policy Brief* (Singapore: S. Rajaratnam School of International Studies, October 2013).

65. Ian Storey and Carlyle A. Thayer, "The South China Sea Dispute: A Review of Developments and Their Implications since the 2002 Declaration on the Conduct of Parties," in *South and Southeast Asia: Responding to Changing Geo-Political and Security Challenges*, ed. K. V. Kesavan and Daljit Singh (Singapore: Institute of Southeast Asian Studies, 2010).

66. Storey and Thayer, "South China Sea Dispute."

67. Dingding Chen and Jianwei Wang, "Lying Low No More? China's New Thinking on the Tao Guang Yang Hui Strategy," *China: An International Journal* 9, no. 2 (2011).

68. Chen and Wang, "Lying Low No More?"

69. Qiushi Journal, "About Qiushi Journal," first viewed March 27, 2014; http://en.qstheory.cn/2020-06/16/c_461019.htm

70. Qiushi Journal, "About Qiushi Journal."

71. Qiushi Journal, "About Qiushi Journal."

72. Fisher and Ury, *Getting to Yes*, 42.

73. Fisher and Ury, *Getting to Yes*, 47.

74. Fisher and Ury, *Getting to Yes*, 32.

75. Laurie R. Weingart and Mara Olekalns, "Communication Processes in Negotiation: Frequencies, Sequences, and Phases," in *The Handbook of Negotiation and Culture*, ed. Michele J. Gelfand and Jeanne M. Brett (Stanford, CA: Stanford Business Books, 2004).

76. David Lax and James Sebenius, *The Manager as Negotiator: Bargaining for Cooperation and Competitive Gain* (New York: Free Press, 1986), 11.

77. Zongze Ruan, "Hexie Shijie Yinling Zhongguo Waijiao Xinshidai" [Harmonious world is leading a new era in Chinese diplomacy], *Liaowang*, January 9, 2006, 3.

78. Jian Zhang, "China's South China Sea Policy: Evolution, Claims and Challenges," in *The South China Sea Maritime Dispute: Political, Legal, and Regional Perspectives*, ed. Leszek Buszynski and Christopher B. Roberts (New York: Routledge, 2015), 61.

79. Geoff Berridge, *Diplomacy: Theory and Practice*, 4th ed. (New York: Palgrave Macmillan, 2010), 1.

80. Brad Glosserman, "China's Smile Diplomacy," *South China Morning Post*, April 1, 2004, http://www.scmp.com/article/450592/chinas-smile-diplomacy; Lai To Lee, *China and the South China Sea Dialogues* (Westport, CT: Praeger, 1999); Lai To Lee, "China, the USA and the South China Sea Conflicts," *Security Dialogue* 34, no. 1 (2003); Sheldon W. Simon, "Evaluating Track II Approaches to Security Diplomacy in the Asia-Pacific: The CSCAP Experience," *Pacific Review* 15, no. 2 (2002).

81. Lo, *China's Policy Towards Territorial Disputes*.

82. Lanteigne, *Chinese Foreign Policy*; Storey and Thayer, "South China Sea Dispute."

83. Fisher and Ury, *Getting to Yes*.

84. Jiye Kim and Daniel Druckman, "Shelved Sovereignty or Invalid Sovereignty? The South China Sea Negotiations, 1992–2016," *Pacific Review* 33, no. 1 (2020).

85. Kristin Asdal and Hilde Reinertsen, *Doing Document Analysis: A Practice-Oriented Method* (London: SAGE, 2022).

86. Fisher and Ury, *Getting to Yes*, 32.

87. Jack S. Levy, "Qualitative Methods in International Relations," in *Millennial Reflections on International Studies*, ed. Michael Brecher and Frank. P Harvey (Ann Arbor: University of Michigan Press, 2002).

88. Keyuan Zou, "Joint Development in the South China Sea: A New Approach," *International Journal of Marine and Coastal Law* 21, no. 2 (2006).

89. Sorin Fetic, "Operationalisation of Defence Diplomacy," *Strategic Impact*, no. 4 (2013).

90. Fetic, "Operationalisation of Defence Diplomacy," 46.

CHAPTER 2

1. Costas M. Constantinou and James Der Derian, "Sustaining Global Hope: Sovereignty, Power and the Transformation of Diplomacy," in *Sustainable Diplomacies*, ed. Costas M. Constantinou and James Der Derian (New York: Palgrave Macmillan, 2010).

2. Fuchang Yang, ed., *Contemporary China and Its Foreign Policy* (Beijing: World Affairs Press, 2003), 181.

3. Information Office of the State Council, *White Paper: China's Peaceful Development*.

4. Ministry of Foreign Affairs of the People's Republic of China, "China's Indisputable Sovereignty over the Xisha and Nansha Islands," full text published in *Beijing Review*, no. 7 (January 30, 1930): 15–24; Ministry of Foreign Affairs of the People's Republic of China, "Statement by Spokesperson Qin Gang of the Ministry of Foreign Affairs of China on the US State Department Issuing a So-called Press Statement on the South China Sea," August 4, 2012, http://www.fmprc.gov.cn/eng/xwfw/s2510/t958226.htm; Ministry of Foreign Affairs, People's Republic of China, "Foreign Ministry Spokesperson Hua Chunying's Regular Press Conference," April 28, 2013, http://www.fmprc.gov.cn/eng/xwfw/s2510/2511/t1035948.shtml

5. Griffiths, "States, Nations, and Territorial Stability."

6. Taylor M. Fravel, "International Relations Theory and China's Rise: Assessing China's Potential for Territorial Expansion," *International Studies Review* 12, no. 4 (2010).

7. A. Doak Barnett, *After Deng, What? Will China Follow the USSR?* (Washington, DC: Foreign Policy Institute, School of Advanced International Studies, Johns Hopkins University, 1991), 22–23.

8. Xinhua, "Xi Eyes More Enabling Int'l Environment for China's Peaceful Development," Xinhua, November 30, 2014, http://news.xinhuanet.com/english/china/2014-11/30/c_133822694_2.htm

9. Quansheng Zhao, "Patterns and Choices of Chinese Foreign Policy," *Asian Affairs* 20, no. 1 (1993).

10. Lucian W. Pye, *The Dynamics of Chinese Politics* (Cambridge, MA: Oelgeschlager, Gunn & Hain, 1981).

11. Lucian W. Pye, "China: Erratic State, Frustrated Society," *Foreign Affairs* 68, no. 4 (1990).

12. Yaqing Qin, "Continuity through Change: Background Knowledge and China's International Strategy," *Chinese Journal of International Politics* 7, no. 3 (2014).

13. Yizhou Wang, introduction to *Transformation of Foreign Affairs and International Relations in China, 1978–2008*, ed. Yizhou Wang (Leiden: Brill, 2011), 1.

14. Tingyang Zhao, *Tianxia Tixi: Shijie Zhidu Zhexue Daolun* [The Tianxia system: An introduction to the philosophy of a world institution] (Nanjing: Jiangsu Jiaoyu Chubanshe, 2005).

15. Zhang, "Rise of Chinese Exceptionalism in International Relations," 311.

16. Ashok Kapur, *China's Changing Approach to Strategy and Negotiations: Past and Present*, Sapru House paper (New Delhi: Indian Council of World Affairs, 2013), 12.

17. Ministry of Foreign Affairs of the People's Republic of China, "China's Initiation of the Five Principles of Peaceful Co-Existence," 2000, https://www.fmprc.gov.cn/mfa_eng/ziliao_665539/3602_665543/3604_665547/t18053.shtml

18. Zedong Mao, "Opening Address to the Eighth National Congress of the Communist Party of China" (Peking: Foreign Languages Press, 1956), http://www.marxists.org/subject/china/documents/cpc/8th_cong_opening.htm

19. Zedong Mao, *Mao Zedong on Diplomacy* (Beijing: Foreign Languages Press, 1954).

20. Jiye Kim, "China's Wars and Strategies: Looking Back at the Korean War and the Sino-Indian War," *Strategic Analysis* 42, no. 2 (2018), https://doi.org/10.1080/09700161.2018.1439329

21. Julia C. Strauss, "The Past in the Present: Historical and Rhetorical Lineages in China's Relations with Africa," *China Quarterly* 199 (2009).

22. Editorial Departments of Renmin Ribao and Hongqi, "Peaceful Coexistence—Two Diametrically Opposed Policies" (Peking: Foreign Languages Press, 1963), http://www.marxists.org/subject/china/documents/polemic/peaceful.htm

23. Zhou Enlai, "Premier Chou En-Lai's Letter to Prime Minister Nehru," in *The Sino-Indian Boundary Question (Enlarged Edition)* (Peking: Foreign Languages Press, 1959).

24. Nianlong Han, ed., *Diplomacy of Contemporary China* (Hong Kong: New Horizon Press, 1990), 415.

25. Lanteigne, *Chinese Foreign Policy*.

26. Information Office of the State Council, *White Paper: China's Policies on Asia-Pacific Security Cooperation* (Beijing: Information Office of the State Council, 2017).

27. Information Office of the State Council, *The Diversified Employment of China's Armed Forces* (Beijing: Information Office of the State Council, 2013).

28. Information Office of the State Council, *2010 China's National Defense* (Beijing: Information Office of the State Council, 2010).

29. Information Office of the State Council, *China: Arms Control and Disarmament* (Beijing: Information Office of the State Council, 1995).

30. Feng Zhang, "Confucian Foreign Policy Traditions in Chinese History," *Chinese Journal of International Politics* 8, no. 2 (2015), https://doi.org/10.1093/cjip/pov004

31. Alastair Iain Johnston, "How New and Assertive Is China's New Assertiveness?," *International Security* 37, no. 4 (2013); Carlyle A. Thayer, "China's New Wave of Aggressive Assertiveness in the South China Sea," *International Journal of China Studies* 2, no. 3 (2011); Michael Yahuda, "China's New Assertiveness in the South China Sea," *Journal of Contemporary China* 22, no. 81 (2013).

32. Enrico Fels and Truong-Minh Vu, eds., *Power Politics in Asia's Contested Waters: Territorial Disputes in the South China Sea* (Cham, Switzerland: Springer International, 2016).

33. Alexandra Sakaki, "Keeping the Dragon at Bay: The South China Sea Dispute in Japan's Security Strategy," in *Power Politics in Asia's Contested Waters: Territorial Disputes in the South China Sea*, ed. Enrico Fels and Truong-Minh Vu, (Cham, Switzer-

land: Springer International, 2016), 426; Srini Sitaraman, "Rising Chinese Power and Territorial Assertiveness in the South China Sea: India-Vietnam Strategic Partnership as a Counterbalancing Endeavor," in *Power Politics in Asia's Contested Waters: Territorial Disputes in the South China Sea*, ed. Enrico Fels and Truong-Minh Vu (Cham, Switzerland: Springer International, 2016), 418.

34. Information Office of the State Council, *White Paper: China's Peaceful Development* (Beijing: Information Office of the State Council, 2011).

35. China News, "Shoulun Zhongmei Jingli Duihua" [First round of China—US strategic and economic dialogue], July 29, 2009, http://www.chinanews.com/gn/news/2009/07-29/1794984.shtml

36. Shambaugh, *China Goes Global*; Yoshihara and Holmes, "Can China Defend?"

37. Jiaxuan Tang, *Heavy Storm and Gentle Breeze* (Beijing: Foreign Languages Press, 2011), 362.

38. Richard Javad Heydarian, "The US-Philippine-China Triangle: From Equi-Balancing to Counter-Balancing amid the South China Sea Disputes," in *Power Politics in Asia's Contested Waters: Territorial Disputes in the South China Sea*, ed. Enrico Fels and Truong Minh Vu, (Cham, Switzerland: Springer International, 2016), 348.

39. Brendon Taylor, "The South China Sea as a 'Crisis,'" in *The South China Sea Maritime Dispute: Political, Legal, and Regional Perspectives*, ed. Leszek Buszynski and Christopher B. Roberts (New York: Routledge, 2015), 174.

40. Michael D. Swaine, "China's Assertive Behavior: On 'Core Interests,'" *China Leadership Monitor* 34 (2011).

41. Swaine, "China's Assertive Behavior."

42. Hillary Clinton, "Interview with Greg Sheridan, Melbourne, Australia," *The Australian*, November 8, 2010, https://2009-2017.state.gov/secretary/20092013clinton/rm/2010/11/150671.htm

43. Xinhua, "Modernizing Navy for Self-Defense," *Xinhuanet*, July 2010, http://news.xinhuanet.com/english2010/indepth/2010-07/13/c_13397060.htm

44. Xi Jinping, "Work Together to Build the Silk Road Economic Belt. 7 September 2013. Speech at Nazarbayev University, Astana, Kazakhstan," in *Governance of China* (2014), 317.

45. Chang Hee Park, "China's Policy on the Border Disputes," paper presented at the 13th Future Northeast Forum, Seoul, April 30, 2014.

46. Han, *Diplomacy of Contemporary China*.

47. Deng Xiaoping, "Zai Zhongyang Guwenweiyuanhui Disanci Quantihuiyishangde Jianghua" [Speech in the Central Advisory Committee at its third plenary session], October 22, 1984, accessed October 26, 2013, http://www.lib.szu.edu.cn/szulibhtm/AD_tqzl/BD_ldrytq/dxp_szu/book3/084.htm; Yilong Li and Ligang Zou, "Gezhi Zhengyi, Gongtongkaifazhengce Zai Nanhaiwentishangde Jiazhifenxi" [The policy of shelving disputes and seeking joint development in value analysis on the South China Sea issue], *Legal System and Society* (April 2010).

48. Lee, *China and the South China Sea Dialogues*; Chen Jing, "Li Said That President Hu Jintao's Trip to Southeast Asian Countries Fruitful," *Xinhuawang*, April 28, 2005, http://news.xinhuanet.com/world/2005-04/28/content_2891208.htm; Ligang Zou and Xinxin Ye, "A View of the Legal System for Joint Development of Marine Resources in the South China Sea," *Journal of Henan Political Management Institute for*

Party Cadre 124 (2011); Ministry of Foreign Affairs of the People's Republic of China, "Waijiabu Buzhang Yang Jiechi Jiu Zhongguo Waijiao Zhengce He Duiwaiguanxi Da Zhongwai Jizhe Wen" [Q&A: Foreign minister Yang Jiechi with domestic/international reporters on China's foreign policy and foreign relations], March 8, 2012, http://www.fmprc.gov.cn/ce/ceph/chn/zgxw/t914106.htm; Shang Lin, "Wang Yi: Nansha Gongtongkaifade Yiyi Bujin Zaiyu Jingjiliyi" [Wang Yi: Spratly joint development is not merely about economic interest], *Beijing Times*, August 4, 2013, http://news.xinhuanet.com/world/2013-08/04/c_125112470.htm

49. Information Office of the State Council, *White Paper: China's Peaceful Development*.

50. Shicun Wu and Keyuan Zou, "Maritime Security in the South China Sea: Cooperation and Implications," in *Maritime Security in the South China Sea: Regional Implications and International Cooperation*, ed. Shicun Wu and Keyuan Zou (Farnham, UK: Ashgate, 2009).

51. Yang, *Contemporary China and Its Foreign Policy*; Communist Party of China, *Constitution of the Communist Party of China (Revised and Adopted at the 19th National Congress of the Communist Party of China on October 24, 2017)* (2017).

52. Yang, *Contemporary China and Its Foreign Policy*.

53. Downs and Saunders, "Legitimacy and the Limits of Nationalism."

54. Andrew Bingham Kennedy, *The International Ambitions of Mao and Nehru: National Efficacy, Beliefs, and the Making of Foreign Policy* (New York: Cambridge University Press, 2012).

55. M. H. Hunt, "Chinese Foreign Relations in Historical Perspective," in *China's Foreign Relations in the 1980s*, ed. Harry Harding and Asia Society (New Haven: Yale University Press, 1984); Alastair I. Johnston, *Cultural Realism: Strategic Culture and Grand Strategy in Chinese History* (Princeton: Princeton University Press, 1995); Arthur Waldron, "Chinese Strategy from the Fourteenth to the Seventeenth Centuries," in *The Making of Strategy: Rulers, States, and War*, ed. Williamson Murray, MacGregor Knox, and Alvin H. Bernstein (Cambridge: Cambridge University Press, 1994).

56. Yaqing Qin, "Development of International Relations Theory in China: Progress through Debates," *International Relations of the Asia-Pacific* 11, no. 2 (2011).

57. Qin, "Development of International Relations Theory."

58. Evan S. Medeiros and Taylor M. Fravel, "China's New Diplomacy," *Foreign Affairs* 82 (2009).

59. Lanteigne, *Chinese Foreign Policy*; Ministry of Foreign Affairs of the People's Republic of China, "The Soviet Union's Stance on the Sino-Indian Boundary Question and Soviet-Indian Relations," April 1963, Wilson Center Digital Archive, PRC FMA 105-01272-01, 1-119.

60. Lanteigne, *Chinese Foreign Policy*.

61. The draft of the Code of Conduct prepared by China in 1999.

62. Leszek Buszynski, "The South China Sea: Oil, Maritime Claims, and U.S.–China Strategic Rivalry," *Washington Quarterly* 35, no. 2 (2012), http://dx.doi.org/10.1080/0163660X.2012.666495

63. Yan, *Lishide Guanxing*.

64. Hsiao and Yang, "Soft Power Politics"; Yves-Heng Lim and Jiye Kim, "Deter-

mining the Determinants: Factors of Change in China's South China Sea Strategy, 1995–2015," *Pacific Focus* 35, no. 2 (2020).

65. Zhao, "Patterns and Choices of Chinese Foreign Policy."

66. Yan, *Lishide Guanxing*; CCTV, "Chinese FM Calls for Respecting 4 Principles on South China Sea Issue," *China Central Television*, September 9, 2014. http://english.cntv.cn/2014/09/08/VIDE1410150001707535.shtml

67. CCTV, "Chinese FM Calls for Respecting 4 Principles."

68. Information Office of the State Council, *White Paper: China's Peaceful Development*.

69. Deng, "Speech in the Central Advisory Committee at Its Third Plenary Session"; Li and Zou, "The Policy of Shelving Disputes."

70. Wang, "China's Multilateral Diplomacy."

71. Marc Lanteigne, "The South China Sea in China's Developing Maritime Strategy," in *Power Politics in Asia's Contested Waters: Territorial Disputes in the South China Sea*, ed. Enrico Fels and Truong-Minh Vu (Cham, Switzerland: Springer International, 2016), 105; K. Noguchi, "Bringing Realism Back In: Explaining China's Strategic Behaviour in the Asia-Pacific," *Asia-Pacific Review* 18, no. 2 (2011); Shambaugh, *China Goes Global*; Yoshihara and Holmes, "Can China Defend."

72. Ministry of Foreign Affairs of the People's Republic of China, "Foreign Minister Yang Jiechi on the South China Sea Issue," July 13, 2012.

73. Ministry of Foreign Affairs of the People's Republic of China, "Wang Yi Expounds on China's Position on Situation of South China Sea," February 14, 2014, http://www.fmprc.gov.cn/mfa_eng/wjb_663304/wjbz_663308/activities_663312/t1129921.shtml

74. Ministry of Foreign Affairs of the People's Republic of China, "Foreign Ministry Spokesperson Hua Chunying's Regular Press Conference"; Ministry of Foreign Affairs, People's Republic of China, "China's Indisputable Sovereignty over the Xisha and Nansha Islands"; Qin, "Statement by Spokesperson Qin Gang of the Ministry of Foreign Affairs of China on the US State Department Issuing a So-Called Press Statement on the South China Sea."

75. UN Division for Ocean Affairs and the Law of the Sea, "United Nations Convention on the Law of the Sea: Declarations Made upon Signature, Ratification, Accession or Succession or Anytime Thereafter," 1996, Upon ratification, Oceans & Law of the Sea, United Nations. http://www.un.org/depts/los/convention_agreements/convention_declarations.htm#China

76. UN Division for Ocean Affairs and the Law of the Sea, "United Nations Convention on the Law of the Sea: Declarations Made Upon Signature, Ratification, Accession or Succession or Anytime Thereafter," 2006, Upon ratification, Oceans & Law of the Sea, United Nations. http://www.un.org/depts/los/convention_agreements/convention_declarations.htm#China

77. Zhang, "The Rise of Chinese Exceptionalism in International Relations."

78. Ying-jeou Ma, "Soar on the Wings of Partnership—President Ma Ying-Jeou's remarks at Center for Strategic and International Studies Video Conference," April 9, 2014; Ying-jeou Ma, "Eight Years of Reform Create a Better Taiwan—President's New Year's Day Message," January 1, 2016.

79. Ma, "Eight Years of Reform."

80. Yann-huei Song and Keyuan Zou, eds., *Major Law and Policy Issues in the South China Sea: European and American Perspectives* (Surrey, UK: Ashgate, 2014), 7.

81. Ministry of Foreign Affairs, Republic of China, "Statement of the Ministry of Foreign Affairs concerning the Declaration on the Conduct of Parties in the South China Sea Signed by the Association of Southeast Asian Nations (ASEAN) and the People's Republic of China (PRC) in Cambodia on November 4, 2002," November 5, 2002.

82. Yann-huei Song, *Managing Potential Conflicts in the South China Sea: Taiwan's Perspectives* (Singapore: Singapore University Press, 1999), 2.

83. Song, *Managing Potential Conflicts*, 2–3; I. Townsend-Gault, "Preventive Diplomacy and Pro-Activity in the South China Sea," *Contemporary Southeast Asia: A Journal of International and Strategic Affairs* 20, no. 2 (1998): 184.

84. N. A. Hu, "South China Sea: Troubled Waters or a Sea of Opportunity?," *Ocean Development and International Law* 41, no. 3 (2010): 206–7.

85. Yann-huei Song, "Conflicting Outer Continental Shelf Claims in the East and South China Seas: Proposals for Cooperation and Peaceful Resolution," *University of Hawai'i Law Review* 35 (2013).

86. Foreign Press Liaison Office of the Ministry of Foreign Affairs (Republic of China), "Press Release: President Ma Addresses Members of News Media on Their Return from Taiping Island," March 23, 2016.

87. Bureau of Oceans and International Environmental and Scientific Affairs, *Limits in the Seas—Taiwan's Maritime Claims*, No. 127 (United States Department of State, November 15, 2005).

88. UNCLOS, *United Nations Convention on the Law of the Sea (Concluded on 10 December 1982. Came into force in 1994)* (1982).

89. Bureau of Oceans and International Environmental and Scientific Affairs, *Limits in the Seas—Taiwan's Maritime Claims*, 10.

90. Bureau of Oceans and International Environmental and Scientific Affairs, *Limits in the Seas—Taiwan's Maritime Claims*, 25.

91. Bureau of Oceans and International Environmental and Scientific Affairs, *Limits in the Seas—China: Maritime Claims in the South China Sea*, No. 143 (United States Department of State, December 5, 2014), 13.

92. Ministry of Foreign Affairs (Republic of China), "The Ministry of Foreign Affairs of the Republic of China Solemnly Declares Statement on the Governments of Malaysia and Vietnam Filed a Joint Submission to the Commission on the Limits of the Continental Shelf of the United Nations, Extending the Outer Limits of Their Respective Continental Shelf 200 Nautical Miles Beyond Their Shorelines," May 11, 2009.

93. MFA (ROC), "The Republic of China (Taiwan) Reiterates Its Position on the South China Sea," April 11, 2012.

94. MFA (ROC), "ROC Government Reiterates its Position on South China Sea Issues," October 31, 2015; MFA (ROC), "Statement on the South China Sea," July 7, 2015.

95. Republic of China (ROC), "Position Paper on ROC South China Sea Policy," March 21, 2016; Li and Li, " Dotted Line," 290; Zou, "Chinese Traditional Maritime Boundary," 32.

96. Wei-I Chang, *Nan-Hai Tsu-Yuan K'ai-Fa yu Chu-Ch'uan Wei-Hu* (Taipei County, Taiwan: P'an Shih Library, December 1994). The Office of Ocean and Polar Affairs estimates the publication date of the map to be between 1946 and 1948, based on studies addressing this question. Bureau of Oceans and International Environmental and Scientific Affairs, *Limits in the Seas—China: Maritime Claims in the South China Sea* (United States Department of State, 2014), 3. Bureau of Oceans and International Environmental and Scientific Affairs, *Limits in the Seas—China: Maritime Claims in the South China Sea*, No. 143 (United States Department of State, December 5, 2014), 3.

97. Li and Li, "Dotted Line," 290.

98. China Ocean News, "Vietnam Severely Violates China's Sovereignty by Insisting Paracel and Spratly Islands in Its Legislation," June 22, 2012.

99. Jinming Li, *South China Sea Dispute and International Law of the Sea* (Beijing: Ocean Press, 2003), 50–52.

100. Republic of China Ministry of Foreign Affairs, "The Government of the Republic of China Lodges Its Protest against the Recent Illegal Occupation of Investigator Shoal and Erica Reef in the Nansha Islands by the Malaysian Government," July 13, 1999; J. Wang, "Daiguo Weihu Haishanf Jiaotong Anqun Chutan" [A preliminary study of approaches to safeguarding sea lanes of communication by big powers], *China Military Science* 2, no. 110 (2010): 245.

101. Bureau of Oceans and International Environmental and Scientific Affairs, *Limits in the Seas—China: Maritime Claims in the South China Sea*, No. 143, 15.

102. Republic of China (ROC), "South China Sea Peace Initiative," May 26, 2015.

103. MFA (ROC), "The Ministry of Foreign Affairs of the Republic of China (Taiwan) Reiterates Its Absolute Sovereignty over Taiping Island," May 12, 2012; MFA (ROC), "The Republic of China (Taiwan) Protests Vietnam Law Claiming South China Sea Islands," January 7, 2013; MFA (ROC), "ROC Government Reiterates Its Position on South China Sea Issues," October 31, 2015; MFA (ROC), "Statement on the South China Sea"; MFA (ROC), "Remarks by President Ma Ying-jeou on Taiping Island," January 28, 2016.

104. Wang, "Daiguo Weihu Haishanf Jiaotong Anqun Chutan" [A preliminary study of approaches to safeguarding sea lanes of communication by big powers], 249.

105. Song, "Conflicting Outer Continental Shelf Claims," 499.

106. UNCLOS, *United Nations Convention on the Law of the Sea*, Article 121.

107. S. L. Ko, "Chen Shui-bian Defends His Visit to Taiping Island," *Taipei Times*, February 4, 2008, 3.

108. Taipei Times, "Minister Leads Group at Opening Rites for Itu Aba Facilities," December 13, 2015, 1.

109. MFA (ROC), "Remarks by President Ma Ying-jeou on Taiping Island."

110. Permanent Court of Arbitration, "Press Release: Arbitration between the Republic of the Philippines and the People's Republic of China," October 29, 2015, http://www.pcacases.com/web/sendAttach/1524

111. MFA (ROC), "Remarks by President Ma Ying-jeou on Taiping Island."

112. Foreign Press Liaison Office of the Ministry of Foreign Affairs (The Republic of China), "Press Release: President Ma Addresses Members of News Media on Their Return from Taiping Island," March 23, 2016.

113. MFA (ROC), "Press Release: President Ma Addresses Members of News Media."

114. MFA (ROC), "Remarks by President Ma Ying-jeou on Taiping Island."

115. MFA (ROC), "Taiping Island Is an Island, Not a Rock, and the ROC Possesses Full Rights Associated with an Exclusive Economic Zone and Continental Shelf in Accordance with UNCLOS," January 23, 2016.

116. MFA (ROC), "Nanhai Zhudao Zhi Zhuquan Shengming Ji Toushu" [Statements and letters on the sovereignty over the South China Sea Islands], March 23, 2016.

117. MFA (ROC), "The Ministry of Foreign Affairs of the Republic of China Solemnly Declares Statement on the Governments of Malaysia and Vietnam," May 11, 2009.

118. MFA (ROC), "Waijiaobu Linian Lai Jiu Nanhai Zhengyiwenti Zhi Shengming Yilanbiao" [Collection of the ministry's statements over the years on the problem of South China Sea dispute], August 11, 2011, 15.

119. MFA (ROC), "The Ministry of Foreign Affairs of the Republic of China (Taiwan) Reiterates Its Absolute Sovereignty over Taiping Island."

120. MFA (ROC), "The Republic of China (Taiwan) Protests Vietnam Law Claiming South China Sea Islands."

121. MFA (ROC), "Waijiaobu Linian Lai Jiu Nanhai Zhengyiwenti Zhi Shengming Yilanbiao" [Collection of the ministry's statements over the years on the problem of South China Sea dispute].

122. MFA (ROC), "Solemn Declaration of the Ministry of Foreign Affairs of the Republic of China concerning the Philippine Senate Bill 2699 and House Bill 3216," February 6, 2009.

123. MFA (ROC), "Philippine Warship, Chinese Vessels in Standoff over Fishermen at South China Sea," April 11, 2012.

124. Permanent Court of Arbitration, "Press Release: Arbitration between the Republic of the Philippines and the People's Republic of China."

125. Ministry of Foreign Affairs, Republic of China, "Taiping Island Is an Island, Not a Rock, and the ROC Possesses Full Rights Associated with an Exclusive Economic Zone and Continental Shelf in Accordance with UNCLOS," January 23, 2016.

126. Asia Maritime Transparency Initiative, "An Interview with Shen Lyu-shun, Representative of the Republic of China to the United States," December 15, 2015, http://amti.csis.org/an-interview-with-shen-lyu-shun-representative-of-the-republic-of-china-to-the-united-states

127. C. C Hsieh and Y. F. Low, "Ma Again Invites Philippine Officials to Visit Taiping Island," *Focus Taiwan News Channel*, April 7, 2016.

128. MFA (ROC), "Statement on the South China Sea."

129. Republic of China (ROC), "South China Sea Peace Initiative."

130. MFA (ROC), "Remarks by President Ma Ying-jeou on Taiping Island."

131. Public Diplomacy Coordination Council, "Taiwan and the Philippines Sign Agreement on Law Enforcement Cooperation in Fisheries Matters," November 19, 2015.

132. D. Y. Lin, "Foreign Minister's Remarks at an International Press Conference," May 17, 2013; Department of Policy Planning, "Foreign Policy Report, 8th Congress of the Legislative Yuan, 5th Session," March 12, 2014.

133. MFA (ROC), "President Ma Proposes the East China Sea Peace Initiative, Calls on All Parties Concerned to Resolve Diaoyutai Dispute Peacefully," August 5, 2012.

134. Committee on Foreign Affairs, *Hearing before the Subcommittee on Asia and the Pacific of the Committee on Foreign Affairs House of Representatives, Serial No. 113–123* (Washington, DC: U.S. Government Printing Office, February 5, 2014), 19.

135. Ma, "Soar on the Wings of Partnership."

136. MFA (ROC), "The Taiwan-Japan Fisheries Agreement—Embodying the Ideals and Spirit of the East China Sea Peace Initiative," August 2013.

137. Ma, "Soar on the Wings of Partnership."

138. H. Y. Lee, "Tsai Ing-wen Backs ROC Sovereignty over Taiping Island," *Focus Taiwan News Channel*, January 29, 2016.

139. Song, "Conflicting Outer Continental Shelf Claims," 485.

CHAPTER 3

1. Ministry of Foreign Affairs of the People's Republic of China, "Wang Yi Stresses 'Four Respects' on South China Sea Issue," August 5, 2022, https://www.fmprc.gov.cn/mfa_eng/zxxx_662805/t1897526.shtml

2. Jooyeon Jeong, *Industrial Relations in Korea: Diversity and Dynamism of Korean Enterprise Unions from a Comparative Perspective* (Abingdon, UK: Routledge, 2007), 17.

3. Urs Luterbacher and Detlef F. Sprinz, *International Relations and Global Climate Change* (Cambridge, MA: MIT Press, 2001), 164.

4. Thomas C. Schelling, *The Strategy of Conflict* (Cambridge: Harvard University Press, 1960), 22.

5. Taylor M. Fravel, "Power Shifts and Escalation: Explaining China's Use of Force in Territorial Disputes," *International Security* 32, no. 3 (2008).

6. Data sourced from Asia Maritime Transparency Initiative, "Island Features Occupation Status in the South China Sea," 2020, https://amti.csis.org/scs-features-map

7. Joshua Kurlantzick, *Charm Offensive: How China's Soft Power Is Transforming the World* (New Haven: Yale University Press, 2007); Joseph S. Nye, *Soft Power: The Means to Success in World Politics* (New York: Public Affairs, 2004).

8. Luterbacher and Sprinz, *International Relations and Global Climate Change*, 164.

9. Schelling, *Strategy of Conflict*, 22.

10. Nicholas Cumming-Bruce, "Beijing Makes More Mischief in South China Sea," *Guardian*, May 22, 1995, 12.

11. Scott Kastner, "Is the Taiwan Strait Still a Flash Point? Rethinking the Prospects for Armed Conflict between China and Taiwan," *International Security* 40, no. 3 (2016).

12. Schelling, *Strategy of Conflict*, 22.

13. Robert Jervis, *The Meaning of the Nuclear Revolution: Statecraft and the Prospect of Armageddon* (Ithaca: Cornell University Press, 1989), 139.

14. Yu Jia, "Arbitral Tribunal Abusing Its Power," *China Daily*, June 3, 2016.

15. Clive H. Schofield, "Trouble over the Starting Line: State Practice concerning Baselines in the South China Sea," in *UN Convention on the Law of the Sea and the South China Sea*, ed. Shicun Wu, Mark J. Valencia, and Nong Hong (Farnham, UK: Ashgate, 2015), 123.

16. Jia, "Arbitral Tribunal Abusing its Power."

17. Ministry of Foreign Affairs of the People's Republic of China, "Foreign Ministry Spokesperson Hong Lei's Remarks on ASEAN Foreign Ministers' Statement on the Six-Point Principles on the South China Sea Issue," July 21, 2012, http://www.fmprc.gov.cn/ce/cedk/eng/fyrth/t955114.htm

18. Permanent Court of Arbitration, "Award on Jurisdiction and Admissibility: In the Matter of an Arbitration before an Arbitral Tribunal Constituted under Annex VII to the 1982 United Nations Convention on the Law of the Sea between the Republic of the Philippines and the People's Republic of China," October 29, 2015.

19. You, "Deciphering Beijing's Maritime Security Policy."

20. Heydarian, "US-Philippine-China Triangle," 350.

21. The draft of the Code of Conduct prepared by China in 1999.

22. Lee, *China and the South China Sea Dialogues*, 25–26.

23. Declaration On Conduct of the Parties in the South China Sea, "Declaration on the Conduct of Parties in the South China Sea, the Governments of the Member States of ASEAN and the Government of the People's Republic of China, done on 4 November 2002, Phnom Penh, the Kingdom of Cambodia," 2002, https://asean.org/declaration-on-the-conduct-of-parties-in-the-south-china-sea-2/

24. Leszek Buszynski and Christopher Roberts, eds., *The South China Sea Maritime Dispute: Political, Legal, and Regional Perspectives* (New York: Routledge, 2015), 210–11.

25. Hasjim Djalal, "'Due Regards' and 'Abuse of Rights' in UNCLOS," in *UN Convention on the Law of the Sea and the South China Sea*, ed. Shicun Wu, Mark J. Valencia, and Nong Hong (Farnham, UK: Ashgate, 2015), 68.

26. United States Department of State, *Limits in the Seas—China: Maritime Claims in the South China Sea* (Bureau of Oceans and International Environmental and Scientific Affairs, 2014).

27. Zhang, "Rise of Chinese Exceptionalism."

28. United States Department of State, *Limits in the Seas—China: Maritime Claims in the South China Sea*, 17.

29. Guifang Xue, "Deep Danger: Intensified Competition in the South China Sea and Implications for China," in *Maritime Security Issues in the South China Sea and the Arctic: Sharpened Competition or Collaboration?*, ed. Gordon Houlden and Nong Hong (Beijing: China Democracy and Legal System Publishing House, 2012).

30. Permanent Mission of the People's Republic of China, "Notes Verbales CML/17/2009 and CML/18/2009," May 7, 2009, http://www.un.org/Depts/los/clcs_new/submissions_files/mysvnm33_09/chn_2009re_mys_vnm_e.pdf

31. Bureau of Oceans and International Environmental and Scientific Affairs, *Limits in the Seas—China*.

32. Enlai Zhou, "Zhou Enlai's Statement about the US-British Draft Peace Treaty with Japan and San Francisco Conference Statement," *People's Daily* (1951), http://news.xinhuanet.com/ziliao/2004-12/15/content_2337746.htm

33. Zhou, "Zhou Enlai's Statement about the US-British Draft Peace Treaty."

34. Leszek Buszynski, "The Origins and Development of the South China Sea Maritime Dispute," in *The South China Sea Maritime Dispute: Political, Legal, and Regional Perspectives*, ed. Leszek Buszynski and Christopher B. Roberts (New York: Routledge, 2015), 6.

35. Bureau of Oceans and International Environmental and Scientific Affairs, *Limits in the Seas—China.*

36. Li Xue, "How China Views the South China Sea Arbitration Case," *The Diplomat*, July 14, 2015.

37. Aaron Friedberg, "Hegemony with Chinese Characteristics," *The National Interest* 114 (2011).

38. Information Office of the State Council, *White Paper: China's Peaceful Development.*

39. Griffiths, "States, Nations, and Territorial Stability."

40. White House, *National Security Strategy* (2022), 37.

41. Secretary of State for Transport, "National Strategy for Maritime Security" (2022), 78.

42. Ministry of Foreign Affairs, Japan, *Diplomatic Bluebook 2023* (2023), 95.

43. Federal Republic of Germany, *Strategy on China of the Government of the Federal Republic of Germany* (2023), 56.

44. Federal Republic of Germany, *Strategy on China of the Government of the Federal Republic of Germany*, 21–22.

45. US Energy Information Administration, "China," last updated February 4, 2014, http://www.eia.gov/countries/analysisbriefs/China/china.pdf

46. US Geological Survey, *World Petroleum Resources Assessment Project: Assessment of Undiscovered Oil and Gas Resources of Southeast Asia, 2010, Fact Sheet 2010–3015* (June 2010).

47. US Energy Information Administration, "China."

48. John Lee, "China's Geostrategic Search for Oil," *Washington Quarterly* 35, no. 3 (2012): 76.

49. US Energy Information Administration, "China."

50. Justin Guay, "China's Coal Imports Drop for the First Time since Country Became Net Coal Importer," *Huffington Post*, November 10, 2014.

51. Jiye Kim and Arpit Raswant, *International Business and Security: Geostrategy in Perspective* (Cham, Switzerland: Palgrave Macmillan, 2022).

52. Bill Hayton, *The South China Sea: The Struggle for Power in Asia* (New Haven: Yale University Press, 2014).

53. Rod Chapman, "Cluff Oil Signs for South China Sea," *The Guardian*, September 6, 1983; Rod Chapman, "BP Abandons First South China Well," *The Guardian*, January 11, 1984.

54. Chapman, "BP Abandons First South China Well."

55. Beijing Xinhua, "PRC Begin Geophysical Surveys in South China Sea," Xinhua (Foreign Broadcast Information Service–China) September 21, 1980.

56. Xinhua, "CNOOC to Kick Off Bidding for Untapped Oil and Gas Resources in South China Sea," Xinhua, March 7, 2007, accessed October 19, 2014, http://english.peopledaily.com.cn/200703/07/eng20070307_355170.html

57. Oil & Gas Journal, "CNOOC Starts Up Oil Field in Pearl River Mouth

Basin," *Oil & Gas Journal*, August 25, 2014, http://www.ogj.com/articles/2014/08/cnooc-starts-up-oil-field-in-pearl-river-mouth-basin.html

58. Hayton, *South China Sea*.

59. Buszynski, "Origins and Development of the South China Sea Maritime Dispute," 11.

60. Selig S. Harrison, *China, Oil and Asia: Conflict Ahead?* (New York: Columbia University Press, 1977); Lo, *China's Policy towards Territorial Disputes*.

61. Dieter Heinzig, *Disputed Islands in the South China Sea: Paracels, Spratlys, Pratas, Macclesfield Bank* (Wiesbaden: Harrassowitz, 1976).

62. Nihon Keizai Shinbun, "Japanese Economic Daily," *Nihon Keizai Shinbun*, August 3, 1976; Choon-ho Park, "The South China Sea Disputes: Who Owns the Islands and the Natural Resources?," *Ocean Development & International Law* 5, no. 1 (1978).

63. Daily Report Asia-Pacific, "SRV Proposal on South China Sea Claim Rejected," *Daily Report Asia-Pacific*, February 11, 1981, (FBIS-APA-81–028), February 8, 1981, N1.

64. John Gittings, "Scramble for Oil in East China Sea," *The Guardian*, December 18, 1970.

65. Gittings, "Scramble for Oil."

66. Daily Report, "Communist China: International Affairs," *Daily Report: People's Republic of China*, January 4, 1971.

67. Michael D. Swaine, "'Understanding the Historical Record," in *Managing Sino-American Crises: Case Studies and Analysis*, ed. Michael D. Swaine, Tuosheng Zhang, and Danielle F. S. Cohen (Washington, DC: Carnegie Endowment for International Peace, 2006); Taylor, "South China Sea as a 'Crisis'."

68. You, "Deciphering Beijing's Maritime Security Policy."

69. You, "Deciphering Beijing's Maritime Security Policy."

70. Hayton, *South China Sea*, xvi.

71. You, "Deciphering Beijing's Maritime Security Policy."

72. Xuetong Yan, *Lishide Guanxing*.

73. Mohan Malik, *Maritime Security in the Indo-Pacific: Perspectives from China, India, and the United States* (Lanham, MD: Rowman & Littlefield, 2014); Rory Medcalf, *Indo-Pacific Empire: China, America and the Contest for the World's Pivotal Region* (Manchester: Manchester University Press, 2020); Thomas Wilkins and Jiye Kim, "Adoption, Accommodation or Opposition? Regional Powers Respond to American-led Indo-Pacific Strategy," *The Pacific Review* 35, no. 3 (2022).

74. Kheng Swe Lim, "China's Nationalist Narrative of the South China Sea: A Preliminary Analysis," in *Power Politics in Asia's Contested Waters: Territorial Disputes in the South China Sea*, ed. Enrico Fels and Truong-Minh Vu (Cham, Switzerland: Springer International, 2016), 162; J. Wang, "Daiguo Weihu Haishanf Jiaotong Anqun Chutan," 134.

75. Ministry of Foreign Affairs of the People's Republic of China, "Foreign Minister Yang Jiechi on the South China Sea Issue," July 13, 2012.

76. Vijay Sakhuja and Institute of Southeast Asian Studies., *Asian Maritime Power in the 21st Century: Strategic Transactions: China, India, and Southeast Asia* (Singapore: Institute of Southeast Asian Studies, 2011), 9.

77. Malik, *Maritime Security in the Indo-Pacific*, 3; Thomas Wilkins and Jiye Kim, "Adoption, Accommodation or Opposition?—Regional Powers Respond to American-Led Indo-Pacific Strategy," *Pacific Review* 35, no. 3 (2022), https://doi.org/10.1080/09512748.2020.1825516

78. Philip Andrews-Speed and Christopher Len, *The Future of the US Security Umbrella for Sea Lines of Communication (SLOCs) between the Middle East and Southeast Asia, and the Future Role of China* (Energy Studies Institute, National University of Singapore, February 2016).

79. Benjamin Goldsmith, "A Liberal Peace in Asia?," *Journal of Peace Research* 44, no. 1 (2007).

80. Shicun Wu, *Solving Disputes for Regional Cooperation and Development in the South China Sea: A Chinese Perspective* (Farnham, UK: Chandos, 2013), 15.

81. Merriden Varrall, *Chinese Worldviews and China's Foreign Policy* (Sydney: Lowy Institute, 2015).

82. Hong, *UNCLOS and Ocean Dispute Settlement*; Zou, "China's U-Shaped Line."

83. CCTV, "Chinese FM Calls for Respecting 4 Principles on South China Sea Issue," China Central Television, September 9, 2014, http://english.cntv.cn/2014/09/08/VIDE1410150001707535.shtml

84. Gungwu Wang, *To Act Is to Know: Chinese Dilemmas* (Singapore: Eastern Universities Press, 2003).

85. Whilliam Choong, "Mistrust Hurts Naval Cooperation in Region," *Straits Times*, May 27, 2011.

86. Zou, "Chinese Traditional Maritime Boundary Line"; Buszynski, "Origins and Development."

87. Li and Li, "Dotted Line on the Chinese Map," 290.

88. Marc Lanteigne, "The South China Sea in China's Developing Maritime Strategy," in *Power Politics in Asia's Contested Waters: Territorial Disputes in the South China Sea*, ed. Enrico Fels and Truong-Minh Vu (Cham, Switzerland: Springer International, 2016), 105.

89. China Ocean News, "Vietnam Severely Violates China's Sovereignty"; Li, *South China Sea Dispute*.

90. Ministry of Foreign Affairs of the People's Republic of China, *Zhou Enlai Waijiao Wenxuan* [Selected diplomatic documents of Zhou Enlai] (Beijing: Zhongyang Wenxian Chubanshe, 1990).

91. Chen and Wang, "Lying Low No More?"

92. Suisheng Zhao, "Shaping the Regional Context of China's Rise: How the Obama Administration Brought Back Hedge in Its Engagement with China," *Journal of Contemporary China* 21, no. 75 (2012); Friedberg, "Hegemony with Chinese Characteristics."

93. Benedict Anderson, *Imagined Communities: Reflections on the Origin and Spread of Nationalism* (London: Verso, 1983); Lim, "China's Nationalist Narrative."

94. Christopher R. Hughes, "After 1989: Nationalism and the New Global Elite," in *Contemporary Chinese Society and Politics: Critical Concepts in Asian Studies*, ed. Andrew Kipnis, Luigi Tomba, and Jonathan Unger (London: Routledge, 2009); Lim, "China's Nationalist Narrative," 160.

95. Zhao, "Patterns and Choices of Chinese Foreign Policy."
96. Zhao, "Patterns and Choices of Chinese Foreign Policy."
97. Lim, "China's Nationalist Narrative of the South China Sea," 161.
98. Hayton, *South China Sea*, 11.
99. Huu Tuc Nguyen, "Vietnam's Position on South China Sea," *RSIS Commentary*, no. 170 (August 27, 2014).
100. Kaihao Wang, "Into the Deep for Relics," *China Daily USA*, September 16, 2014, 8.
101. Le Zou, "South China Sea Mapping Underway," *Global Times*, March 27, 2012, http://www.globaltimes.cn/content/702256.shtml
102. Wu, *Solving Disputes*.
103. Wu, *Solving Disputes*, 30.
104. Gerardo Valero, "Spratly Archipelago Dispute: Is the Question of Sovereignty Still Relevant?," *Marine Policy* 18, no. 4 (1994): 323.
105. Y. Ru and Y. Gong, "Dongya Chaogong Tixi De Wenhua Neihan—Yu Xifang Zhimin Tixi De Bijiao" [Cultural connotation of the tributary system of East Asia—A comparison with the western colonial system], *Journal of Binzhou University (Binzhou xueyuan xuebao)* 25, no. 2 (2009): 51–52.
106. Wu, *Solving Disputes for Regional Cooperation*.
107. Buszynski, "Origins and Development of the South China Sea Maritime Dispute," xxiii.
108. Buszynski, "Origins and Development of the South China Sea Maritime Dispute."
109. Buszynski, "Origins and Development of the South China Sea Maritime Dispute," 4–5.
110. Buszynski, "Origins and Development of the South China Sea Maritime Dispute," 4–5.
111. Buszynski, "Origins and Development of the South China Sea Maritime Dispute."
112. Information Office of the State Council, *White Paper: China's Peaceful Development*.
113. Lim, "China's Nationalist Narrative," 159.
114. Wu, *Solving Disputes*.
115. Jing Huang and Sharinee Jagtiani, "Introduction: Unknotting Tangled Lines in the South China Sea Dispute," in *Territorial Disputes in the South China Sea*, ed. Jing Huang and Andrew Billo (New York: Palgrave Macmillan, 2015), 1.
116. Chen and Wang, "Lying Low No More?"
117. Xiaodong Wang et al., eds., *Zhongguo Bu Gaoxing* [China Is not Happy] (Jiangsu: Phoenix Publishing, 2009).
118. Suisheng Zhao, "Foreign Policy Implications of Chinese Nationalism Revisited: The Strident Turn," *Journal of Contemporary China* 22, no. 82 (2013).
119. Zhao, "Foreign Policy Implications of Chinese Nationalism Revisited," 5.
120. Zhao, "Foreign Policy Implications of Chinese Nationalism Revisited."
121. Kerry Brown, "Foreign Policy Making under Xi Jinping: The Case of the South China Sea," *Journal of Political Risk* 4, no. 2 (2016): 2.
122. Lanteigne, "South China Sea in China's Developing Maritime Strategy," 97.

123. Brown, "Foreign Policy Making under Xi Jinping," 17.

124. Lim, "China's Nationalist Narrative of the South China Sea," 165.

125. David Scott, *The Chinese Century? The Challenge to Global Order* (Basingstoke, UK: Palgrave Macmillan, 2008).

126. Zenel Garcia and Christine Bianco, "The Impact of Chinese History on Perceptions of the Law of the Sea in the South China Sea," *Territory, Politics, Governance* (July 5, 2023): 15, https://doi.org/10.1080/21622671.2023.2218427

127. Xi Jinping, "President Xi Jinping Holds Talks with President Truong Tan Sang of Vietnam, Stressing China and Vietnam Should Unswervingly March along Path of Friendly Cooperation," September 15, 2015, http://www.fmprc.gov.cn/ce/cena/eng/zgxw/t1052303.htm

128. Zhao, "Patterns and Choices of Chinese Foreign Policy," 12.

129. P. K. Ghosh, "Artificial Islands in the South China Sea," *The Diplomat*, September 23, 2014, http://thediplomat.com/2014/09/artificial-islands-in-the-south-china-sea

130. Chang Hee Park, "China and the South China Sea," a conference paper presented at the Northeast Future Forum, Seoul, April 30, 2014.

131. Leszek Buszynski, "The South China Sea: Oil, Maritime Claims, and U.S.–China Strategic Rivalry," *Washington Quarterly* 35, no. 2 (2012): 139, https://doi.org/10.1080/0163660X.2012.666495

132. Teddy Ng, "Deng Xiaoping's Guiding Principles Are Still in Play Today," *South China Morning Post*, August 22, 2014, http://www.scmp.com/print/news/china/article/1578761/deng-xiaopings-guiding-principles-are-still-play-today

133. International Strategy and Security Research Center, *Zhongguo Guojia Anquan Yanjiu Baogao (2014)* [The national security blue paper: The research report on national security of China] (Beijing: University of International Relations of China, May 6, 2014).

134. Yi Wang, "Speech by Foreign Minister Wang Yi at the Brookings Institution: Toward a New Model of Major-Country Relations Between China and the United States," September 20, 2013, https://www.mfa.gov.cn/eng/xw/zyjh/202405/t20240530_11340621.html

135. The United States Department of Defense, *Annual Freedom of Navigation Report: Fiscal Year 2020* (The United States Department of Defense, 2020).

136. Michael R. Pompeo, "U.S. Position on Maritime Claims in the South China Sea," July 13, 2020, https://2017-2021.state.gov/u-s-position-on-maritime-claims-in-the-south-china-sea/index.html

137. Chun Yao, "China Vows to Make South China Sea Safe," Xinhua, December 15, 2011, http://www.mfa.gov.cn/ce/ceindo/eng/gdxw/t887657.htm

138. Ding Gang, "Why Does Speculation Grow in South China Sea," *People's Daily Online*, August 3, 2011, accessed October 17, 2014, http://english.peopledaily.com.cn/90780/91342/7458582.html

139. Yan, *Lishide Guanxing*, 58–59.

140. Nathan and Scobell, *China's Search for Security*, xvii.

141. Yoshihara and Holmes, "Can China Defend a 'Core Interest'?"

142. James R. Holmes, "Strategic Features of the South China Sea: A Tough Neighborhood for Hegemons," *Naval War College Review* 67, no. 2 (2014); Robert Kaplan,

Asia's Cauldron: The South China Sea and the End of a Stable Pacific (New York: Random House, 2014).

143. Hongtu Zhao, "Maliujia Kunju Yu Zhongguo Nengyuan Anquan Zaisikao" [Malacca dilemma and rethinking on China's energy security], *Xiandai Guoji Guanxi* 6 (2007).

144. Kaplan, *Asia's Cauldron*, xx.

145. Kaplan, *Asia's Cauldron*, 13.

146. Kaplan, *Asia's Cauldron*.

147. Jiaxuan Tang, *Heavy Storm and Gentle Breeze* (Beijing: Foreign Languages Press, 2011).

148. Tang, *Heavy Storm and Gentle Breeze*, 320.

149. Ke Xu, "Anti-Piracy Cooperation Dilemma: ASEAN and China," in *China-ASEAN Relations: Economic and Legal Dimensions*, ed. John Wong, Keyuan Zou, and Huaqun Zeng (Hackensack, NJ: World Scientific, 2006).

150. Yoshihara and Holmes, "Can China Defend a 'Core Interest'?"

CHAPTER 4

1. Ab Tan, "Manila Annexes Much of Disputed Spratly Islands," *Washington Post*, September 7, 1979.

2. Daily Report, "Moscow Radio Peace and Progress in Mandarin to Southeast Asia," December 3, 1980, B1.

3. William Zartman and Guy Olivier Faure, "The Dynamics of Escalation and Negotiation," in *Escalation and Negotiation in International Conflicts*, ed. William Zartman and Guy Olivier Faure (Cambridge: Cambridge University Press, 2005), 4.

4. Zartman and Faure, "Dynamics of Escalation and Negotiation."

5. Zaiqian Wang, "Wu Shicun: Nanhaiwenti Bushi Zhongguoyu Dongmengjiande Wenti" [Wu Shicun: The South China Sea dispute is not a problem between China and ASEAN], *Zhongguo Xinwenwang*, May 20, 2014, accessed September 20, 2014, http://news.china.com.cn/2014-05/20/content_32440431.htm

6. Guoxiu Wu, "Chinese Scholars Say South China Sea Dispute Negatively Impacts Maritime Security," *CCTV America*, August 23, 2014, http://www.cctv-america.com/2014/08/23/chinese-scholars-speak-about-the-china-philippines-dispute

7. Kheng Swe Lim, "China-ASEAN Relations: Hamstrung Soft Power in South China Sea?," *RSIS Commentary*, no. 174 (September 3, 2014).

8. Joseph Y. S. Cheng and Stephanie Paladini, "China's Ocean Development Strategy and Its Handling of the Territorial Conflicts in the South China Sea," *Philippine Political Science Journal* 35, no. 2 (2014), https://doi.org/10.1080/01154451.2014.965476

9. Ramses Amer and Jianwei Li, "Recent Developments in the South China Sea—an Assessment of the Core Bilateral Relationship between China and Vietnam," in *Maritime Security Issues in the South China Sea and the Arctic: Sharpened Competition or Collaboration?*, ed. Gordon Houlden and Nong Hong (Beijing: China Democracy and Legal System Publishing House, 2012); Hu Chen, "Motives behind US Talk of 'Freedom of Navigation'," *People's Daily Online*, June 30, 2011, http://english.peopledaily.com.cn/90001/90780/91342/7425457.html

10. Ministry of Foreign Affairs of the People's Republic of China, "Wang Yi Met with Vietnamese Deputy Prime Minister and Foreign Minister Pham Binh Minh," August 9, 2014, http://www.fmprc.gov.cn/mfa_eng/zxxx_662805/t1181545.shtml

11. Keyuan Zou, "The Sino-Vietnamese Agreement on Maritime Boundary Delimitation in the Gulf of Tonkin," *Ocean Development & International Law* 36, no. 1 (2005): 22–24.

12. People's Daily, "Two China-Vietnam Beibu Gulf Agreements Take Effect," *People's Daily Online*, July 1, 2004, accessed May 2, 2016, http://en.people.cn/200407/01/eng20040701_148157.html

13. Buszynski, "Origins and Development," 3.

14. Zou, "Sino-Vietnamese Agreement on Maritime Boundary."

15. People's Daily, "Hu Jintao Meets Vietnamese President," *People's Daily*, April 20, 2001, http://en.people.cn/english/200104/19/eng20010419_68128.html

16. *People's Daily*, "Hu Jintao Meets Vietnamese President."

17. Ministry of Foreign Affairs of the People's Republic of China, "President Hu Jintao Meets with His Vietnamese Counterpart Tran Duc Luong," November 20, 2004, http://www.fmprc.gov.cn/mfa_eng/topics_665678/huvisit_665888/t171290.shtml

18. The 16-word principle consists of 16 Chinese letters—*chang, qi, wen, ding, mian, xiang, wei, lai, mu, lin, you, hao, quan, mian, he, zuo*—which form four phrases that translate to long-term stability, future-oriented, good-neighborliness, and comprehensive cooperation. Ministry of Foreign Affairs of the People's Republic of China, "President Hu Jintao Meets with His Vietnamese Counterpart Tran Duc Luong."

19. Ministry of Foreign Affairs of the People's Republic of China, "Chinese President Hu Jintao Holds Talks with Vietnamese President Tran Duc Luong," July 19, 2005, http://www.fmprc.gov.cn/mfa_eng/wjb_663304/zzjg_663340/yzs_663350/gjlb_663354/2792_663578/2794_663582/t204259.shtml

20. Ministry of Foreign Affairs of the People's Republic of China, Department of Policy Planning, *China's Foreign Affairs* (Beijing: World Affairs Press, 2008), 409.

21. Ministry of Foreign Affairs of the People's Republic of China, *China's Foreign Affairs*, 409; Ministry of Foreign Affairs of the People's Republic of China, Department of Policy Planning, *China's Foreign Affairs* (Beijing: World Affairs Press, 2009), 466.

22. Ministry of Foreign Affairs of the People's Republic of China, *China's Foreign Affairs*, 466.

23. Xinhua, "China, Vietnam to Promote Closer Friendly, Cooperative Ties," Xinhua, March 21, 2006, http://news.xinhuanet.com/english/2006-03/22/content_4328698.htm

24. Ministry of Foreign Affairs of the People's Republic of China, Department of Policy Planning, *China's Foreign Affairs* (Beijing: World Affairs Press, 2007), 525.

25. Ministry of Foreign Affairs of the People's Republic of China, *China's Foreign Affairs* (2007), 525.

26. Ministry of Foreign Affairs of the People's Republic of China, *China's Foreign Affairs* (2007), 524; Ministry of Foreign Affairs of the People's Republic of China, *China's Foreign Affairs* (2008), 408; Ministry of Foreign Affairs of the People's Republic of China, *China's Foreign Affairs* (2009), 466.

27. Ministry of Foreign Affairs of the People's Republic of China, *China's Foreign Affairs* (2007), 420.

28. Ministry of Foreign Affairs of the People's Republic of China, *China's Foreign Affairs* (2008), 306.

29. Ministry of Foreign Affairs of the People's Republic of China, *China's Foreign Affairs* (2009), 341; Ministry of Foreign Affairs of the People's Republic of China, Department of Policy Planning, *China's Foreign Affairs* (Beijing: World Affairs Press, 2010), 316.

30. Ministry of Foreign Affairs of the People's Republic of China, "Hu Jintao Holds Talks with Nong Duc Manh," May 30, 2008, http://lt.china-office.gov.cn/eng/xwdt/200806/t20080603_2690582.htm

31. Ministry of Foreign Affairs of Vietnam, "Agreement on the Basic Principles Guiding the Settlement of Sea-Related Matters between the Socialist Republic of Viet Nam and the People's Republic of China," October 11, 2011, https://vietnamembassy-usa.org/news/2011/10/vn-china-basic-principles-settlement-sea-issues

32. Ministry of Foreign Affairs of the People's Republic of China, "Vice President Xi Jinping Meets with Vietnamese President Truong Tan Sang," December 22, 2011, http://nl.china-embassy.gov.cn/eng/zgyw/201112/t20111226_10043134.htm

33. Ministry of Foreign Affairs of the People's Republic of China, "Vice President Xi Jinping Meets with Vietnamese Army Chief," April 13, 2012, http://www.fmprc.gov.cn/mfa_eng/wjb_663304/zzjg_663340/yzs_663350/gjlb_663354/2792_663578/2794_663582/t923082.shtml

34. Ministry of Foreign Affairs of the People's Republic of China, "President Xi Jinping Vows to Consolidate and Develop Inter-party and Inter-governmental Ties with Vietnam for the Benefit of Both Peoples during Phone Talks with General Secretary of the CPV Central Committee," March 21, 2013, http://www.fmprc.gov.cn/mfa_eng/wjb_663304/zzjg_663340/yzs_663350/gjlb_663354/2792_663578/2794_663582/t1024384.shtml

35. Ministry of Foreign Affairs of the People's Republic of China, "President Xi Jinping Holds Talks with President Truong Tan Sang of Vietnam, Stressing China and Vietnam Should Unswervingly March along Path of Friendly Cooperation," June 19, 2013, http://www.fmprc.gov.cn/ce/cena/eng/zgxw/t1052303.htm

36. Ministry of Foreign Affairs of the People's Republic of China, "President Xi Jinping Holds Talks with President Truong Tan Sang of Vietnam."

37. Technavio, *Global Sonobuoy Market 2016–2020 (WGR390273)*, April 7, 2016, accessed April 9, 2016, https://www.wiseguyreports.com/reports/global-sonobuoy-market-2016-2020

38. Song, "Conflicting Outer Continental Shelf Claims," 485.

39. Daniel J. Dzurek, "Maritime Briefing—the Spratly Islands Dispute: Who's on First?," *International Boundaries Research Unit* 2, no. 1 (1996).

40. Leszek Buszynski and Christopher B. Roberts, "Stabilisation and Resolution," in *The South China Sea Maritime Dispute: Political, Legal, and Regional Perspectives*, ed. Leszek Buszynski and Christopher B. Roberts (New York: Routledge, 2015), 188.

41. Rodolfo Severino and Institute of Southeast Asian Studies, *Southeast Asia in Search of an ASEAN Community: Insights from the Former ASEAN Secretary-General* (Singapore: Institute of Southeast Asian Studies, 2006), 186.

42. Association of Southeast Asian Nations, "Statement by the ASEAN Foreign Ministers on the Recent Development in the South China Sea, Singapore, March 18, 1995," in *ASEAN Documents Series 1994–1995*, ed. ASEAN Secretariat (Jakarta: Association of Southeast Asian Nations, 1995).

43. Department of Foreign Affairs of the Philippines, "Response of the DFA Spokesperson to the Recent Statement of the Chinese Ministry of Foreign Affairs on the West Philippines Sea Issue," July 15, 2013, https://www.dfa.gov.ph/index.php/2013-06-27-21-50-36/dfa-releases/332

44. Lim, "China's Nationalist Narrative," 164.

45. Ministry of Foreign Affairs of the People's Republic of China, *China's Foreign Affairs* (2007), 317.

46. Ministry of Foreign Affairs of the People's Republic of China, *China's Foreign Affairs* (2008), 233.

47. Ministry of Foreign Affairs of the People's Republic of China, *China's Foreign Affairs* (2009); Ministry of Foreign Affairs of the People's Republic of China, *China's Foreign Affairs* (2010); Ministry of Foreign Affairs of the People's Republic of China, *China's Foreign Affairs* (2014).

48. US Department of State, Bureau of East Asian and Pacific Affairs, *Fact Sheet: U.S. Relations with the Philippines*, November 13, 2015, http://www.state.gov/r/pa/ei/bgn/2794.htm

49. Richard Javad Heydarian, "The US-Philippine-China Triangle: From Equi-Balancing to Counter-Balancing amid the South China Sea Disputes," in *Power Politics in Asia's Contested Waters: Territorial Disputes in the South China Sea*, ed. Enrico Fels and Truong Minh Vu (Cham, Switzerland: Springer International, 2016), 340.

50. US Department of State, "Daily Press Briefing," Briefer: Christine Shelly (May 10, 1995).

51. Chen, "Motives behind US Talk of 'Freedom of Navigation'."

52. Pascal Abb, "Punish the Philippines, Forgive Vietnam? The South China Sea Disputes in the Eyes of Chinese Experts," in *Power Politics in Asia's Contested Waters: Territorial Disputes in the South China Sea*, ed. Enrico Fels and Truong-Minh Vu (Cham, Switzerland: Springer International, 2016), 155.

53. Andrew Higgins, "In Philippines, Banana Growers Feel Effect of South China Sea Dispute," *Washington Post*, June 11, 2012; Suisheng Zhao, "Foreign Policy Implications of Chinese Nationalism Revisited: The Strident Turn," *Journal of Contemporary China* 22, no. 82 (2013).

54. Buszynski and Roberts, eds., *South China Sea Maritime Dispute*, 213.

55. Bruno Hellendorff, "'Coopetition' and Risk Tolerance in the South China Sea: Indonesia and Malaysia's Middle Power Strategies," in *Power Politics in Asia's Contested Waters: Territorial Disputes in the South China Sea*, ed. Enrico Fels and Truong-Minh Vu (Cham, Switzerland: Springer International, 2016), 312.

56. Buszynski and Roberts, *South China Sea Maritime Dispute*, 213; Christopher B. Roberts, "ASEAN: The Challenge of Unity in Diversity," in *The South China Sea Maritime Dispute: Political, Legal, and Regional Perspectives*, ed. Leszek Buszynski and Christopher B. Roberts (Oxford: Routledge, 2015).

57. Roberts, "ASEAN: The Challenge of Unity in Diversity."

58. Lanteigne, "South China Sea," 102.

59. For discussion on definition of middle power, see Jiye Kim, "Between a Regional Hegemon and a Middle Power: The Case of Nigeria," in *Awkward Powers: Escaping Traditional Great and Middle Power Theory*, ed. Gabriel Abbondanza and Thomas Wilkins (Palgrave Macmillan, 2022).

60. Scott Bentley, "Mapping the Nine-Dash Line: Recent Incidents Involving Indonesia in the South China Sea," *The Strategist*, October 29, 2013, http://www.aspistrategist.org.au/mapping-the-nine-dash-line-recent-incidents-involving-indonesia-in-the-south-china-sea/

61. Shofwan Al Banna Choiruzzad, "Indonesia forges Stronger Ties with China to Boost Economy," *The Conversation*, November 19, 2014, https://theconversation.com/indonesia-forges-stronger-ties-with-china-to-boost-economy-34004

62. Hellendorff, "'Coopetition' and Risk Tolerance in the South China Sea," 313.

63. Wu, "Chinese Scholars Say South China Sea Dispute Negatively Impacts Maritime Security."

64. Ernest Z. Bower, "The JMSU: A Tale of Bilateralism and Secrecy in the South China Sea," Center for Strategic and International Studies, July 27, 2010; Barry Wain, "Manila's Bungle in the South China Sea," *Far Eastern Economic Review*, January 2008.

65. Wain, "Manila's Bungle in the South China Sea."

66. Wain, "Manila's Bungle in the South China Sea"; Heydarian, "US-Philippine-China Triangle."

67. Heydarian, "US-Philippine-China Triangle."

68. Ministry of Foreign Affairs of the People's Republic of China, *China's Foreign Affairs* (2007), 524.

69. Ministry of Foreign Affairs of the People's Republic of China, *China's Foreign Affairs* (2007), 317.

70. Ministry of Foreign Affairs of the People's Republic of China, *China's Foreign Affairs* (2008), 408.

71. Ministry of Foreign Affairs of the People's Republic of China, *China's Foreign Affairs* (2009), 233.

72. Huaigao Qi, "Joint Development in the South China Sea: China's Incentives and Policy Choices," *Journal of Contemporary East Asia Studies* 8, no. 2 (2019): 221, https://doi.org/https://doi.org/10.1080/24761028.2019.1685427

73. Wain, "Manila's Bungle in the South China Sea."

74. Qi, "Joint Development in the South China Sea."

75. Information Office of the State Council, *White Paper: China's Peaceful Development*; Ministry of Foreign Affairs of the People's Republic of China, "Hu Jintao Holds Talks with Nong Duc Manh"; Zemin Zheng, "Asia and the Pacific."

76. Srikanth Kondapalli, "Interview with Rajya Sabha TV," Rajya Sabha TV, January 16, 2017.

77. Li Xue, "How China Views the South China Sea Arbitration Case," *The Diplomat*, July 14, 2015.

78. Xue, "How China Views the South China Sea Arbitration Case."

79. Chun Yao, "China Vows to Make South China Sea Safe," Xinhua, December 15, 2011, http://www.mfa.gov.cn/ce/ceindo/eng/gdxw/t887657.htm

80. Keyuan Zou, "Can China Respect the Law of the Seas?, 42.

81. Sam Bateman, "Maritime Boundary Delimitation, Excessive Claims and

Effective Regime Building in the South China Sea," in *Major Law and Policy Issues in the South China Sea: European and American Perspectives*, ed. Yann-huei Song and Keyuan Zou (Farnham, UK: Ashgate, 2014), 131.

82. Yao, "China Vows to Make South China Sea Safe."

83. Wang Yi, "Foreign Minister Wang Yi: Build an Even Closer China-ASEAN Community of Common Destiny," Ministry of Foreign Affairs of the People's Republic of China, August 9, 2014, http://www.fmprc.gov.cn/mfa_eng/zxxx_662805/t1181521.shtml

84. Rory Medcalf, "China's Premature Power Play Goes Very Wrong," *The National Interest*, June 3, 2014, http://nationalinterest.org/feature/chinas-premature-power-play-goes-very-wrong-10587

85. Association of Southeast Asian Nations, "Statement by the ASEAN Foreign Ministers on the Recent Development in the South China Sea, Singapore, March 18, 1995."

86. Sheldon W. Simon, "ASEAN Regional Forum," in *Asian Security Handbook: An Assessment of Political-Security Issues in the Asia-Pacific Region*, ed. William M. Carpenter and David G. Wiencek (New York: M. E. Sharpe, 1996).

87. Lanteigne, *Chinese Foreign Policy*.

88. Ji You, "Chinese Response to the a la Carte Maritime Disorder in the Indo-Pacific Region," paper presented to the 16th Asian Security Conference, Institute for Defence Studies and Analyses, New Delhi, February 19–21, 2014.

89. Buszynski and Roberts, "Stabilisation and Resolution," 190.

90. Jiaxuan Tang, "Speech by Chinese Foreign Minister Tang Jiaxuan at the Meeting of China-ASEAN Dialogue," Ministry of Foreign Affairs of the People's Republic of China, July 26, 2001, updated April 19, 2004, http://www.fmprc.gov.cn/ce/cegv/eng/ljzg/zgwjzc/t85864.htm

91. Tang, "Speech by Chinese Foreign Minister Tang Jiaxuan at the Meeting of China-ASEAN Dialogue."

92. China-ASEAN Summit, "Chairman's Statement of the 17th ASEAN-China Summit," November 13, 2014, Nay Pyi Taw, Myanmar; Wang, "Foreign Minister Wang Yi: Build an Even Closer China-ASEAN Community."; Xinhua, "China's Defence Minister Urges Not to Play Up South China Sea Issues," *Xinhuanet*, November 4, 2015.

93. Tang, "Speech by Chinese Foreign Minister Tang Jiaxuan at the Meeting of China-ASEAN Dialogue."

94. Wang, "Foreign Minister Wang Yi: Build an Even Closer China-ASEAN Community."

95. Wang, "Foreign Minister Wang Yi: Build an Even Closer China-ASEAN Community."

96. Jiye Kim, "Finding the Common Ground with South Korea," in *One Belt One Road: China's Global Outreach*, ed. Srikanth Kondapalli and Xiaowen Hu (New Delhi: Pentagon Press, 2017).

97. Lanteigne, "The South China Sea in China's Developing Maritime Strategy."

98. "Joint Statement between Republic of the Philippines and People's Republic of China Consultations on the South China Sea and on Other Areas of Cooperation" (Code of Conduct between China and the Philippines), signed on August 9–10, 1995.

99. "Joint Statement between Republic of the Philippines and People's Republic of China."

100. Tang, "Speech by Chinese Foreign Minister Tang Jiaxuan at the Meeting of China-ASEAN Dialogue."

101. G. John Ikenberry, "The Rise of China, the United States, and the Future of the Liberal International Order," in *Tangled Titans: The United States and China*, ed. David L. Shambaugh (Lanham, MD: Rowman and Littlefield, 2013).

102. Jiaxuan Tang, "Speech by Foreign Minister Tang Jiaxuan at the ASEAN-China Dialogue (August 1, Bandar Seri Begawan)," 2002.

103. Buszynski, "ASEAN, the Declaration of Conduct."

104. Buszynski, "ASEAN, the Declaration of Conduct," 343.

105. James Hookway, "Philippine Warship in Standoff with China Vessels," *Wall Street Journal*, April 11, 2012, http://www.wsj.com/articles/SB10001424052702303815404577336550439399694

106. Ministry of Foreign Affairs of the People's Republic of China, "Foreign Ministry Spokesperson Hong Lei's Remarks on ASEAN Foreign Ministers' Statement on the Six-Point Principles on the South China Sea Issue," July 21, 2012, http://www.fmprc.gov.cn/ce/cedk/eng/fyrth/t955114.htm

107. Ministry of Foreign Affairs of the People's Republic of China, "Foreign Ministry Spokesperson Hong Lei's Remarks on ASEAN Foreign Ministers' Statement on the Six-Point Principles on the South China Sea Issue," 25; UNCLOS, *United Nations Convention on the Law of the Sea.*

108. Ministry of Foreign Affairs of the People's Republic of China, "Foreign Ministry Spokesperson Hong Lei's Remarks."

109. Times of India, "ASEAN Leaves Last Word on Sea Disputes Draft to China," November 26, 1999.

110. Declaration On the Conduct of Parties in the South China Sea, "Declaration on the Conduct of Parties in the South China Sea" 2002, https://asean.org/declaration-on-the-conduct-of-parties-in-the-south-china-sea-2/

111. China-ASEAN Summit, "Chairman's Statement of the 17th ASEAN-China Summit."

112. China-ASEAN Summit, "Chairman's Statement of the 17th ASEAN-China Summit."

113. Zou, "Can China Respect the Law of the Seas?," 41.

114. Information Office of the State Council, *White Paper: China's Peaceful Development.*

115. Shicun Wu and Keyuan Zou, "Maritime Security in the South China Sea," 9–10.

116. B. Creutzfeldt, "Theory Talk #45: Qin Yaqing on Rules vs. Relations, Drinking Coffee and Tea, and a Chinese Approach to Global Governance," *Theory Talks*, November 30, 2011. https://www.files.ethz.ch/isn/155106/Theory%20Talk45_Yaqing.pdf

117. Yao, "China Vows to Make South China Sea Safe."

118. Declaration On the Conduct of the Parties, "Declaration on the Conduct of Parties in the South China Sea."

119. Yi Wang, "Wang Yi Talks about China's Four-Point Consensus on South

China Sea Issue with Brunei, Cambodia and Laos," April 23, 2016, Ministry of Foreign Affairs of the People's Republic of China, http://www.fmprc.gov.cn/mfa_eng/zxxx_662805/t1358478.shtml

120. Association of Southeast Asian Nations, "Association of Southeast Asian Nations-China Senior Officials' Meeting: Terms of Reference of the ASEAN-China Joint Working Group on the Implementation of the Declaration on the Conduct of Parties in the South China Sea, December 7, Kuala Lumpur," 2004, https://asean.org/asean-china-senior-officials-meeting-on-the-implementation-of-the-declaration-on-the-conduct-of-parties-in-the-south-china-sea-kuala-lumpur

121. Ministry of Foreign Affairs of the People's Republic of China, *China's Foreign Affairs* (2007), 525.

122. Ministry of Foreign Affairs of the People's Republic of China, *China's Foreign Affairs* (2008), 410; Ministry of Foreign Affairs of the People's Republic of China, *China's Foreign Affairs* (2008), 467.

123. Xi Jinping, "Work Together to Build the Silk Road Economic Belt. September 7, 2013. Speech at Nazarbayev University, Astana, Kazakhstan," in *Governance of China* (2014), 317.

CHAPTER 5

1. Shambaugh, *China Goes Global*; Chan, *China Engages Global Health Governance*.

2. Shambaugh, *China Goes Global*.

3. Chan, *China Engages Global Health Governance*.

4. Chan, *China Engages Global Health Governance*, 125.

5. Geneva Convention, *Convention on the Territorial Sea and the Contiguous Zone*, completed at Geneva, April 29, 1958, entered into force, September 10, 1964, http://legal.un.org/ilc/texts/instruments/english/conventions/8_1_1958_territorial_sea.pdf; UNCLOS, *United Nations Convention on the Law of the Sea (Concluded on 10 December 1982. Came into force in 1994)* (1982).

6. Kim and Druckman, "Shelved Sovereignty or Invalid Sovereignty?," 45.

7. Vesselin Popovski, "UNCLOS and the Peaceful Use of the Sea," in *UN Convention on the Law of the Sea and the South China Sea*, ed. Shicun Wu, Mark J. Valencia, and Nong Hong (Farnham, UK: Ashgate, 2015), 73.

8. International Union for Conservation of Nature, "Conventional Law/Customary Law," October 25, 2012, https://www.iucn.org/content/conventional-law-customary-law

9. Sam Bateman, "Maritime Security Governance in the Indian Ocean Region," *Journal of the Indian Ocean Region* 12, no. 1 (2016).

10. *The Economist*, "Terrific Pacific," July 20, 1996.

11. Audra Mitchell, "Outer Space," in *Security Studies: An Introduction*, ed. Paul D Williams and Matt McDonald (New York: Routledge, 2018), 575.

12. Hong, *UNCLOS and Ocean Dispute Settlement*; Shicun Wu, Mark J. Valencia, and Nong Hong, *UN Convention on the Law of the Sea and the South China Sea* (Farnham, UK: Ashgate, 2015).

13. Buszynski, "Origins and Development of the South China Sea Maritime Dispute," 7.

14. Feng Zhang, "Assessing China's Response to the South China Sea Arbitration Ruling," *Australian Journal of International Affairs* 71, no. 4 (2017), https://doi.org/https://doi.org/10.1080/10357718.2017.1287876

15. Zhang, "Assessing China's Response to the South China Sea Arbitration Ruling."

16. Zhang, "Assessing China's Response to the South China Sea Arbitration Ruling."

17. Djalal, "'Due Regards' and 'Abuse of Rights'," 65.

18. Djalal, "'Due Regards' and 'Abuse of Rights'," 67.

19. Buszynski and Roberts, "Stabilisation and Resolution," 210–11.

20. Griffiths, "States, Nations, and Territorial Stability," 530.

21. Wu, Valencia, and Hong, "The South China Sea: UNCLOS and State Practice"; Clive H. Schofield, "Trouble over the Starting Line: State Practice concerning Baselines in the South China Sea," in *UN Convention on the Law of the Sea and the South China Sea*, ed. Shicun Wu, Mark J. Valencia, and Nong Hong (Farnham, UK: Ashgate, 2015).

22. Heydarian, "US-Philippine-China Triangle."

23. Jiye Kim and Arpit Raswant, "Indo-Pacific Powers: Internalization, Interpretation, and Implementation of International Law," *The Pacific Review* 36, no. 4 (2022), https://doi.org/https://doi.org/10.1080/09512748.2022.2046629

24. UN Division for Ocean Affairs and the Law of the Sea, "United Nations Convention on the Law of the Sea: Declarations Made upon Signature, Ratification, Accession or Succession or Anytime Thereafter," 1996, Oceans & Law of the Sea, United Nations, http://www.un.org/depts/los/convention_agreements/convention_declarations.htm#China

25. Joseph S. Nye, "Avoiding Conflict in the South China Sea," *Project Syndicate*, June 3, 2015, http://www.project-syndicate.org/commentary/south-china-sea-conflict-by-joseph-s--nye-2015-06

26. US Government, "South China Sea, Map and Gazetteer, US Government, 803425AI (G02257) 1–10, January," (2010).

27. Guoxing Ji, "Rough Waters in the South China Sea: Navigation Issues and Confidence-Building Measures," *Asia Pacific Issues (Analysis from the East-West Center)*, no. 53 (2001): 3.

28. U.S. Navy, U.S. Marine Corps, U.S. Coast Guard, *The Commander's Handbook on the Law of Naval Operations* (Norfolk, VA: Department of the Navy Office of the Chief of Naval Operations, U.S. Marine Corps, Department of Transportation U.S. Coast Guard, 1995). See page indicated as 1-6.

29. Sean O'Keefe (Secretary of the Navy), Frank B. Kelso II (Chief of Naval Operations), Carl E. Mundy Jr. (Commandant of the Marine Corps), ". . . From the Sea Preparing the Naval Service for the 21st Century," *Proceedings* 118 (November 1992), https://www.usni.org/magazines/proceedings/1992/november/sea-preparing-naval-service-21st-century

30. Ministry of Foreign Affairs of the People's Republic of China, "Foreign Minister Yang Jiechi on the South China Sea Issue," July 13, 2012.

31. UN Division for Ocean Affairs and the Law of the Sea, "United Nations Convention on the Law of the Sea: Declarations."

32. UN Division for Ocean Affairs and the Law of the Sea, "United Nations Convention on the Law of the Sea: Declarations."

33. UN Division for Ocean Affairs and the Law of the Sea, "United Nations Convention on the Law of the Sea: Declarations."

34. Permanent Court of Arbitration, "Award on Jurisdiction and Admissibility: In the Matter of an Arbitration before an Arbitral Tribunal Constituted under Annex VII to the 1982 United Nations Convention on the Law of the Sea between the Republic of the Philippines and the People's Republic of China," October 29, 2015.

35. Data sourced from Ministry of Foreign Affairs of the People's Republic of China, *China's Foreign Affairs* (2007); Ministry of Foreign Affairs of the People's Republic of China, *China's Foreign Affairs* (2008); Ministry of Foreign Affairs of the People's Republic of China, *China's Foreign Affairs* (2009); Ministry of Foreign Affairs of the People's Republic of China, *China's Foreign Affairs* (2010); Ministry of Foreign Affairs of the People's Republic of China, *China's Foreign Affairs* (2014). In this table, UNCLOS meeting refers to the Meeting of States Parties to the United Nations Convention on the Law of the Sea. The meeting is regularly held at the UN headquarters in New York and China sends its delegation that consists of the Ministry of Foreign Affairs, the State Oceanic Administration, and the Permanent Mission to the United Nations.

36. Ministry of Foreign Affairs of the People's Republic of China, *China's Foreign Affairs* (2007), 528–29.

37. Ministry of Foreign Affairs of the People's Republic of China, *China's Foreign Affairs* (2008), 410–11.

38. Ministry of Foreign Affairs of the People's Republic of China, *China's Foreign Affairs* (2009), 467.

39. Ministry of Foreign Affairs of the People's Republic of China, *China's Foreign Affairs* (2010), 432.

40. John Kemp, "East and South China Sea Disputes need Creative Diplomacy," Reuters, August 26, 2014, http://uk.reuters.com/article/2014/08/26/southchinasea-oil-kemp-idUKL5N0QW40A20140826

41. Gregory Poling, "The South China Sea in Focus: Clarifying the Limits of Maritime Dispute," A Report of the CSIS Sumitro Chair for Southeast Asian Studies (Washington, DC: Center for Strategic and International Studies, 2014), ix.

42. Greg Sheridan, "Bishop-Plibersek Debate: Bipartisan Line on South China Sea," *The Australian*, June 23, 2016.

43. Haiqing Li, "Woguo Dongyahai Diqu Haiyang Fazhanzhuanluede Sikao" [Reflections on our strategy for ocean development in East Asian seas], *Haiyang Fazhan Yu Guanli (Journal of Maritime Development and Management)* 1 (2005).

44. Zou, "Can China Respect the Law of the Seas?," 40.

45. Park, "South China Sea Disputes," 28.

46. Wu and Zou, "Maritime Security in the South China Sea."

47. Bateman, "Maritime Security Governance in the Indian Ocean Region."

48. You, "Test Case for China's Defence."

49. Survey and Mapping Law of the People's Republic of China, Presidential

Order No. 75, August 29, 2002, http://www.china.org.cn/china/LegislationsForm2001-2010/2011-02/14/content_21916711.htm; Law of the People's Republic of China on the Territorial Sea and the Contiguous Zone, Order No. 55 of the President, February 25, 1992, http://www.npc.gov.cn/zgrdw/englishnpc/Law/2007-12/12/content_1383846.htm

50. Stuart Kaye, "Marine Scientific Research and Military Survey: Law and State Practice," in *UN Convention on the Law of the Sea and the South China Sea*, ed. Shicun Wu, Mark J. Valencia, and Nong Hong (Farnham, UK: Ashgate, 2015), 92.

51. CCTV, "Chinese FM Calls for Respecting 4 Principles on South China Sea Issue," *China Central Television*, September 9, 2014, http://english.cntv.cn/2014/09/08/VIDE1410150001707535.shtml (no longer available).

52. Zhang, "Rise of Chinese Exceptionalism," 317.

53. Xuetong Yan et al., *Ancient Chinese Thought.*

54. Nye, *Soft Power.*

55. Yan et al., *Ancient Chinese Thought.*

56. Lanteigne, "South China Sea in China's Developing Maritime Strategy"; Nan Li, "The Evolution of China's Naval Strategy and Capability: From 'Near Coast' and 'Near Seas' to 'Far Seas,'" *Asian Security* 5, no. 2 (2009).

57. Andrew Cheon and Johannes Urpelainen, "Escaping Oil's Stranglehold: When Do States Invest in Energy Security?," *Journal of Conflict Resolution* 59, no. 6 (2015).

58. "Riau Islands Police Beefed Up to 12,000 to Anticipate South China Sea Tension," *Jakarta Post*, January 20, 2017.

59. Lanteigne, "South China Sea in China's Developing Maritime Strategy"; K. Noguchi, "Bringing Realism Back In: Explaining China's Strategic Behaviour in the Asia-Pacific," *Asia-Pacific Review* 18, no. 2 (2011); Shambaugh, *China Goes Global*; Yoshihara and Holmes, "Can China Defend a 'Core Interest'?"

60. Yan, *Lishide Guanxing*, 58–59.

61. Heydarian, "US-Philippine-China Triangle," 348.

62. Heydarian, "US-Philippine-China Triangle," 348.

63. Tommy Koh, "The Exclusive Economic Zone," *Malaya Law Review* 30, no. 1 (1988): 25.

64. Kim and Druckman, "Shelved Sovereignty or Invalid Sovereignty?," 46. Original map from Wei-I Chang, *Nan-Hai Tsu-Yuan K'ai-Fa yu Chu-Ch'uan Wei-Hu* (Taipei County, Taiwan: P'an Shih Library, December 1994); Bureau of Oceans and International Environmental and Scientific Affairs, United States Department of State, *Limits in the Seas—China.*

65. Lanteigne, "South China Sea in China's Developing Maritime Strategy," 101.

66. Liu, *Liu Huaqing Huiyilu* [Memoirs of Liu Huaqing].

67. Evan Jones, "Steel Hulls and High-Stakes: Prospect Theory and China's Use of Military Force in the South China Sea," in *Power Politics in Asia's Contested Waters: Territorial Disputes in the South China Sea*, ed. Enrico Fels and Truong-Minh Vu (Cham, Switzerland: Springer International, 2016).

68. John Gittings, "South China Seizure," *The Guardian*, January 21, 1974, 11; Nicholas Cumming-Bruce, "Beijing Makes More Mischief in South China Sea," *The Guardian*, May 22, 1995, 12.

69. Lanteigne, "South China Sea in China's Developing Maritime Strategy."

70. Data sourced from Ministry of Foreign Affairs of People's Republic of China and Asia Maritime Transparency Initiative.

71. Zhao, "Foreign Policy Implications of Chinese Nationalism."

72. Ben Blanchard, "China Says It Followed Rules in U.S. Aircraft Intercept," *Reuters*, May 26, 2016.

73. You, "Deciphering Beijing's Maritime Security Policy."

74. You, "Deciphering Beijing's Maritime Security Policy."

75. David Brunnstrom, "US to Press for South China Sea Freeze despite China Rejection," *Sydney Morning Herald*, August 5, 2014, http://www.smh.com.au/world/us-to-press-for-south-china-sea-freeze-despite-china-rejection-20140805-100gva.html

76. Victor Beattie, "Will Regional Ties Prevent South China Sea Conflict?," *Voice of America*, June 25, 2014, http://www.voanews.com/content/singapore-pm-regional-ties-will-prevent-south-china-sea-conflict/1944515.html

77. Cumming-Bruce, "Beijing Makes More Mischief."

78. US Army, Training and Doctrine Command, *The U.S. Army Operating Concept: Win in a Complex World 2020–2040*, October 7, 2014, 10.

79. Meng Yan and Jun Liang, "Maneuver 5 Exercise Enters Stage of Actual-Troop Confrontation," People's Daily Online and China Military Online, October 29, 2013, http://english.peopledaily.com.cn/90786/8439923.html

80. US Department of Defense, Office of the Secretary, *Annual Report to Congress: Military and Security Developments Involving the People's Republic of China 2014* (Washington, DC: US Department of Defense, April 24, 2014), i.

81. Robert D. Kaplan, "How We Would Fight China," *The Atlantic*, June 1, 2005.

82. Frank C. Borik, "Sub Tzu & the Art of Submarine Warfare," *Naval Institute Proceedings*, November 1995.

83. Greg Torode, "Insight—Vietnam Building Deterrent against China in Disputed Seas with Submarines," Reuters (Hong Kong), September 7, 2014, http://uk.reuters.com/article/2014/09/07/uk-vietnam-submarines-china-insight-idUKKBN0H20T720140907

84. John Ruwitch, "Satellites and Seafood: China Keeps Fishing Fleet Connected in Disputed Waters," Reuters, July 27, 2014, http://www.reuters.com/article/2014/07/27/us-southchinasea-china-fishing-insight-idUSKBN0FW0QP20140727

85. Kapur, *China's Changing Approach to Strategy and Negotiations.*

86. Andrew Erickson and G. B. Collins, "China's Oil Security Pipe Dream: The Reality and Strategic Consequences of Seaborne Imports," *Naval War College Review* 63 (2010).

87. Dennis Blair and Kenneth Lieberthal,"Smooth Sailing: The World's Shipping Lanes Are Safe," *Foreign Affairs* 86 (2007): 12; Taylor, "South China Sea as a 'Crisis'," 175.

88. Bruce A. Elleman and S. C. M. Paine, *Naval Power and Expeditionary Wars: Peripheral Campaigns and New Theatres of Naval Warfare* (London: Routledge, 2010).

89. Elleman and Paine, *Naval Power and Expeditionary Wars.*

90. Mark T. Esper, "Remarks by Secretary Esper at an International Institute for Strategic Studies Webinar on the U.S. Vision for Security in the Indo-Pacific Region," July 21, 2020.

91. Rex Li, "China's Sea Power Aspirations and Strategic Behaviour in the South China Sea from the Theoretical Perspective of Identity Construction," in *Power Politics in Asia's Contested Waters: Territorial Disputes in the South China Sea*, ed. Enrico Fels and Truong-Minh Vu (Cham, Switzerland: Springer International, 2016).

92. Abb, "Punish the Philippines, Forgive Vietnam?"

CHAPTER 6

1. Jiye Kim and Arpit Raswant, "Australian Perspective on Engaging with South Korea in the Indo-Pacific," *Asian Politics & Policy* 15, no. 1 (2023), https://doi.org/10.1111/aspp.12672

2. Ministry of Foreign Affairs of the People's Republic of China, "Wang Yi Stresses 'Four Respects' on South China Sea Issue."

3. You, "Deciphering Beijing's Maritime Security Policy."

4. Liu Xuanzun and Guo Yuandan, "Interview with South China Sea Think Tank Head Shows Three Possibilities Risking China-US Military Conflict," *Global Times*, August 2, 2020, https://www.globaltimes.cn/content/1196426.shtml

5. Tan, "Manila Annexes Much of Disputed Spratly Islands."

6. US Department of State, "Daily Press Briefing."

7. US Department of Defense, *Summary of the 2018 National Defense Strategy of the United States of America: Sharpening the American Military's Competitive Edge* (Washington, DC, 2018), 1; US Department of Defense, *Indo-Pacific Strategy Report: Preparedness, Partnerships, and Promoting a Networked Region* (Washington, DC: Department of Defense, June 1, 2019), 8; US Department of Defense, *Defense Space Strategy Summary* (Washington, DC, 2020), 3; Arpit Raswant, Jiye Kim, and Tim Mahlberg, "Space Is Going Commercial in Asia, but There's a Rocky Road Ahead," *The Diplomat*, January 20, 2023.

8. Pompeo, "U.S. Position on Maritime Claims in the South China Sea."

9. US Department of State, "Press Statement: On the Situation in the South China Sea," November 19, 2021, https://www.state.gov/on-the-situation-in-the-south-china-sea/

10. Rodrigo Roa Duterte, "Fifth State of the Nation Address by the President of the Philippines," July 27, 2020, https://mirror.officialgazette.gov.ph/2020/07/27/rodrigo-roa-duterte-fifth-state-of-the-nation-address-july-27-2020/

11. Ministry of Foreign Affairs of the People's Republic of China, "Position Paper: China Adheres to the Position of Settling through Negotiation the Relevant Disputes between China and the Philippines in the South China Sea," July 13, 2016, https://www.fmprc.gov.cn/nanhai/eng/snhwtlcwj_1/201607/t20160713_8527301.htm

12. Ministry of Foreign Affairs of the People's Republic of China, "Position Paper: China Adheres to the Position of Settling through Negotiation."

13. Srikanth Kondapalli, "SAARC Summit: China's Role Will Be Keenly Watched by the South Asian Countries," *Economic Times*, November 26, 2014, http://blogs.economictimes.indiatimes.com/et-commentary/saarc-summit-chinas-role-will-be-keenly-watched-by-the-south-asian-countries

14. Xi Jinping, "New Asian Security Concept for New Progress in Security Coop-

eration (Remarks at the Fourth Summit of the Conference on Interaction and Confidence Building Measures in Asia, Shanghai)," May 21, 2014.

15. Xi Jinping, "Speech by Chinese President Xi Jinping to Indonesian Parliament," October 2, 2013, http://www.asean-china-center.org/english/2013-10/03/c_133062675.htm

16. Xinhua, "21 Asian Countries Sign MOU on Establishing Asian Infrastructure Investment Bank," *Xinhuanet*, October 24, 2014, http://english.peopledaily.com.cn/business/n/2014/1024/c90778-8799681.html

17. Jong Wha Lee, "China's New World Order," *Project Syndicate*, November 12, 2014, http://www.project-syndicate.org/commentary/china-global-governance-by-lee-jong-wha-2014-11; Shashi Tharoor, "China's Silk Road Revival," *Project Syndicate*, October 14, 2014, http://www.project-syndicate.org/commentary/china-silk-road-economic-belt-goals-by-shashi-tharoor-2014-10

18. Lee, "China's New World Order."

19. Gungwu Wang, "The Nanhai Trade: A Study of the Early History of Chinese Trade in the South China Sea," *Journal of the Malayan Branch of the Royal Asiatic Society* 31, no. 2 (182) (1958): 6.

20. Jiye Kim, Arpit Raswant, and Thomas Wilkins, "Threat Perception Variation in the Indo-Pacific," *Journal of East Asian Studies* 24, no. 3 (Nov. 2024): 286–304, https://doi.org/10.1017/jea.2024.16

21. Ministry of Foreign Affairs of the People's Republic of China, "Wang Yi Attends the ASEAN-China Ministerial Meeting," August 3, 2021, https://www.fmprc.gov.cn/mfa_eng/zxxx_662805/t1897344.shtml

22. South China Sea Strategic Situation Probing Initiative, "US Reconnaissance Aircraft Operating over the South China Sea amid the PLA's Paracel Training," August 4, 2020; South China Sea Strategic Situation Probing Initiative, "US Reconnaissance Aircraft Operating over the South China Sea, July 2020," August 4, 2020.

23. Esper, "Remarks by Secretary Esper."

Bibliography

Abb, Pascal. "Punish the Philippines, Forgive Vietnam? The South China Sea Disputes in the Eyes of Chinese Experts." In *Power Politics in Asia's Contested Waters: Territorial Disputes in the South China Sea*, edited by Enrico Fels and Truong-Minh Vu. Cham, Switzerland: Springer International, 2016.

Amer, Ramses, and Jianwei Li. "Recent Developments in the South China Sea—an Assessment of the Core Bilateral Relationship between China and Vietnam." In *Maritime Security Issues in the South China Sea and the Arctic: Sharpened Competition or Collaboration?*, edited by Gordon Houlden and Nong Hong, 41–75. Beijing: China Democracy and Legal System Publishing House, 2012.

Anderson, Benedict. *Imagined Communities: Reflections on the Origin and Spread of Nationalism*. London: Verso, 1983.

Andrews-Speed, Philip, and Christopher Len. *The Future of the US Security Umbrella for Sea Lines of Communication (SLOCs) between the Middle East and Southeast Asia, and the Future Role of China*. Singapore: Energy Studies Institute, National University of Singapore, February 2016.

Asdal, Kristin, and Hilde Reinertsen. *Doing Document Analysis: A Practice-Oriented Method*. London: SAGE, 2022.

Asia Maritime Transparency Initiative. "An Interview with Shen Lyu-Shun, Representative of the Republic of China to the United States." December 15, 2015. http://amti.csis.org/an-Interview-with-Shen-Lyu-Shun-Representative-of-the-Republic-of-China-to-the-United-States

Asia Maritime Transparency Initiative. "Island Features Occupation Status in the South China Sea." 2020. https://amti.csis.org/scs-features-map

Association of Southeast Asian Nations. "Association of Southeast Asian Nations–China Senior Officials' Meeting: Terms of Reference of the ASEAN-China Joint Working Group on the Implementation of the Declaration on the Conduct of Parties in the South China Sea, December 7, Kuala Lumpur." 2004. http://www.asean.org/news/item/terms-of-reference-of-the-asean-china-joint-working-group-on-the-implementation-of-the-declaration-on-the-conduct-of-parties-in-the-south-china-sea

Association of Southeast Asian Nations. "Statement by the ASEAN Foreign Ministers on the Recent Development in the South China Sea, Singapore, March 18, 1995." In *ASEAN Documents Series 1994–1995*, edited by ASEAN Secretariat. Jakarta: Association of Southeast Asian Nations, 1995.

Barnett, A. Doak. *After Deng, What? Will China Follow the USSR?* Washington, DC: Foreign Policy Institute, School of Advanced International Studies, Johns Hopkins University, 1991.

Bateman, Sam. "Cooperation or Trust: What Comes First in the South China Sea?" *RSIS Commentary*, no. 167, September 17, 2013. Singapore: S. Rajaratnam School of International Studies. https://rsis.edu.sg/rsis-publication/idss/2055-cooperation-or-trust-what-com/

Bateman, Sam. "Maritime Boundary Delimitation, Excessive Claims and Effective Regime Building in the South China Sea." In *Major Law and Policy Issues in the South China Sea: European and American Perspectives*, edited by Yann-huei Song and Keyuan Zou. Farnham, UK: Ashgate, 2014.

Bateman, Sam. "Maritime Security Governance in the Indian Ocean Region." *Journal of the Indian Ocean Region* 12, no. 1 (2016): 5–23.

Beattie, Victor. "Will Regional Ties Prevent South China Sea Conflict?" *Voice of America*, June 25, 2014. http://www.voanews.com/content/singapore-pm-regional-ties-will-prevent-south-china-sea-conflict/1944515.html

Beijing Xinhua. "PRC Begin Geophysical Surveys in South China Sea." Xinhua (Foreign Broadcast Information Service–China), September 21, 1980.

Bentley, Scott. "Mapping the Nine-Dash Line: Recent Incidents Involving Indonesia in the South China Sea." *The Strategist*, October 29, 2013. http://www.aspistrategist.org.au/mapping-the-nine-dash-line-recent-incidents-involving-indonesia-in-the-south-china-sea/

Berridge, Geoff. *Diplomacy: Theory and Practice*. 4th ed. New York: Palgrave Macmillan, 2010.

Blair, Dennis, and Kenneth Lieberthal. "Smooth Sailing: The World's Shipping Lanes Are Safe." *Foreign Affairs* 86 (2007).

Blanchard, Ben. "China Says It Followed Rules in U.S. Aircraft Intercept." Reuters, May 26, 2016.

Borik, Frank C. "Sub Tzu & the Art of Submarine Warfare." *Naval Institute Proceedings* (November 1995): 64–72.

Bouchat, Clarence J. *The Paracel Islands and U.S. Interests and Approaches in the South China Sea*. Carlisle Barracks, PA: Strategic Studies Institute and U.S. Army War College Press, 2014.

Bower, Ernest Z. "The JMSU: A Tale of Bilateralism and Secrecy in the South China Sea." Center for Strategic and International Studies. July 27, 2010.

Brown, Kerry. "Foreign Policy Making under Xi Jinping: The Case of the South China Sea." *Journal of Political Risk* 4, no. 2 (2016).

Brunnstrom, David. "US to Press for South China Sea Freeze despite China Rejection." *Sydney Morning Herald*, August 5, 2014. http://www.smh.com.au/world/us-to-press-for-south-china-sea-freeze-despite-china-rejection-20140805-100gva.html

Bureau of Oceans and International Environmental and Scientific Affairs. *Limits in the Seas—China: Maritime Claims in the South China Sea, No. 143*. United States Department of State, December 5, 2014.

Bureau of Oceans and International Environmental and Scientific Affairs. *Limits in the Seas—Taiwan's Maritime Claims.* No. 127. United States Department of State, November 15, 2005.

Buszynski, Leszek. "ASEAN, the Declaration of Conduct, and the South China Sea." *Contemporary Southeast Asia* 25, no. 3 (2003): 343–62.

Buszynski, Leszek. "The Origins and Development of the South China Sea Maritime Dispute." In *The South China Sea Maritime Dispute: Political, Legal, and Regional Perspectives*, edited by Leszek Buszynski and Christopher B. Roberts. New York: Routledge, 2015.

Buszynski, Leszek. "The South China Sea: Oil, Maritime Claims, and U.S.–China Strategic Rivalry." *Washington Quarterly* 35, no. 2 (2012): 139–56. https://doi.org/10.1080/0163660X.2012.666495

Buszynski, Leszek, and Christopher Roberts, eds. *The South China Sea Maritime Dispute: Political, Legal, and Regional Perspectives*. New York: Routledge, 2015.

Buszynski, Leszek, and Christopher B. Roberts. "Stabilisation and Resolution." In *The South China Sea Maritime Dispute: Political, Legal, and Regional Perspectives*, edited by Leszek Buszynski and Christopher B. Roberts. New York: Routledge, 2015.

Buszynski, Leszek, and Iskandar Sazlan. "Maritime Claims and Energy Cooperation in the South China Sea." *Contemporary Southeast Asia* 29, no. 1 (2007): 143–71.

CCTV. "Chinese FM Calls for Respecting 4 Principles on South China Sea Issue." *China Central Television*, September 9, 2014.

Chan, Lai-Ha. *China Engages Global Health Governance: Responsible Stakeholder or System-Transformer?* New York: Palgrave Macmillan, 2010.

Chang, Wei-I. *Nan-Hai tsu-yuan k'ai-fa yu chu-ch'uan wei-hu* [South China Sea resource development and sovereignty protection]. Taipei County, Taiwan: P'an Shih Library, December 1994.

Chapman, Rod. "BP Abandons First South China Well." *Guardian*, January 1984, 18.

Chapman, Rod. "Cluff Oil Signs for South China Sea." *Guardian*, September 6, 1983.

Chen, Caiyun, and Zhouping Deng. "Lun Nanhaifenzheng De Zhongguo Duice" [Discussion on China's response to the South China Sea disputes]. *Jiangsu Kejidaxue Xuebao* 11, no. 3 (2011): 79–84.

Chen, Dingding, and Jianwei Wang. "Lying Low No More? China's New Thinking on the Tao Guang Yang Hui Strategy." *China: An International Journal* 9, no. 2 (2011): 195–216.

Chen, Hu. "Motives behind US Talk of 'Freedom of Navigation'." *People's Daily Online*, June 30, 2011. Accessed October 17, 2014. http://english.peopledaily.com.cn/90001/90780/91342/7425457.html

Cheng, Joseph Y. S., and Stephanie Paladini. "China's Ocean Development Strategy and Its Handling of the Territorial Conflicts in the South China Sea." *Philippine Political Science Journal* 35, no. 2 (2014): 185–202. https://doi.org/10.1080/01154451.2014.965476

Cheon, Andrew, and Johannes Urpelainen. "Escaping Oil's Stranglehold: When Do States Invest in Energy Security?" *Journal of Conflict Resolution* 59, no. 6 (2015): 953–83.

China-ASEAN Summit. "Chairman's Statement of the 17th ASEAN-China Summit." November 13, 2014. Nay Pyi Taw, Myanmar.

China News. "Shoulun Zhongmei Jingli Duihua" [First round of China—US strategic and economic dialogue]. July 29, 2009. http://www.chinanews.com/gn/news/2009/07-29/1794984.shtml

China Ocean News. "Vietnam Severely Violates China's Sovereignty by Insisting Paracel and Spratly Islands in Its Legislation." June 22, 2012. Accessed May 16, 2014. http://www.oceanol.com/redian/shiping/19614.html

Choiruzzad, Shofwan Al Banna. "Indonesia Forges Stronger Ties with China to Boost Economy." *The Conversation*, November 19, 2014. https://theconversation.com/indonesia-forges-stronger-ties-with-china-to-boost-economy-34004

Choong, Whilliam. "Mistrust Hurts Naval Cooperation in Region." *Straits Times*, May 27, 2011.

Clinton, Hillary. "Interview with Greg Sheridan, Melbourne, Australia." *The Australian*, November 8, 2010. https://2009-2017.state.gov/secretary/20092013clinton/rm/2010/11/150671.htm

Cole, Bernard D. *The Great Wall at Sea: China's Navy in the Twenty-First Century*. Annapolis, MD: Naval Institute Press, 2010.

Committee on Foreign Affairs. *Hearing before the Subcommittee on Asia and the Pacific of the Committee on Foreign Affairs House of Representatives, Serial No. 113–123*. Washington, DC: US Government Printing Office, February 5, 2014.

Communist Party of China. *Constitution of the Communist Party of China (Revised and Adopted at the 19th National Congress of the Communist Party of China on October 24, 2017)*. 2017.

Constantinou, Costas M., and James Der Derian. "Sustaining Global Hope: Sovereignty, Power and the Transformation of Diplomacy." In *Sustainable Diplomacies*, edited by Costas M. Constantinou and James Der Derian. New York: Palgrave Macmillan, 2010.

Creutzfeldt, B. "Theory Talk #45: Qin Yaqing on Rules vs. Relations, Drinking Coffee and Tea, and a Chinese Approach to Global Governance." *Theory Talks*, November 30, 2011. https://www.files.ethz.ch/isn/155106/Theory%20Talk45_Yaqing.pdf

Cumming-Bruce, Nicholas. "Beijing Makes More Mischief in South China Sea." *The Guardian*, May 22, 1995, 12.

Daily Report. "Communist China: International Affairs." *Daily Report: People's Republic of China*, January 4, 1971.

Daily Report. "Moscow Radio Peace and Progress in Mandarin to Southeast Asia." December 3, 1980.

Daily Report Asia-Pacific. "SRV Proposal on South China Sea Claim Rejected." *Daily Report Asia-Pacific* (FBIS-APA-81–028), February 8, 1981, 1.

Declaration on the Conduct of Parties in the South China Sea. "Declaration on the Conduct of Parties in the South China Sea, the Governments of the Member States of ASEAN and the Government of the People's Republic of China, Done on November 4, 2002, Phnom Penh, the Kingdom of Cambodia." 2002. https://asean.org/declaration-on-the-conduct-of-parties-in-the-south-china-sea-2/

Deng Xiaoping. "Zai Zhongyang Guwenweiyuanhui Disanci Quantihuiyishangde Jianghua" [Speech in the Central Advisory Committee at its third plenary session]. October 22, 1984.

Department of Foreign Affairs of the Philippines. "Response of the DFA Spokesperson to the Recent Statement of the Chinese Ministry of Foreign Affairs on the

West Philippines Sea Issue." July 15, 2013. https://www.dfa.gov.ph/index.php/2013-06-27-21-50-36/dfa-releases/332

Department of Policy Planning. "Foreign Policy Report, 8th Congress of the Legislative Yuan, 5th Session." March 12, 2014.

Djalal, Hasjim. "'Due Regards' and 'Abuse of Rights' in UNCLOS." In *UN Convention on the Law of the Sea and the South China Sea*, edited by Shicun Wu, Mark J. Valencia, and Nong Hong, 65–72. Farnham, UK: Ashgate, 2015.

Downs, Erica Strecker, and Phillip C. Saunders. "Legitimacy and the Limits of Nationalism: China and the Diaoyu Islands." *International Security* 23, no. 3 (1998): 114–46.

Duterte, Rodrigo Roa. "Fifth State of the Nation Address by the President of the Philippines." July 27, 2020. https://mirror.officialgazette.gov.ph/2020/07/27/rodrigo-roa-duterte-fifth-state-of-the-nation-address-july-27-2020/

Dzurek, Daniel J. "Maritime Briefing—the Spratly Islands Dispute: Who's on First?" *International Boundaries Research Unit* 2, no. 1 (1996).

The Economist. "Terrific Pacific." *The Economist*, July 20, 1996, 29–30.

Editorial Departments of Renmin Ribao and Hongqi. "Peaceful Coexistence—Two Diametrically Opposed Policies." Peking: Foreign Languages Press, 1963. http://www.marxists.org/subject/china/documents/polemic/peaceful.htm

Elleman, Bruce A., and S. C. M. Paine. *Naval Power and Expeditionary Wars: Peripheral Campaigns and New Theatres of Naval Warfare*. London: Routledge, 2010.

Erickson, Andrew, and G. B. Collins. "China's Oil Security Pipe Dream: The Reality and Strategic Consequences of Seaborne Imports." *Naval War College Review* 63 (2010).

Esper, Mark T. "Remarks by Secretary Esper at an International Institute for Strategic Studies Webinar on the U.S. Vision for Security in the Indo-Pacific Region." July 21, 2020.

Federal Republic of Germany. *Strategy on China of the Government of the Federal Republic of Germany*. 2023.

Fels, Enrico, and Truong-Minh Vu, eds. *Power Politics in Asia's Contested Waters: Territorial Disputes in the South China Sea*. Cham, Switzerland: Springer International, 2016.

Fetic, Sorin. "Operationalisation of Defence Diplomacy." *Strategic Impact*, no. 4 (2013): 44–52.

Fisher, Roger, and William Ury. *Getting to Yes: Negotiating Agreement without Giving In*. New York: Penguin Books, 1991.

Foreign Press Liaison Office of the Ministry of Foreign Affairs (Republic of China). "Press Release: President Ma Addresses Members of News Media on Their Return from Taiping Island." March 23, 2016.

Fravel, Taylor M. "International Relations Theory and China's Rise: Assessing China's Potential for Territorial Expansion." *International Studies Review* 12, no. 4 (2010): 505–32.

Fravel, Taylor M. "Power Shifts and Escalation: Explaining China's Use of Force in Territorial Disputes." *International Security* 32, no. 3 (2008): 44–83.

Fravel, Taylor M. *Strong Borders, Secure Nation: Cooperation and Conflict in China's Territorial Disputes*. Princeton: Princeton University Press, 2008.

Friedberg, Aaron. "Hegemony with Chinese Characteristics." *National Interest* 114 (2011): 18–27.

Gang, Ding. "Why Does Speculation Grow in South China Sea." *People's Daily Online*, August 3, 2011. Accessed October 17, 2014. http://english.peopledaily.com.cn/90780/91342/7458582.html

Garcia, Zenel, and Christine Bianco. "The Impact of Chinese History on Perceptions of the Law of the Sea in the South China Sea." *Territory, Politics, Governance* (2023):1–21. https://doi.org/10.1080/21622671.2023.2218427

Garver, John W. "China's Push through the South China Sea: The Interaction of Bureaucratic and National Interests." *China Quarterly* (1992).

Geneva Convention. *Convention on the Territorial Sea and the Contiguous Zone*. Done at Geneva on April 29, 1958. Entered into force on September 10, 1964. http://legal.un.org/ilc/texts/instruments/english/conventions/8_1_1958_territorial_sea.pdf

Ghosh, P. K. "Artificial Islands in the South China Sea." *The Diplomat*, September 23, 2014. http://thediplomat.com/2014/09/artificial-islands-in-the-south-china-sea

Gilpin, Robert. *War and Change in World Politics*. Cambridge: Cambridge University Press, 1981.

Gittings, John. "Scramble for Oil in East China Sea." *The Guardian*, December 18, 1970.

Gittings, John. "South China Seizure." *The Guardian*, January 21, 1974, 11.

Glosserman, Brad. "China's Smile Diplomacy." *South China Morning Post*, April 1, 2004. http://www.scmp.com/article/450592/chinas-smile-diplomacy

Goldsmith, Benjamin. "A Liberal Peace in Asia?" *Journal of Peace Research* 44, no. 1 (2007): 5–27.

Griffiths, Ryan D. "States, Nations, and Territorial Stability: Why Chinese Hegemony Would Be Better for International Order." *Security Studies* 25, no. 3 (2016): 519–45.

Guay, Justin. "China's Coal Imports Drop for the First Time since Country Became Net Coal Importer." *Huffington Post*, November 10, 2014.

Han, Nianlong, ed. *Diplomacy of Contemporary China*. Edited by Nianlong Han. Hong Kong: New Horizon Press, 1990.

Harrison, Selig S. *China, Oil and Asia: Conflict Ahead?* New York: Columbia University Press, 1977.

Hayton, Bill. *The South China Sea: The Struggle for Power in Asia*. New Haven: Yale University Press, 2014.

Heinzig, Dieter. *Disputed Islands in the South China Sea: Paracels, Spratlys, Pratas, Macclesfield Bank*. Wiesbaden: Harrassowitz, 1976.

Hellendorff, Bruno. "'Coopetition' and Risk Tolerance in the South China Sea: Indonesia and Malaysia's Middle Power Strategies." In *Power Politics in Asia's Contested Waters: Territorial Disputes in the South China Sea*, edited by Enrico Fels and Truong-Minh Vu. Cham, Switzerland: Springer International, 2016.

Heydarian, Richard Javad. "The US-Philippine-China Triangle: From Equi-Balancing to Counter-Balancing amid the South China Sea Disputes." In *Power Politics in Asia's Contested Waters: Territorial Disputes in the South China Sea*, edited by Enrico Fels and Truong Minh Vu. Cham, Switzerland: Springer International, 2016.

Higgins, Andrew. "In Philippines, Banana Growers Feel Effect of South China Sea Dispute." *Washington Post*, June 11, 2012.

Holmes, James R. "Strategic Features of the South China Sea: A Tough Neighborhood for Hegemons." *Naval War College Review* 67, no. 2 (2014): 1–22.

Hong, Nong. *UNCLOS and Ocean Dispute Settlement: Law and Politics in the South China Sea*. Abingdon, UK: Routledge, 2012.

Hookway, James. "Philippine Warship in Standoff with China Vessels." *Wall Street Journal*, April 11, 2012. http://www.wsj.com/articles/SB10001424052702303815404577336550439399694

Hsiao, Michael, and Alan Yang. "Soft Power Politics in the Asia Pacific: Chinese and Japanese Quests for Regional Leadership." *Asia-Pacific Journal* 8 (2009).

Hsieh, C. C., and Y. F. Low. "Ma Again Invites Philippine Officials to Visit Taiping Island." *Focus Taiwan News Channel*, April 7, 2016.

Hu, N. A. "South China Sea: Troubled Waters or a Sea of Opportunity?" *Ocean Development and International Law* 41, no. 3 (2010): 203–13.

Hua, Judy, and Aizhu Chen. "China, US to Cooperate on Strategic Oil Reserves." *Reuters UK Edition*, July 11, 2014. http://uk.reuters.com/article/2014/07/11/china-usa-oil-idUKL4N0PM3IE20140711

Huang, Jing, and Sharinee Jagtiani. "Introduction: Unknotting Tangled Lines in the South China Sea Dispute." In *Territorial Disputes in the South China Sea*, edited by Jing Huang and Andrew Billo. New York: Palgrave Macmillan, 2015.

Hughes, Christopher R. "After 1989: Nationalism and the New Global Elite." In *Contemporary Chinese Society and Politics: Critical Concepts in Asian Studies*, edited by Andrew Kipnis, Luigi Tomba, and Jonathan Unger. London: Routledge, 2009.

Hunt, M. H. "Chinese Foreign Relations in Historical Perspective." In *China's Foreign Relations in the 1980s*, edited by Harry Harding and the Asia Society. New Haven: Yale University Press, 1984.

Ikenberry, G. John. "The Rise of China, the United States, and the Future of the Liberal International Order." In *Tangled Titans: The United States and China*, edited by David L. Shambaugh, 53–74. Lanham, MD: Rowman and Littlefield, 2013.

Information Office of the State Council. *2010 China's National Defense*. Beijing: Information Office of the State Council, 2010.

Information Office of the State Council. *China: Arms Control and Disarmament*. Beijing: Information Office of the State Council, 1995.

Information Office of the State Council. *The Diversified Employment of China's Armed Forces*. Beijing: Information Office of the State Council, 2013.

Information Office of the State Council. *White Paper: China's Peaceful Development*. Beijing: Information Office of the State Council, 2011.

Information Office of the State Council. *White Paper: China's Policies on Asia-Pacific Security Cooperation*. Beijing: Information Office of the State Council, 2017.

International Strategy and Security Research Center. *Zhongguo Guojia Anquan Yanjiu Baogao (2014)* [The national security blue paper: The research report on national security of China]. Beijing: University of International Relations of China, May 6, 2014.

International Union for Conservation of Nature. "Conventional Law/Customary Law." International Union for Conservation of Nature. October 25, 2012.

Jakarta Post. "Riau Islands Police Beefed Up to 12,000 to Anticipate South China Sea Tension." *Jakarta Post*, January 20, 2017.

Jeong, Jooyeon. *Industrial Relations in Korea: Diversity and Dynamism of Korean Enterprise Unions from a Comparative Perspective*. Abingdon, UK: Routledge, 2007.

Jervis, Robert. *The Meaning of the Nuclear Revolution: Statecraft and the Prospect of Armageddon*. Ithaca: Cornell University Press, 1989.

Ji, Guoxing. "Rough Waters in the South China Sea: Navigation Issues and Confidence-Building Measures." *Asia Pacific Issues (Analysis from the East-West Center)*, no. 53 (2001).

Jia, Yu. "Arbitral Tribunal Abusing Its Power." *China Daily*, June 3, 2016.

Jing, Chen. "Li Zhaoxing Shuo Hu Jintao Zhuxi Dongnanya Sanguozhixingchengguo Fengshuo" [Li said that President Hu Jintao's trip to Southeast Asian countries was fruitful]. *Xinhuawang*, April 28, 2005. http://news.xinhuanet.com/world/2005-04/28/content_2891208.htm

Johnston, Alastair I. *Cultural Realism: Strategic Culture and Grand Strategy in Chinese History*. Princeton: Princeton University Press, 1995.

Johnston, Alastair Iain. "How New and Assertive Is China's New Assertiveness?" *International Security* 37, no. 4 (2013): 7–48.

"Joint Statement between Republic of the Philippines and People's Republic of China Consultations on the South China Sea and on Other Areas of Cooperation." (Code of Conduct between China and the Philippines), signed on August 9–10, 1995.

Jones, Evan. "Steel Hulls and High-Stakes: Prospect Theory and China's Use of Military Force in the South China Sea." In *Power Politics in Asia's Contested Waters: Territorial Disputes in the South China Sea*, edited by Enrico Fels and Truong-Minh Vu. Cham, Switzerland: Springer International, 2016.

Ju, Hailong. "Heping Jiejue Nanhai Wentide Xianshi Sikao" [Realistic thought of peaceful settlement of the South China Sea issue]. *Dongnanya Yanjiu* 5 (2006): 58–61.

Kaplan, Robert. *Asia's Cauldron: The South China Sea and the End of a Stable Pacific*. New York: Random House, 2014.

Kaplan, Robert D. "How We Would Fight China." *The Atlantic*, June 1, 2005.

Kapur, Ashok. *China's Changing Approach to Strategy and Negotiations: Past and Present*. Sapru House Paper. New Delhi: Indian Council of World Affairs, 2013.

Kastner, Scott. "Is the Taiwan Strait Still a Flash Point? Rethinking the Prospects for Armed Conflict between China and Taiwan." *International Security* 40, no. 3 (2016): 54–92.

Kaye, Stuart. "Marine Scientific Research and Military Survey: Law and State Practice." In *UN Convention on the Law of the Sea and the South China Sea*, edited by Shicun Wu, Mark J. Valencia, and Nong Hong. Farnham, UK: Ashgate, 2015.

Keith, Ronald C. "New History Inside Hu Jintao's Foreign Policy: 'Harmony' versus 'Hegemony.'" In *China: A New Stage of Development for an Emerging Superpower*, edited by Joseph Y. S. Cheng. Hong Kong: City University of Hong Kong Press, 2012.

Kemp, John. "East and South China Sea Disputes Need Creative Diplomacy." Reuters, August 26, 2014. http://uk.reuters.com/article/2014/08/26/southchinasea-oil-kemp-idUKL5N0QW40A20140826

Kennedy, Andrew Bingham. *The International Ambitions of Mao and Nehru: National Efficacy Beliefs and the Making of Foreign Policy*. New York: Cambridge University Press, 2012.

Keohane, Robert. "Neoliberal Institutionalism." In *After Hegemony: Cooperation and Discord in the World Political Economy*, edited by Robert Keohane: Princeton: Princeton University Press, 1984.

Kim, Jiye. "Between a Regional Hegemon and a Middle Power: The Case of Nigeria." In *Awkward Powers: Escaping Traditional Great and Middle Power Theory*, edited by Gabriel Abbondanza and Thomas Wilkins, 221–41. Palgrave Macmillan, 2022.

Kim, Jiye. "China's Wars and Strategies: Looking Back at the Korean War and the Sino-Indian War." *Strategic Analysis* 42, no. 2 (2018): 119–33. https://doi.org/10.1080/09700161.2018.1439329

Kim, Jiye. "Disputed Waters, Contested Norms: Framing Discourses on the South China Sea Disputes." *Pacific Affairs* 90, no. 2 (2017): 297–305. https://doi.org/10.5509/2017902297

Kim, Jiye. "Finding the Common Ground with South Korea." In *One Belt One Road: China's Global Outreach*, edited by Srikanth Kondapalli and Xiaowen Hu, 310–22. New Delhi: Pentagon Press, 2017.

Kim, Jiye, and Daniel Druckman. "Shelved Sovereignty or Invalid Sovereignty? The South China Sea Negotiations, 1992–2016." *Pacific Review* 33, no. 1 (2020): 32–60.

Kim, Jiye, and Arpit Raswant. "Australian Perspective on Engaging with South Korea in the Indo-Pacific." *Asian Politics & Policy* 15, no. 1 (2023): 1–15. https://doi.org/https://doi.org/10.1111/aspp.12672

Kim, Jiye, and Arpit Raswant. "Indo-Pacific Powers: Internalization, Interpretation, and Implementation of International Law." *Pacific Review* 36, no. 4 (2022): 871–96. https://doi.org/https://doi.org/10.1080/09512748.2022.2046629

Kim, Jiye, and Arpit Raswant. *International Business and Security: Geostrategy in Perspective*. Cham, Switzerland: Palgrave Macmillan, 2022.

Kim, Jiye, Arpit Raswant, and Thomas Wilkins. "Threat Perception Variation in the Indo-Pacific." *Journal of East Asian Studies* 24, no. 3 (2025): 286–304. https://doi.org/10.1017/jea.2024.16

Ko, S. L. "Chen Shui-Bian Defends His Visit to Taiping Island." *Taipei Times*, February 4, 2008.

Koh, Tommy. "The Exclusive Economic Zone." *Malaya Law Review* 30, no. 1 (1988).

Kondapalli, Srikanth. "Interview with Rajya Sabha TV." Rajya Sabha TV, January 16, 2017.

Kondapalli, Srikanth. "SAARC Summit: China's Role Will Be Keenly Watched by the South Asian Countries." *Economic Times*, November 26, 2014. http://blogs.economictimes.indiatimes.com/et-commentary/saarc-summit-chinas-role-will-be-keenly-watched-by-the-south-asian-countries

Kurlantzick, Joshua. *Charm Offensive: How China's Soft Power Is Transforming the World*. New Haven: Yale University Press, 2007.

Kurlantzick, Joshua. "The South China Sea in China's Developing Maritime Strategy." In *Power Politics in Asia's Contested Waters: Territorial Disputes in the South China Sea*, edited by Enrico Fels and Truong-Minh Vu. Cham, Switzerland: Springer International, 2016.

Lanteigne, Marc. *Chinese Foreign Policy: An Introduction*. Abingdon, UK: Routledge, 2009.

Lanteigne, Marc. "The South China Sea in China's Developing Maritime Strategy." In *Power Politics in Asia's Contested Waters: Territorial Disputes in the South China Sea*, ed. Enrico Fels and Truong-Minh Vu. Cham, Switzerland: Springer International, 2016.

Law of the People's Republic of China on the Territorial Sea and the Contiguous Zone. Order No. 55 of the President, February 25, 1992. http://www.npc.gov.cn/zgrdw/englishnpc/Law/2007-12/12/content_1383846.htm

Lax, David, and James Sebenius. *The Manager as Negotiator: Bargaining for Cooperation and Competitive Gain*. New York: Free Press, 1986.

Lee, H. Y. "Tsai Ing-Wen Backs ROC Sovereignty over Taiping Island." *Focus Taiwan News Channel*, January 29, 2016.

Lee, John. "China's Geostrategic Search for Oil." *Washington Quarterly* 35, no. 3 (2012): 75–92.

Lee, Jong Wha. "China's New World Order." *Project Syndicate*, November 12, 2014. http://www.project-syndicate.org/commentary/china-global-governance-by-lee-jong-wha-2014-11

Lee, Lai To. *China and the South China Sea Dialogues*. Westport, CT: Praeger, 1999.

Lee, Lai To. "China, the USA and the South China Sea Conflicts." *Security Dialogue* 34, no. 1 (2003): 25–39.

Lee, Seokwoo. "Territorial Disputes among Japan, China and Taiwan concerning the Senkaku Islands." *Boundary & Territory Briefing*, International Boundaries Research Unit, 2002.

Levy, Jack S. "Qualitative Methods in International Relations." In *Millennial Reflections on International Studies*, edited by Michael Brecher and Frank P. Harvey. Ann Arbor: University of Michigan Press, 2002.

Li, Haiqing. "Woguo Dongyahai Diqu Haiyang Fazhanzhuanluede Sikao" [Reflections on our strategy for ocean development in East Asian seas]. *Haiyang Fazhan Yu Guanli* [Journal of Maritime Development and Management] 1 (2005).

Li, Jinming. *South China Sea Dispute and International Law of the Sea*. Beijing: Ocean Press, 2003.

Li, Jinming, and Dexia Li. "The Dotted Line on the Chinese Map of the South China Sea: A Note." *Ocean Development & International Law* 34, nos. 3–4 (2003): 287–95.

Li, Nan. "The Evolution of China's Naval Strategy and Capability: From 'Near Coast' and 'Near Seas' to 'Far Seas.'" *Asian Security* 5, no. 2 (2009): 144–69.

Li, Rex. "China's Sea Power Aspirations and Strategic Behaviour in the South China Sea from the Theoretical Perspective of Identity Construction." In *Power Politics in Asia's Contested Waters: Territorial Disputes in the South China Sea*, edited by Enrico Fels and Truong-Minh Vu. Cham, Switzerland: Springer International, 2016.

Li, Yilong, and Ligang Zou. "Gezhi zhengyi, gongtongkaifazhengce zai nanhaiwentishangde jiazhifenxi" [The policy of shelving disputes and seeking joint development in value analysis on the South China Sea issue]. *Legal System and Society* (April 2010).

Lim, Kheng Swe. "China-ASEAN Relations: Hamstrung Soft Power in South China Sea?" *RSIS Commentary*, no. 174 (September 3, 2014).

Lim, Kheng Swe. "China's Nationalist Narrative of the South China Sea: A Preliminary Analysis." In *Power Politics in Asia's Contested Waters: Territorial Disputes in the South China Sea*, edited by Enrico Fels and Truong-Minh Vu. Cham, Switzerland: Springer International, 2016.

Lim, Yves Heng, and Jiye Kim. "Determining the Determinants: Factors of Change in

China's South China Sea Strategy, 1995–2015." *Pacific Focus* 35, no. 2 (2020): 200–228. https://doi.org/https://doi.org/10.1111/pafo.12167

Lin, D. Y. "Foreign Minister's Remarks at an International Press Conference." May 17, 2013.

Lin, Shang. "Wang Yi: Nansha gongtongkaifade yiyi bujin zaiyu jingjiliyi" [Wang Yi: Spratly joint development is not merely about economic interest]. *Beijing Times*, August 4, 2013. http://news.xinhuanet.com/world/2013-08/04/c_125112470.htm

Liu, Huaqing. *Liu Huaqing Huiyilu* [Memoirs of Liu Huaqing]. Beijing: Jiefangjun Chubanshe, 2004.

Lo, Chi-kin. *China's Policy towards Territorial Disputes: The Case of the South China Sea Islands*. Edited by Michael Leifer. London: Routledge, 1989.

Luo, Guoqiang. "Duobian Lujing Zai Jiejue Nanhai Zhengduan Zhong De Zuoyong Jiqi Goujian Jian Ping—Nanhai Gefang Xingwei Xuanyan" [Multilateral approach in the South China Sea dispute settlement: Effects and its constructions—with respect to the Declaration on the Conduct of Parties in the South China Sea]. *Faxue Luntan* 4, no. 25 (2010): 93–99.

Luterbacher, Urs, and Detlef F. Sprinz. *International Relations and Global Climate Change*. Cambridge, MA: MIT Press, 2001.

Ma, Ying-jeou. "Eight Years of Reform Create a Better Taiwan—President's New Year's Day Message." January 1, 2016.

Ma, Ying-jeou. "Soar on the Wings of Partnership—President Ma Ying-Jeou's Remarks at Center for Strategic and International Studies Video Conference." April 9, 2014.

Malik, Mohan. *Maritime Security in the Indo-Pacific: Perspectives from China, India, and the United States*. Lanham, MD: Rowman & Littlefield, 2014.

Mandsager, Dennis. "The U.S. Freedom of Navigation Program: Policy, Procedure, and Future." In *The Law of Military Operations*, edited by Michael N. Schmitt, 113–28. Newport, RI: Naval War College Press, 1998.

Mao, Zedong. *Mao Zedong on Diplomacy*. Beijing: Foreign Languages Press, 1954.

Mao, Zedong. "Opening Address to the Eighth National Congress of the Communist Party of China." Peking: Foreign Languages Press, 1956. http://www.marxists.org/subject/china/documents/cpc/8th_cong_opening.htm

Mearsheimer, John J. *The Tragedy of Great Power Politics*. New York: Norton, 2001.

Medcalf, Rory. "China's Premature Power Play Goes Very Wrong." *National Interest*, June 3, 2014. http://nationalinterest.org/feature/chinas-premature-power-play-goes-very-wrong-10587

Medcalf, Rory. *Indo-Pacific Empire: China, America and the Contest for the World's Pivotal Region*. Manchester: Manchester University Press, 2020.

Medeiros, Evan S., and Taylor M. Fravel. "China's New Diplomacy." *Foreign Affairs* 82 (2009).

Ministry of Foreign Affairs, Japan. *Diplomatic Bluebook 2023*. 2023.

Ministry of Foreign Affairs, People's Republic of China. *China's Foreign Affairs*. Department of Policy Planning. Beijing: World Affairs Press, 2007.

Ministry of Foreign Affairs, People's Republic of China. *China's Foreign Affairs*. Department of Policy Planning. Beijing: World Affairs Press, 2008.

Ministry of Foreign Affairs, People's Republic of China. *China's Foreign Affairs*. Department of Policy Planning. Beijing: World Affairs Press, 2009.

Ministry of Foreign Affairs, People's Republic of China. *China's Foreign Affairs*. Department of Policy Planning. Beijing: World Affairs Press, 2010.

Ministry of Foreign Affairs, People's Republic of China. *China's Foreign Affairs*. Department of Policy Planning. Beijing: World Affairs Press, 2014.

Ministry of Foreign Affairs, People's Republic of China. "China's Indisputable Sovereignty over the Xisha and Nansha Islands." January 30, 1980. Full text published in *Beijing Review*, no. 7 (February 18, 1980): 15–24.

Ministry of Foreign Affairs, People's Republic of China. "China's Initiation of the Five Principles of Peaceful Co-Existence." Established in 1954. See https://www.mfa.gov.cn/eng/zy/wjls/3604_665547/202405/t20240531_11367542.html

Ministry of Foreign Affairs, People's Republic of China. "Chinese President Hu Jintao Holds Talks with Vietnamese President Tran Duc Luong." July 19, 2005.

Ministry of Foreign Affairs, People's Republic of China. "Foreign Ministry Spokesperson Hong Lei's Remarks on ASEAN Foreign Ministers' Statement on the Six-Point Principles on the South China Sea Issue." July 21, 2012. http://www.fmprc.gov.cn/ce/cedk/eng/fyrth/t955114.htm

Ministry of Foreign Affairs, People's Republic of China. "Foreign Ministry Spokesperson Hua Chunying's Regular Press Conference." April 28, 2013. http://www.fmprc.gov.cn/eng/xwfw/s2510/2511/t1035948.shtml

Ministry of Foreign Affairs, People's Republic of China. "Foreign Minister Yang Jiechi on the South China Sea Issue." July 13, 2012. http://ph.china-embassy.gov.cn/eng/xwdt/201207/t20120713_1157331.htm

Ministry of Foreign Affairs, People's Republic of China. "Hu Jintao Holds Talks with Nong Duc Manh." May 30, 2008. http://lt.china-office.gov.cn/eng/xwdt/200806/t20080603_2690582.htm

Ministry of Foreign Affairs, People's Republic of China. "Position Paper: China Adheres to the Position of Settling through Negotiation the Relevant Disputes between China and the Philippines in the South China Sea." July 13, 2016. https://www.fmprc.gov.cn/nanhai/eng/snhwtlcwj_1/201607/t20160713_8527301.htm

Ministry of Foreign Affairs, People's Republic of China. "President Hu Jintao Meets with His Vietnamese Counterpart Tran Duc Luong." November 20, 2004. http://www.fmprc.gov.cn/mfa_eng/topics_665678/huvisit_665888/t171290.shtml

Ministry of Foreign Affairs, People's Republic of China. "President Xi Jinping Holds Talks with President Truong Tan Sang of Vietnam, Stressing China and Vietnam Should Unswervingly March along Path of Friendly Cooperation." June 19, 2013. http://www.fmprc.gov.cn/ce/cena/eng/zgxw/t1052303.htm

Ministry of Foreign Affairs, People's Republic of China. "President Xi Jinping Vows to Consolidate and Develop Inter-Party and Inter-Governmental Ties with Vietnam for the Benefit of Both Peoples during Phone Talks with General Secretary of the CPV Central Committee Nguyen Phu Trong." March 21, 2013. http://www.fmprc.gov.cn/mfa_eng/wjb_663304/zzjg_663340/yzs_663350/gjlb_663354/2792_663578/2794_663582/t1024384.shtml

Ministry of Foreign Affairs, People's Republic of China. "Statement by Spokesperson Qin Gang of the Ministry of Foreign Affairs of China on the US State Department Issuing a So-Called Press Statement on the South China Sea." August 4, 2012. http://www.fmprc.gov.cn/eng/xwfw/s2510/t958226.htm

Ministry of Foreign Affairs, People's Republic of China. "Vice President Xi Jinping Meets with Vietnamese Army Chief." April 13, 2012. http://www.fmprc.gov.cn/mfa_eng/wjb_663304/zzjg_663340/yzs_663350/gjlb_663354/2792_663578/2794_663582/t923082.shtml

Ministry of Foreign Affairs, People's Republic of China. "Vice President Xi Jinping Meets with Vietnamese President Truong Tan Sang." December 22, 2011. http://www.fmprc.gov.cn/mfa_eng/wjb_663304/zzjg_663340/yzs_663350/gjlb_663354/2792_663578/2794_663582/t889949.shtml

Ministry of Foreign Affairs, People's Republic of China. "Waijiabu Buzhangyang Jiechi Jiu Zhongguo Waijiao Zhengce He Duiwaiguanxi Da Zhongwai Jizhe Wen" [Q&A: Foreign Minister Yang Jiechi with domestic/international reporters on China's foreign policy and foreign relations]. March 8, 2012. http://www.fmprc.gov.cn/ce/ceph/chn/zgxw/t914106.htm

Ministry of Foreign Affairs, People's Republic of China. "Wang Yi Attends the ASEAN-China Ministerial Meeting." August 3, 2021. https://www.fmprc.gov.cn/mfa_eng/zxxx_662805/t1897344.shtml

Ministry of Foreign Affairs, People's Republic of China. "Wang Yi Expounds on China's Position on Situation of South China Sea." February 14, 2014. http://www.fmprc.gov.cn/mfa_eng/wjb_663304/wjbz_663308/activities_663312/t1129921.shtml

Ministry of Foreign Affairs, People's Republic of China. "Wang Yi Met with Vietnamese Deputy Prime Minister and Foreign Minister Pham Binh Minh." August 9, 2014. http://www.fmprc.gov.cn/mfa_eng/zxxx_662805/t1181545.shtml

Ministry of Foreign Affairs, People's Republic of China. "Wang Yi Stresses 'Four Respects' on South China Sea Issue." August 5, 2021. https://www.fmprc.gov.cn/mfa_eng/zxxx_662805/t1897526.shtml

Ministry of Foreign Affairs, People's Republic of China. *Zhou Enlai Waijiao Wenxuan* [Selected diplomatic documents of Zhou Enlai]. Beijing: Zhongyang Wenxian Chubanshe, 1990.

Ministry of Foreign Affairs, Republic of China. "The Government of the Republic of China Lodges Its Protest against the Recent Illegal Occupation of Investigator Shoal and Erica Reef in the Nansha Islands by the Malaysian Government." July 13, 1999.

Ministry of Foreign Affairs, Republic of China. "The Ministry of Foreign Affairs of the Republic of China (Taiwan) Reiterates Its Absolute Sovereignty over Taiping Island." May 12, 2012.

Ministry of Foreign Affairs, Republic of China. "The Ministry of Foreign Affairs of the Republic of China Solemnly Declares Statement on the Governments of Malaysia and Vietnam Filed a Joint Submission to the Commission on the Limits of the Continental Shelf of the United Nations, Extending the Outer Limits of Their Respective Continental Shelf 200 Nautical Miles beyond Their Shorelines." May 11, 2009.

Ministry of Foreign Affairs, Republic of China. "Nanhai Zhudao Zhi Zhuquan Shengming Ji Toushu" [Statements and letters on the sovereignty over the South China Sea islands]. March 23, 2016.

Ministry of Foreign Affairs, Republic of China. "Philippine Warship, Chinese Vessels in Standoff over Fishermen at South China Sea." April 11, 2012.

Ministry of Foreign Affairs, Republic of China. "President Ma Proposes the East China Sea Peace Initiative, Calls on All Parties Concerned to Resolve Diaoyutai Dispute Peacefully." August 5, 2012.

Ministry of Foreign Affairs, Republic of China. "Press Release: President Ma Addresses Members of News Media on Their Return from Taiping Island." March 23, 2016.

Ministry of Foreign Affairs, Republic of China. "Remarks by President Ma Ying-Jeou on Taiping Island." January 28, 2016.

Ministry of Foreign Affairs, Republic of China. "The Republic of China (Taiwan) Protests Vietnam Law Claiming South China Sea Islands." January 7, 2013.

Ministry of Foreign Affairs, Republic of China. "The Republic of China (Taiwan) Reiterates Its Position on the South China Sea." April 11, 2012.

Ministry of Foreign Affairs, Republic of China. "ROC Government Reiterates Its Position on South China Sea Issues." October 31, 2015.

Ministry of Foreign Affairs, Republic of China. "Solemn Declaration of the Ministry of Foreign Affairs of the Republic of China Concerning the Philippine Senate Bill 2699 and House Bill 3216." February 6, 2009.

Ministry of Foreign Affairs, Republic of China. "Statement of the Ministry of Foreign Affairs Concerning the Declaration on the Conduct of Parties in the South China Sea Signed by the Association of Southeast Asian Nations (ASEAN) and the People's Republic of China (PRC) in Cambodia on November 4, 2002." November 5, 2002.

Ministry of Foreign Affairs, Republic of China. "Statement on the South China Sea." July 7, 2015.

Ministry of Foreign Affairs, Republic of China. "Taiping Island Is an Island, Not a Rock, and the ROC Possesses Full Rights Associated with an Exclusive Economic Zone and Continental Shelf in Accordance with UNCLOS." January 23, 2016.

Ministry of Foreign Affairs, Republic of China. "The Taiwan-Japan Fisheries Agreement—Embodying the Ideals and Spirit of the East China Sea Peace Initiative." Catalogue Card No.: Mofa-En-Fo-102–006-I-1. August 2013.

Ministry of Foreign Affairs, Republic of China. "Waijiaobu Linian Lai Jiu Nanhai Zhengyiwenti Zhi Shengming Yilanbiao" [Collection of the ministry's statements over the years on the problem of the South China Sea dispute]. August 11, 2011.

Ministry of Foreign Affairs, Vietnam. "Agreement on the Basic Principles Guiding the Settlement of Sea-Related Matters between the Socialist Republic of Viet Nam and the People's Republic of China." October 11, 2011. https://vietnamembassy-usa.org/news/2011/10/vn-china-basic-principles-settlement-sea-issues

Mitchell, Audra. "Outer Space." In *Security Studies: An Introduction*, edited by Paul D. Williams and Matt McDonald, 569–81. London: Routledge, 2018.

Morgenthau, Hans J. *Politics among Nations: The Struggle for Power and Peace*. New York: Knopf, 1961.

Nathan, Andrew J., and Andrew Scobell. *China's Search for Security*. New York: Columbia University Press, 2012.

Ng, Teddy. "Deng Xiaoping's Guiding Principles Are Still in Play Today." *South China Morning Post*, August 22, 2014. http://www.scmp.com/print/news/china/article/1578761/deng-xiaopings-guiding-principles-are-still-play-today

Nguyen, Huu Tuc. "Vietnam's Position on South China Sea." *RSIS Commentary*, no. 170 (August 27, 2014).

Nihon Keizai Shinbun. "Japanese Economic Daily." *Nihon Keizai Shinbun*, August 3, 1976.

Noguchi, K. "Bringing Realism Back In: Explaining China's Strategic Behaviour in the Asia-Pacific." *Asia-Pacific Review* 18, no. 2 (2011): 60–85.

Nye, Joseph S. "Avoiding Conflict in the South China Sea." *Project Syndicate*, June 3, 2015. http://www.project-syndicate.org/commentary/south-china-sea-conflict-by-joseph-s--nye-2015-06

Nye, Joseph S. *Soft Power: The Means to Success in World Politics*. New York: Public Affairs, 2004.

Nye, Joseph S., and David Welch. *Understanding Global Conflict and Cooperation: An Introduction to Theory and History*. 10th ed. London: Pearson, 2017.

Oil & Gas Journal. "CNOOC Starts Up Oil Field in Pearl River Mouth Basin." *Oil & Gas Journal*, August 25, 2014. http://www.ogj.com/articles/2014/08/cnooc-starts-up-oil-field-in-pearl-river-mouth-basin.html

Pan, Junwu. *Toward a New Framework for Peaceful Settlement of China's Territorial and Boundary Disputes*. Leiden: Martinus Nijhoff, 2009.

Park, Chang Hee. "China and the South China Sea." A conference paper presented at the Northeast Future Forum, Seoul, April 30, 2014.

Park, Chang Hee. "China's Policy on the Border Disputes." Paper presented at the 13th Future Northeast Forum, Seoul, April 30, 2014.

Park, Choon-ho. "The South China Sea Disputes: Who Owns the Islands and the Natural Resources?" *Ocean Development & International Law* 5, no. 1 (1978): 27–59.

People's Daily. "Hu Jintao Meets Vietnamese President." *People's Daily*, April 20, 2001. http://en.people.cn/english/200104/19/eng20010419_68128.html

People's Daily. "Two China-Vietnam Beibu Gulf Agreements Take Effect." *People's Daily Online*, July 1, 2004.

Permanent Court of Arbitration. "Award on Jurisdiction and Admissibility: In the Matter of an Arbitration before an Artibral Tribunal Constituted under Annex VII to the 1982 United Nations Convention on the Law of the Sea between the Republic of the Philippines and the People's Republic of China." October 29, 2015.

Permanent Court of Arbitration. "Press Release: Arbitration between the Republic of the Philippines and the People's Republic of China." October 29, 2015. http://www.pcacases.com/web/sendAttach/1524

Permanent Mission of the People's Republic of China. "Notes Verbales Cml/17/2009 and Cml/18/2009." May 7, 2009. http://www.un.org/Depts/los/clcs_new/submissions_files/mysvnm33_09/chn_2009re_mys_vnm_e.pdf

Poling, Gregory. "The South China Sea in Focus: Clarifying the Limits of Maritime Dispute." A Report of the CSIS Sumitro Chair for Southeast Asian Studies, Center for Strategic and International Studies, 2014.

Pompeo, Michael R. "U.S. Position on Maritime Claims in the South China Sea." July 13, 2020, https://2017-2021.state.gov/u-s-position-on-maritime-claims-in-the-south-china-sea/index.html

Popovski, Vesselin. "UNCLOS and the Peaceful Use of the Sea." In *UN Convention on the Law of the Sea and the South China Sea*, edited by Shicun Wu, Mark J. Valencia, and Nong Hong, xvi. Farnham, UK: Ashgate, 2015.

Public Diplomacy Coordination Council. "Taiwan and the Philippines Sign Agreement on Law Enforcement Cooperation in Fisheries Matters." November 19, 2015.

Pye, Lucian W. "China: Erratic State, Frustrated Society." *Foreign Affairs* 68, no. 4 (1990).

Pye, Lucian W. *The Dynamics of Chinese Politics*. Cambridge, MA: Oelgeschlager, Gunn & Hain, 1981.

Qi, Huaigao. "Joint Development in the South China Sea: China's Incentives and Policy Choices." *Journal of Contemporary East Asia Studies* 8, no. 2 (2019): 220–39. https://doi.org/https://doi.org/10.1080/24761028.2019.1685427

Qin, Yaqing. "Continuity through Change: Background Knowledge and China's International Strategy." *Chinese Journal of International Politics* 7, no. 3 (2014): 285–314.

Qin, Yaqing. "Development of International Relations Theory in China: Progress through Debates." *International Relations of the Asia-Pacific* 11, no. 2 (2011): 231–57.

Qin, Yaqing. "Relationality and Processual Construction: Bringing Chinese Ideas into International Relations Theory." *Social Sciences in China* 30, no. 4 (2009): 5–20.

Qin, Yaqing. "Zhongguo Guoji Guanxi Lilun" [Chinese theory of International Relations]. In *Zhongguo Duiwai Guanxi Zhuanxing 30 Nian* [Thirty years of transformation in Chinese foreign relations], edited by Yizhou Wang. Beijing: Shehui Kexue Wenxian Chubanshe, 2008.

Qiushi Journal. "About Qiushi Journal." http://en.qstheory.cn/2020-06/16/c_461019.htm

Raswant, Arpit, Jiye Kim, and Tim Mahlberg. "Space Is Going Commercial in Asia, but There's a Rocky Road Ahead." *The Diplomat*, January 20, 2023.

Republic of China. "Position Paper on ROC South China Sea Policy." March 21, 2016.

Republic of China. "South China Sea Peace Initiative." May 26, 2015.

Roberts, Christopher B. "ASEAN: The Challenge of Unity in Diversity." In *The South China Sea Maritime Dispute: Political, Legal, and Regional Perspectives*, edited by Leszek Buszynski and Christopher B. Roberts. Abingdon, UK: Routledge, 2015.

Ru, Y., and Y. Gong. "Dongya chaogong tixi de wenhua neihan—yu xifang zhimin tixi de bijiao" [Cultural connotation of the tributary system of East Asia—A comparison with the western colonial system]. *Journal of Binzhou University (Binzhou xueyuan xuebao)* 25, no. 2 (2009): 51–56.

Ruan, Zongze. "Hexie Shijie Yinling Zhongguo Waijiao Xinshidai" [Harmonious world is leading a new era in Chinese diplomacy]. *Liaowang*, January 9, 2006.

Ruwitch, John. "Satellites and Seafood: China Keeps Fishing Fleet Connected in Disputed Waters." Reuters, July 27, 2014. http://www.reuters.com/article/2014/07/27/us-southchinasea-china-fishing-insight-idUSKBN0FW0QP20140727

Sakaki, Alexandra. "Keeping the Dragon at Bay: The South China Sea Dispute in Japan's Security Strategy." In *Power Politics in Asia's Contested Waters: Territorial Disputes in the South China Sea*, edited by Enrico Fels and Truong-Minh Vu. Cham, Switzerland: Springer International, 2016.

Sakhuja, Vijay, and Institute of Southeast Asian Studies. *Asian Maritime Power in the 21st Century: Strategic Transactions; China, India, and Southeast Asia*. Singapore: Institute of Southeast Asian Studies, 2011.

Samuels, Marwyn S. *Contest for the South China Sea*. New York: Methuen, 1982.

Schelling, Thomas C. *The Strategy of Conflict*. Cambridge: Harvard University Press, 1960.

Schofield, Clive H. "Trouble over the Starting Line: State Practice concerning Baselines in the South China Sea." In *UN Convention on the Law of the Sea and the South China Sea*, edited by Shicun Wu, Mark J. Valencia, and Nong Hong. Farnham, UK: Ashgate, 2015.

Scott, David. *The Chinese Century? The Challenge to Global Order*. Basingstoke, UK: Palgrave Macmillan, 2008.

Secretary of State for Transport of the United Kingdom. "National Strategy for Maritime Security." 2022.

Severino, Rodolfo, and Institute of Southeast Asian Studies. *Southeast Asia in Search of an ASEAN Community: Insights from the Former ASEAN Secretary-General*. Singapore: Institute of Southeast Asian Studies, 2006.

Shambaugh, David L. *China Goes Global: The Partial Power*. Oxford: Oxford University Press, 2013.

Sheridan, Greg. "Bishop-Plibersek Debate: Bipartisan Line on South China Sea." *The Australian*, June 23, 2016.

Simon, Sheldon W. "ASEAN Regional Forum." In *Asian Security Handbook: An Assessment of Political-Security Issues in the Asia-Pacific Region*, edited by William M. Carpenter and David G. Wiencek. New York: M. E. Sharpe, 1996.

Simon, Sheldon W. "Evaluating Track II Approaches to Security Diplomacy in the Asia-Pacific: The CSCAP Experience." *Pacific Review* 15, no. 2 (2002): 167–200.

Sitaraman, Srini. "Rising Chinese Power and Territorial Assertiveness in the South China Sea: India-Vietnam Strategic Partnership as a Counterbalancing Endeavor." In *Power Politics in Asia's Contested Waters: Territorial Disputes in the South China Sea*, edited by Enrico Fels and Truong-Minh Vu. Cham, Switzerland: Springer International, 2016.

Snyder, Scott, Brad Glosserman, and Ralph A. Cossa. "Confidence Building Measures in the South China Sea." *Issues & Insights*, no. 2–01. Honolulu: Pacific Forum, Center for Strategic and International Studies, 2001. https://csis-website-prod.s3.amazonaws.com/s3fs-public/legacy_files/files/publication/issuesinsightsv01n02.pdf

Song, Yann-huei. "Conflicting Outer Continental Shelf Claims in the East and South China Seas: Proposals for Cooperation and Peaceful Resolution." *University of Hawai'i Law Review* 35 (2013): 484–538.

Song, Yann-huei. *Managing Potential Conflicts in the South China Sea: Taiwan's Perspectives*. Singapore: Singapore University Press, 1999.

Song, Yann-huei, and Keyuan Zou, eds. *Major Law and Policy Issues in the South China Sea: European and American Perspectives*. Surrey, UK: Ashgate, 2014.

South China Sea Strategic Situation Probing Initiative. "US Reconnaissance Aircraft Operating over the South China Sea, July 2020." August 4, 2020.

South China Sea Strategic Situation Probing Initiative. "US Reconnaissance Aircraft Operating over the South China Sea amid the PLA's Paracel Training." August 4, 2020.

Storey, Ian, and Carlyle A. Thayer. "The South China Sea Dispute: A Review of Developments and Their Implications since the 2002 Declaration on the Conduct of Parties." In *South and Southeast Asia: Responding to Changing Geo-Political and Security Challenges*, edited by K. V. Kesavan and Daljit Singh, 57–72. Singapore: Institute of Southeast Asian Studies, 2010.

Strauss, Julia C. "The Past in the Present: Historical and Rhetorical Lineages in China's Relations with Africa." *China Quarterly* 199 (2009): 777–95.

Survey and Mapping Law of the People's Republic of China. Presidential Order No. 75, August 29, 2002. http://www.china.org.cn/china/LegislationsForm2001-2010/2011-02/14/content_21916711.htm

Swaine, Michael D. "China's Assertive Behavior: On 'Core Interests.'" *China Leadership Monitor* 34 (2011).

Swaine, Michael D. "Understanding the Historical Record." In *Managing Sino-American Crises: Case Studies and Analysis*, edited by Michael D. Swaine, Tuosheng Zhang, and Danielle F. S. Cohen. Washington, DC: Carnegie Endowment for International Peace, 2006.

Taipei Times. "Minister Leads Group at Opening Rites for Itu Aba Facilities." December 13, 2015.

Tan, Ab. "Manila Annexes Much of Disputed Spratly Islands." *Washington Post*, September 7, 1979.

Tang, Jiaxuan. *Heavy Storm and Gentle Breeze*. Beijing: Foreign Languages Press, 2011.

Tang, Jiaxuan. "Speech by Foreign Minister Tang Jiaxuan at the ASEAN-China Dialogue (August 1, Bandar Seri Begawan)." 2002.

Tang, Jiaxuan. "Speech by Chinese Foreign Minister Tang Jiaxuan at the Meeting of China-ASEAN Dialogue." Ministry of Foreign Affairs, People's Republic of China, July 26, 2001. http://www.fmprc.gov.cn/ce/cegv/eng/ljzg/zgwjzc/t85864.htm

Taylor, Brendon. "The South China Sea as a 'Crisis'." In *The South China Sea Maritime Dispute: Political, Legal, and Regional Perspectives*, edited by Leszek Buszynski and Christopher B. Roberts. New York: Routledge, 2015.

Technavio. *Global Sonobuoy Market 2016–2020 (WGR390273. 7 April)*. 2016. Accessed April 9, 2016. ttps://www.wiseguyreports.com/reports/global-sonobuoy-market-2016-2020

Tharoor, Shashi. "China's Silk Road Revival." *Project Syndicate*, October 14, 2014. http://www.project-syndicate.org/commentary/china-silk-road-economic-belt-goals-by-shashi-tharoor-2014-10

Thayer, Carlyle A. "China's New Wave of Aggressive Assertiveness in the South China Sea." *International Journal of China Studies* 2, no. 3 (2011).

Thucydides. *The Peloponnesian War*. Translated by Martin Hammond. Oxford: Oxford University Press, 2009.

Times of India. "ASEAN Leaves Last Word on Sea Disputes Draft to China." *Times of India*, November 26, 1999, 14.

Torode, Greg. "Insight—Vietnam Building Deterrent against China in Disputed Seas with Submarines." Reuters (Hong Kong), September 7, 2014. http://uk.reuters.com/article/2014/09/07/uk-vietnam-submarines-china-insight-idUKKBN0H20T720140907

Townsend-Gault, I. "Preventive Diplomacy and Pro-Activity in the South China Sea."

Contemporary Southeast Asia: A Journal of International and Strategic Affairs 20, no. 2 (1998): 171–90.

UN Division for Ocean Affairs and the Law of the Sea. "United Nations Convention on the Law of the Sea: Declarations Made upon Signature, Ratification, Accession or Succession or Anytime Thereafter." 1996. Upon ratification, Oceans & Law of the Sea, United Nations. http://www.un.org/depts/los/convention_agreements/convention_declarations.htm#China

UN Division for Ocean Affairs and the Law of the Sea. "United Nations Convention on the Law of the Sea: Declarations Made upon Signature, Ratification, Accession or Succession or Anytime Thereafter." 2006. Upon ratification, Oceans & Law of the Sea, United Nations. http://www.un.org/depts/los/convention_agreements/convention_declarations.htm#China

United Nations Convention on the Law of the Sea. *United Nations Convention on the Law of the Sea (Concluded on 10 December 1982. Came into Force in 1994)*. 1982.

US Army, Training and Doctrine Command (TRADOC). *The U.S. Army Operating Concept: Win in a Complex World 2020–2040*. October 7, 2014.

US Department of Defense. *Defense Space Strategy Summary*. Washington, DC: US Department of Defense, 2020.

US Department of Defense. *Indo-Pacific Strategy Report: Preparedness, Partnerships, and Promoting a Networked Region*. Washington, DC: Department of Defense, June 1, 2019.

US Department of Defense. *Summary of the 2018 National Defense Strategy of the United States of America: Sharpening the American Military's Competitive Edge*. Washington, DC, 2018.

US Department of Defense, Office of the Secretary. *Annual Report to Congress: Military and Security Developments Involving the People's Republic of China 2014*. Washington, DC: US Department of Defense, April 24, 2014.

US Department of State. "Daily Press Briefing." Briefer: Christine Shelly (May 10, 1995).

US Department of State. *Fact Sheet: U.S. Relations with the Philippines*. Bureau of East Asian and Pacific Affairs. November 13, 2015. http://www.state.gov/r/pa/ei/bgn/2794.htm

US Department of State. *Limits in the Seas—China: Maritime Claims in the South China Sea*. Bureau of Oceans and International Environmental and Scientific Affairs, 2014.

US Department of State. "Press Statement: On the Situation in the South China Sea." November 19, 2021. https://2021-2025.state.gov/on-the-situation-in-the-south-china-sea/

US Department of State, Office of the Geographer. South China Sea, Map and Gazetteer, US Government, 803425AI (G02257) 1–10. January 2010. Available at https://cil.nus.edu.sg/research/ocean-law-policy/south-china-sea/maps/

US Energy Information Administration. "China." Last updated February 4, 2014. http://www.eia.gov/countries/analysisbriefs/China/china.pdf

US Geological Survey. *World Petroleum Resources Assessment Project: Assessment of Undiscovered Oil and Gas Resources of Southeast Asia, 2010, Fact Sheet 2010–3015*. June 2010.

Valero, Gerardo. "Spratly Archipelago Dispute: Is the Question of Sovereignty Still Relevant?" *Marine Policy* 18, no. 4 (1994): 314–44.

Varrall, Merriden. *Chinese Worldviews and China's Foreign Policy*. Sydney: Lowy Institute, 2015.

Wain, Barry. "Manila's Bungle in the South China Sea." *Far Eastern Economic Review*, January 2008.

Waldron, A. "Chinese Strategy from the Fourteenth to the Seventeenth Centuries." In *The Making of Strategy: Rulers, States, and War*, edited by Williamson Murray, MacGregor Knox, and Alvin H. Bernstein. Cambridge: Cambridge University Press, 1994.

Waltz, Kenneth. *Theory of International Politics*. Reading, MA: Addison-Wesley, 1979.

Wang, Gungwu. "The Nanhai Trade: A Study of the Early History of Chinese Trade in the South China Sea." *Journal of the Malayan Branch of the Royal Asiatic Society* 31, no. 2 (182) (1958): 3–135.

Wang, Gungwu. *To Act Is to Know: Chinese Dilemmas*. Singapore: Eastern Universities Press, 2003.

Wang, J. "Daiguo Weihu Haishanf Jiaotong Anqun Chutan" [A preliminary study of approaches to safeguarding sea-lanes of communication by big powers]. *China Military Science* 2, no. 110 (2010).

Wang, Jianwei. "China's Multilateral Diplomacy in the New Millennium." In *China Rising: Power and Motivation in Chinese Foreign Policy*, edited by Yong Deng and Feiling Wang. Lanham, MD: Rowman & Littlefield, 2005.

Wang, Kaihao. "Into the Deep for Relics." *China Daily USA*, September 16, 2014, 8.

Wang, Xiaodong, Shaojun Song, Jilao Huang, and Qiang Song, eds. *Zhongguo Bu Gaoxing* [China is not happy]. Jiangsu: Phoenix Publishing, 2009.

Wang, Yi. "Foreign Minister Wang Yi: Build an Even Closer China-ASEAN Community of Common Destiny." Ministry of Foreign Affairs, People's Republic of China, August 9, 2014. http://www.fmprc.gov.cn/mfa_eng/zxxx_662805/t1181521.shtml

Wang, Yi. "Wang Yi Talks about China's Four-Point Consensus on South China Sea Issue with Brunei, Cambodia and Laos." Ministry of Foreign Affairs, People's Republic of China, April 23, 2016. http://www.fmprc.gov.cn/mfa_eng/zxxx_662805/t1358478.shtml

Wang, Yizhou. Introduction to *Transformation of Foreign Affairs and International Relations in China, 1978–2008*, edited by Yizhou Wang, 1–36. Leiden: Brill, 2011.

Wang, Zaiqian. "Wu Shicun: Nanhaiwenti Bushi Zhongguoyu Dongmengjiande Wenti" [Wu Shicun: The South China Sea dispute is not a problem between China and ASEAN]. *Zhongguo Xinwenwang*, May 20, 2014. https://www.nanhai.org.cn/review_c/19.html

Weingart, Laurie R., and Mara Olekalns. "Communication Processes in Negotiation: Frequencies, Sequences, and Phases." In *The Handbook of Negotiation and Culture*, edited by Michele J. Gelfand and Jeanne M. Brett, 143–57. Stanford, CA: Stanford Business Books, 2004.

Wendt, Alexander E. "The Agent–Structure Problem in International Relations Theory." *International Organisation* 41, no. 3 (1987): 335–70.

Wendt, Alexander E. *Social Theory of International Politics*. Cambridge: Cambridge University Press, 1999.

White House. *National Security Strategy*. Washington, DC, 2022.

Wilkins, Thomas, and Jiye Kim. "Adoption, Accommodation or Opposition?—Regional Powers Respond to American-Led Indo-Pacific Strategy." *The Pacific Review* 35, no. 3 (2022): 415–45. https://doi.org/ https://doi.org/10.1080/09512748.2020.1825516

Wu, Guoxiu. "Chinese Scholars Say South China Sea Dispute Negatively Impacts Maritime Security." *CCTV America*, August 23, 2014. http://www.cctv-america.com/2014/08/23/chinese-scholars-speak-about-the-china-philippines-dispute

Wu, Shicun. *Solving Disputes for Regional Cooperation and Development in the South China Sea: A Chinese Perspective*. Hull, UK: Chandos, 2013.

Wu, Shicun, and Huaifeng Ren. "More Than a Declaration: A Commentary on the Background and the Significance of the Declaration on the Conduct of the Parties in the South China Sea." *Chinese Journal of International Law* 2, no. 1 (2003): 311–19.

Wu, Shicun, Mark J. Valencia, and Nong Hong. "The South China Sea: UNCLOS and State Practice." In *UN Convention on the Law of the Sea and the South China Sea*, edited by Shicun Wu, Mark J. Valencia, and Nong Hong. Farnham, UK: Ashgate, 2015.

Wu, Shicun, Mark J. Valencia, and Nong Hong. *UN Convention on the Law of the Sea and the South China Sea*. Farnham, UK: Ashgate, 2015.

Wu, Shicun, and Keyuan Zou. "Maritime Security in the South China Sea: Cooperation and Implications." In *Maritime Security in the South China Sea: Regional Implications and International Cooperation*, edited by Shicun Wu and Keyuan Zou. Farnham, UK: Ashgate, 2009.

Xi Jinping. "New Asian Security Concept for New Progress in Security Cooperation (Remarks at the Fourth Summit of the Conference on Interaction and Confidence Building Measures in Asia, Shanghai)." May 21, 2014.

Xi Jinping. "President Xi Jinping Holds Talks with President Truong Tan Sang of Vietnam, Stressing China and Vietnam Should Unswervingly March along Path of Friendly Cooperation." September 15, 2015. http://www.fmprc.gov.cn/ce/cena/eng/zgxw/t1052303.htm

Xi Jinping. "Speech by Chinese President Xi Jinping to Indonesian Parliament." October 2, 2013. http://www.asean-china-center.org/english/2013-10/03/c_133062675.htm

Xi Jinping. "Work Together to Build the Silk Road Economic Belt." September 7, 2013. Speech delivered at Nazarbayev University, Astana, Kazakhstan. Reprinted in *Governance of China*. Foreign Languages Press, 2014.

Xinhua. "21 Asian Countries Sign MOU on Establishing Asian Infrastructure Investment Bank." *Xinhuanet*, October 24, 2014. http://english.peopledaily.com.cn/business/n/2014/1024/c90778-8799681.html

Xinhua. "China, Vietnam to Promote Closer Friendly, Cooperative Ties." Xinhua, March 21, 2006. http://news.xinhuanet.com/english/2006-03/22/content_4328698.htm

Xinhua. "China's Defence Minister Urges Not to Play Up South China Sea Issues." *Xinhuanet*, November 4, 2015.

Xinhua. "CNOOC to Kick Off Bidding for Untapped Oil and Gas Resources in South China Sea." Xinhua, March 7, 2007.

Xinhua. "Modernizing Navy for Self-Defense." *Xinhuanet*, July 13, 2010. http://news.xinhuanet.com/english2010/indepth/2010-07/13/c_13397060.htm

Xinhua. "Xi Eyes More Enabling Int'l Environment for China's Peaceful Development." Xinhua, November 30, 2014. http://news.xinhuanet.com/english/china/2014-11/30/c_133822694_2.htm

Xiong, Tao. "Nanhai Gefang Xingwei Xuanyande Qiyuan, Kunjing Yu Chulu" [The Declaration on the Conduct of Parties in the South China Sea: Origin, plight, future]. Master's thesis, Jinan University, 2012.

Xu, Ke. "Anti-Piracy Cooperation Dilemma: ASEAN and China." In *China-ASEAN Relations: Economic and Legal Dimensions*, edited by John Wong, Keyuan Zou, and Huaqun Zeng. Hackensack, NJ: World Scientific, 2006.

Xuanzun, Liu, and Guo Yuandan. "Interview with South China Sea Think Tank Head Shows Three Possibilities Risking China-US Military Conflict." *Global Times*, August 2, 2020. https://www.globaltimes.cn/content/1196426.shtml

Xue, Guifang. "Deep Danger: Intensified Competition in the South China Sea and Implications for China." In *Maritime Security Issues in the South China Sea and the Arctic: Sharpened Competition or Collaboration?*, edited by Gordon Houlden and Nong Hong, xv. Beijing: China Democracy and Legal System Publishing House, 2012.

Xue, Li. "How China Views the South China Sea Arbitration Case." *The Diplomat*, July 14, 2015.

Xue, Li, and Huanrong Xiao. "Zhongguo De Jiangou Zhuyi Guojiguanxi Yanjiu (1998–2004): Chengjiu Yu Buzu" [Research on constructivist international relations theory in China]. *Shijie Jingji yu Zhengzhi* 8 (2006).

Yahuda, Michael. "China's New Assertiveness in the South China Sea." *Journal of Contemporary China* 22, no. 81 (2013): 446–59.

Yan, Meng, and Jun Liang. "Maneuver 5 Exercise Enters Stage of Actual-Troop Confrontation." People's Daily Online and China Military Online, October 29, 2013. http://english.peopledaily.com.cn/90786/8439923.html

Yan, Xuetong. *Analysis of China's National Interests*. Translated by the East Asia Nonproliferation Program, James Martin Center for Nonproliferation Studies, Monterey Institute of International Studies, 2002.

Yan, Xuetong. *Lishide Guanxing: Weilai Shiniande Zhongguo Yu Shijie* [Inertia of history: China and the world in the next years]. Beijing: Zhongxin Chubanshe, 2013.

Yan, Xuetong, Daniel Bell, Zhe Sun, and Edmund Ryden. *Ancient Chinese Thought, Modern Chinese Power*. Princeton: Princeton University Press, 2013.

Yang, Fuchang, ed. *Contemporary China and Its Foreign Policy*. Beijing: World Affairs Press, 2003.

Yang, Yi. "Modernizations of China's National Defense." In *Transformation of Foreign Affairs and International Relations in China, 1978–2008*, edited by Yizhou Wang, 239–82. Leiden: Brill, 2011.

Yao, Chun. "China Vows to Make South China Sea Safe." Xinhua, December 15, 2011. http://www.mfa.gov.cn/ce/ceindo/eng/gdxw/t887657.htm

Yoshihara, Toshi, and James R. Holmes. "Can China Defend a 'Core Interest' in the South China Sea?" *Washington Quarterly* 34, no. 2 (2011): 45–59.

You, Ji. "Chinese Response to the a la Carte Maritime Disorder in the Indo-Pacific Region." Paper presented to 16th Asian Security Conference, Institute for Defence Studies and Analyses, New Delhi, February 19–21, 2014.

You, Ji. "Deciphering Beijing's Maritime Security Policy and Strategy in Managing Sovereignty Disputes in the China Seas." *Policy Brief.* Singapore: S. Rajaratnam School of International Studies, October 2013.

You, Ji. "A Test Case for China's Defence and Foreign Policies." *Contemporary Southeast Asia* 16, no. 4 (1995): 375–403.

Yu, Xiaofeng. "The Emergence of Non-Traditional Security Issues in China and Corresponding Strategies." In *Transformation of Foreign Affairs and International Relations in China, 1978–2008*, edited by Yizhou Wang. Leiden: Brill, 2011.

Yu, Yan. "Bridge over Troubled Water." *Beijing Review* 54, no. 31 (2011): 10–13.

Yuan, Jingdong. "Emerging Maritime Rivalry in the South China Sea: Territorial Disputes, Sea-Lane Security, and the Pursuit of Power." Paper prepared for the International Security Research and Outreach Programme, 2012. Accessed June 2, 2013. http://www.international.gc.ca/arms-armes/isrop-prisi/research-recherche/intl_security-securite_int/Report-South_China_Sea.aspx

Zartman, William, and Guy Olivier Faure. "The Dynamics of Escalation and Negotiation." In *Escalation and Negotiation in International Conflicts,* edited by William Zartman and Guy Olivier Faure. Cambridge: Cambridge University Press, 2005.

Zhang, Feng. "Assessing China's Response to the South China Sea Arbitration Ruling." *Australian Journal of International Affairs* 71, no. 4 (2017): 440–59. https://doi.org/https://doi.org/10.1080/10357718.2017.1287876

Zhang, Feng. "Confucian Foreign Policy Traditions in Chinese History." *Chinese Journal of International Politics* 8, no. 2 (2015): 197–218. https://doi.org/10.1093/cjip/pov004

Zhang, Feng. "The Rise of Chinese Exceptionalism in International Relations." *European Journal of International Relations* 19, no. 2 (2013): 305–28.

Zhang, Jian. "China's South China Sea Policy: Evolution, Claims and Challenges." In *The South China Sea Maritime Dispute: Political, Legal, and Regional Perspectives,* edited by Leszek Buszynski and Christopher B. Roberts. New York: Routledge, 2015.

Zhao, Hongtu. "Maliujia Kunju Yu Zhongguo Nengyuan Anquan Zaisikao" [Malacca dilemma and rethinking China's energy security]. *Xiandai Guoji Guanxi* 6 (2007): 36–42.

Zhao, Quansheng. "Patterns and Choices of Chinese Foreign Policy." *Asian Affairs* 20, no. 1 (1993): 3–15.

Zhao, Suisheng. "Foreign Policy Implications of Chinese Nationalism Revisited: The Strident Turn." *Journal of Contemporary China* 22, no. 82 (2013): 535–53.

Zhao, Suisheng. "Shaping the Regional Context of China's Rise: How the Obama Administration Brought Back Hedge in Its Engagement with China." *Journal of Contemporary China* 21, no. 75 (2012).

Zhao, Tingyang. *Tianxia Tixi: Shijie Zhidu Zhexue Daolun* [The Tianxia system: An introduction to the philosophy of a world institution]. Nanjing: Jiangsu Jiaoyu Chubanshe, 2005.

Zheng, Zemin. "Asia and the Pacific under the South China Sea Dispute Pattern." PhD diss., Central Party School, 2004.

Zhou, Enlai. "Premier Chou En-Lai's Letter to Prime Minister Nehru." In *The Sino-Indian Boundary Question (Enlarged Edition)*, 47–50. Peking: Foreign Languages Press, 1959.

Zhou, Enlai. "Zhou Enlai's Statement about the US-British Draft Peace Treaty with Japan and San Francisco Conference Statement." *People's Daily*, 1951. http://news.xinhuanet.com/ziliao/2004-12/15/content_2337746.htm

Zou, Keyuan. "Can China Respect the Law of the Seas? An Assessment of Maritime Agreements between China and Its Neighbors." *Harvard Asia Quarterly* 12, no. 3 (2010): 39–45.

Zou, Keyuan. "China's U-Shaped Line in the South China Sea Revisited." *Ocean Development and International Law* 43, no. 1 (2012): 18–34.

Zou, Keyuan. "The Chinese Traditional Maritime Boundary Line in the South China Sea and Its Legal Consequences for the Resolution of the Dispute over the Spratly Islands." *International Journal of Marine and Coastal Law* 14, no. 1 (1999): 27–55.

Zou, Keyuan. "Joint Development in the South China Sea: A New Approach." *International Journal of Marine and Coastal Law* 21, no. 2 (2006): 83–109.

Zou, Keyuan. *Law of the Sea in East Asia: Issues and Prospects*. London: Routledge, 2005.

Zou, Keyuan. "The Sino-Vietnamese Agreement on Maritime Boundary Delimitation in the Gulf of Tonkin." *Ocean Development and International Law* 36, no. 1 (2005): 13–24.

Zou, Le. "South China Sea Mapping Underway." *Global Times*, March 27, 2012. http://www.globaltimes.cn/content/702256.shtml

Zou, Ligang, and Xinxin Ye. "Nanhai ziyuan gongtongkaifade falu jizhi goujian luelun" [A view on the legal system for joint development of marine resources in the South China Sea]. *Journal of Henan Political Management Institute for Party Cadre* 124 (2011): 59–63.

Index